THE FRENZIED POETS

ANDREY BIELY AND THE RUSSIAN SYMBOLISTS

ANDREY
BIELY

ANDREY BIELY AN

B

The
FRENZIED POETS

THE RUSSIAN SYMBOLISTS

OLEG A. MASLENIKOV

UNIVERSITY OF CALIFORNIA PRESS
BERKELEY AND LOS ANGELES

1952

University of California Press · Berkeley and Los Angeles, California
Cambridge University Press · London, England

Copyright 1952
by the Regents of the University of California

designed by Ward Ritchie

To George Rapall Noyes

PREFACE

THE SYMBOLIST MOVEMENT in Russia was one of the outstanding and most complex phenomena in the cultural history of that country. Yet, up to the present few studies on that subject have appeared in print. No large work has been published on Andrey Biely, who was among the most significant symbolist writers. Perhaps the reason for such neglect has been that the mystical trends of symbolism run counter to Marxist philosophy and are, therefore, deemed alien to Soviet Russian mentality.

The slight accounts of the movement that are scattered in histories of Russian literature, in special studies discussing literary phenomena in general, as well as in a few critical and semicritical monographs, approach the problem from varying points of view; and each interpretation of symbolism differs with each individual writer's own philosophy. Thus, the Marxists interpret the symbolist movement exclusively in the light of socioeconomic factors and stress class struggle as the determining element; the formalists seek to analyze the techniques of the writers; the psychologists approach the works of symbolist writers from the point of view of their own theories of creative art—whether Freudian, anti-Freudian, or a-Freudian; comparatists strive to account for literary phenomena by establishing similarities between the works of various writers; proponents of the biographic school submit their own version of "the truth." Every method of literary scholarship, if it be sufficiently exhaustive, will prove valid to a greater or lesser degree. Yet no single method can provide a complete, all-embracing explanation of even so much as a single piece of literature. Literature, like all art, like culture itself, is so complex a phenomenon as to demand a many-sided illumination to bring out all its facets.

It is not surprising, therefore, that the various presentations of the Russian symbolist movement show diverse and at times even conflicting interpretations. Moreover, the term "symbolism" embraces a number of different connotations, because it describes not a single, homogeneous current, but rather several, parallel streams. This adds to the confusion. A writer who perhaps best reflects these various streams is Andrey Biely (pseudonym of Boris Nikolayevich Bugayev, 1880–1934). He was one of the leaders of the "younger" symbolists, who claimed that a symbolist poet was a superior being, a forerunner of a new race of artists—of men who could intuitively divine Plato's ideal world and interpret the truth through the temporal symbols that are accessible to the average man.

The life and works of a symbolist writer are inseparably connected, for his writings reflect his inner experiences insofar as they enable him to glimpse, in moments of creative ecstasy, the absolute that lies beyond the veil of Isis. The present study will, consequently, seek to establish certain biographical data in the life of Andrey Biely, and to point out how his experiences may have affected his works and those of his literary colleagues. Furthermore, since his biography and writings reflect the "symbolist mentality" (to borrow a term from Professor Janko Lavrin), a study of Biely's life and work may help to illuminate the essence of the symbolist movement in Russia.

I feel that a word about the verses quoted is necessary. The translations into English of some examples of modern Russian poems (several of which appear without a title in the original), seek to convey primarily the "feeling" of the Russian verse. Their aim is to preserve the meaning and the rhythm of the Russian. The translations, therefore, seek to duplicate such

Preface ix

deviations from the classical poetic forms as occur in the symbolist verses, especially the lame or varying meters found in some poems of Blok, Biely, and Balmont. For the same reason they retain the peculiar system of capitalization in Biely's early verses. I am aware of the differences between good Russian and good English poetry. Yet in these translations I have occasionally sacrificed poetic value, especially good rhymes, to preserve the inner rhythm of the Russian, which was the main concern of the symbolist poets. In their rebellion against tradition they regarded themselves primarily as "bearers of rhythm," paying less attention to good rhymes and resorting also to assonances, which they infinitely preferred to trite, hackneyed, "acceptable" forms. I also followed the authors in their occasional use of three periods where we would ordinarily expect dashes. These periods are set close, to distinguish them from the spaced periods indicating missing words.

I might add a word about the nonchronological order of the book. I have preferred to present Biely from several sides, in his relations with other members of the Russian symbolist movement, and thus attempted to reconstruct a general picture of that fascinating period in the history of Russian culture. I have, therefore, been obliged to discuss events in Biely's life from several angles, and on occasion to repeat myself. I trust that this flaw is offset by the advantages of the approach selected for this study.

Various persons have shared with me their reminiscences and materials pertaining to this study. I am grateful to many, among them to Anna Alexeyevna Turgenev, the late Vladislav Felicianovich Hodasevich, and especially to the late Mikhail Andreyevich Osorgin. I should like also to express my appreciation for the guidance and inspiration that I owe to my teachers, colleagues, and friends: the late Professors Alexander S. Kaun and George Z. Patrick; Professor Robert J. Kerner; and, particularly, Professor George R. Noyes, to whom I am deeply

Preface

indebted for his invaluable and ever-patient criticism of the manuscript, and to whom this work is dedicated. I should like to thank also Professors Rudolf Altrocchi, Clarence D. Brenner, Jacqueline E. de La Harpe, Waclaw Lednicki, Lawrence M. Price, and Robert K. Spaulding, for their helpful criticism and suggestions; and Professor Gleb P. Struve for his constructive interest.

Finally I should like to acknowledge my debt to two members of the editorial staff of the University of California Press: to Professor William Hardy Alexander for his aid in improving a number of my translations (to his efforts I owe the rhymed version of Bryusov's poem "To the City"); and to Mr. Maxwell E. Knight for his numerous helpful suggestions in editing the final version of the book.

Oleg A. Maslenikov

BERKELEY, CALIFORNIA

CONTENTS

PART I: THE BACKGROUND
1. *The Origins of the Russian Symbolist Movement*   3
2. *The Early Phases of the Symbolist Movement*   9

PART II: BORIS NIKOLAYEVICH BUGAYEV
3. *Childhood*   33
4. *Boris Bugayev and the Solovyovs*   45
5. *Boris Bugayev as Man and Artist*   65

PART III: ANDREY BIELY AND "LA MÊLÉE SYMBOLISTE"
6. *Andrey Biely and Valeri Bryusov*   99
7. *Andrey Biely and the Merezhkovskys*   128
8. *Andrey Biely and Alexander Blok*   146
9. *Andrey Biely and Vyacheslav Ivanov*   197
10. *Conclusion*   217
    Bibliography   225
    Index   231

ILLUSTRATIONS

Andrey Biely	*frontispiece*
Constantin Balmont	139
Zinaida Hippius	139
Dmitri Merezhkovsky	139
Valeri Bryusov	139
Vladimir Solovyov	151
Alexander Blok	151
Vyacheslav Ivanov	151
Andrey Biely	151

TRANSLITERATION

THROUGHOUT THE TEXT phonetic spelling, familiar to the English-speaking public, and in general use in nonscientific literature, has been used for Russian names and words. The transliteration in the footnotes and in the bibliography, however, corresponds to that of the Library of Congress. This system has been widely adopted throughout the United States, and was adhered to in order to facilitate referring to the sources quoted.

Russian	Bibliography	Text	Russian	Bibliography	Text
а	a	a	т	t	t
б	b	b	у	u	u
в	v	v	ф	f	f
г	g	g / h*	х	kh	kh / h†
д	d	d	ц	ts	ts
е	e	e / ye**	ч	ch	ch
ё	e	yo	ш	sh	sh
ж	zh	zh	щ	shch	shch
з	z	z	ъ	"	(omit)
и	i	i	ы	y	y
й	i	y	ь	'	(omit)
к	k	k	э	e	e
л	l	l	ѣ	e	e / ie‡
м	m	m	ю	iu	yu
н	n	n	я	ia	ya
о	o	o	-ый	-yi	-y
п	p	p	-ий	-ii	-i / -y following g, k, kh
р	r	r			
с	s	s			

* initial, when h is transliterated
** initial and intervocalic; but e after i or y
† initial
‡ when accented, except when following g, k, kh

ABBREVIATIONS USED IN THE FOOTNOTES

Arabeski: Andrei Belyi, *Arabeski* (Moscow, 1911), 504 pp.
Nachalo veka: Andrei Belyi, *Nachalo veka* (Moscow, 1933), 503 pp.
Na rubezhe: Andrei Belyi, *Na rubezhe dvukh stoletii* (Moscow, 1930), 496 pp.
Nekropol': Vladislav Khodasevich, *Nekropol'* (Bruxelles, 1939), 280 pp.
Omut: Andrei Belyi, *Mezhdu dvukh revoliutsii*, Part I (Leningrad, 1934), 409 pp.
Perepiska: Aleksandr Blok and Andrei Belyi, *Perepiska* (ed. by V. N. Orlov). In *Letopisi Gosudarstvennogo literaturnogo muzeia*, vol. VII (Moscow, 1940), lxiv, 370 pp.
Simvolizm: Andrei Belyi, *Simvolizm* (Moscow, 1910), 635 pp.
Vengerov: S. A. Vengerov (ed.), *Russkaia literatura XX veka* (Moscow, 1914–1916), 3 vols. Incomplete.
Zhivyia litsa: Z. N. Gippius, *Zhivyia litsa* (Praha, 1925), 2 vols.
Literaturnoe Nasledstvo: Literaturnoe Nasledstvo, vols. 27–28 (Moscow, 1937), 693 pp.

PART I

THE BACKGROUND

1

THE ORIGINS OF THE RUSSIAN SYMBOLIST MOVEMENT

IF ENVIRONMENT HELPS shape the life, thought, and art of a society, the symbolist movement in Russian literature was certainly a legitimate product of its time. It arose at a period when certain groups of Russian society came to realize that they faced a new era. Symbolism expressed the thoughts and feelings of those intellectuals who could neither accept nor transform the reality that loomed before them. Symbolism was their reaction to the harassing social, political, economic, and purely intellectual changes of their time. Because these changes resembled those that western Europe had been experiencing since the industrial revolution, the intellectuals in Russia responded similarly to the impulses that had produced first "romanticism" and then "decadence" or "symbolism" in the West. Russian symbolism was a protest against the forces that seemed to debase and degrade an individual in his own eyes. As such it had its immediate roots in the Russian scene of the 1880's.

The 1880's were a drab and stagnant decade in Russian social and intellectual history.[1] The assassination of Alexander

[1] See for example T. G. Masaryk, *Rusko a Evropa* (Praha, 1933), II, 179–698. P. N. Miliukov, *Le mouvement intellectuel russe* (Paris, 1918); *Ocherki po istorii russkoi kul'tury* (Jubilee ed.; Paris, 1931), II, 345–385; *Russia and Its Crisis* (Chicago, 1908). D. S. Mirsky, *Contemporary Russian Literature, 1881–1925* (New York, 1926), pp. 3–96. D. N. Ovsianiko-Kulikovskii, ed., *Istoriia russkoi literatury XIX veka* (Moscow, 1910), IV, 335–371; V, 1–440. S. A. Vengerov, ed., *Russkaia literatura XX veka, 1890–1910* (Moscow, 1914–1917), I, 1–56; II, 22–240.

II (March 1, 1881) had led the government to adopt a vigorously reactionary course, and during the ensuing quarter century, Konstantin Pobedonostsev (1827–1907), procurateur of the holy synod and former tutor of Tsar Alexander III, dominated the spiritual life of Russia. His forceful personality came to symbolize the almost physically oppressive power of the state, which obtruded upon every phase of Russian life. Against this background of political reaction, Russia began undergoing vital economic changes, which in turn brought about unavoidable social readjustments.

The 1880's marked the beginning of Russia's industrialization, a period when she embarked upon what amounted to a belated industrial revolution with its inevitable concomitant—urbanization and rise of a capitalistic economy. The landowning class, long on the decline, all at once became aware that it had lost its leadership in Russian society and that thereafter the upstart bourgeoisie (though still a minor factor in governmental policy), would dictate in matters of literary and artistic taste.

As Russia's industrialization progressed and her social profile changed, the materialistic system of philosophy grew in prestige, until it had become completely dominant. Contemporaneously with this rising tide of materialism, the Russian intellectuals found that the new currents of biological thought tended further to depress their self-esteem. The doctrine of Darwinism, which was beginning successfully to penetrate the consciousness of the average educated Russian, added to his spiritual discomfiture. Darwinism seemed to rob a reasoning individual of his belief in man's divine origin and consequently in the immortality of his soul: the notions which, as the exponents of contemporary scientific thought insisted, he had invented and to which he had clung for ages in an attempt to overcome the finality of the oblivion that was death. In its popularized version, Darwinism shattered the link between man and god and forged in its place one that bound man and ape, thus further undermining man's self-importance and self-assurance.[2] Hence, toward the end of the nineteenth century, the political, economic, and social changes in Russian life, as well as the philosophic doctrines that came from abroad, tended to depress the self-esteem of Russian intellectuals, and to undermine their sense of security and well-being. Consequently they found themselves exposed not only to the forces that underlay the romantic rebellion in western Europe, but also to those that determined the modernist movement.

It is not strange, therefore, that in Russian symbolism traits of French symbolism are blended with those that hark back to German romanticism of an earlier generation. Spiritually the Russian symbolists stood closer to the German romantics[3] (Schleiermacher, the Schlegels, Novalis, Schelling, and their successors, Schopenhauer and Nietzsche), than they did to the French symbolists (Verlaine, Rimbaud, Mallarmé). The basis of Russian symbolism lay first and foremost in the idealistic philosophy, which was the direct negation of modern materialism.

The Russian poets ostensibly accepted the artistic creed of their French contemporaries. Yet by so doing they were actually acknowledging their debt to German thought, which they translated to fit their own philosophic beliefs. To the Russians symbolism meant more than a literary method that employed

---

[2] Already by 1870 Darwin's *Origin of Species* had evoked a protest from the populist critic N. K. Mikhailovskii, whose work *Teoriia Darvina i obshchestvennaia nauka* (St. Petersburg, 1870–1873, 2 vols.) argues against Darwin. Another anti-Darwinist was N. IA. Danilevskii, *Darvinism* (St. Petersburg, 1885–1889, 3 vols.). During the 1890's Darwinism evoked considerable journalistic comment, which included translations as well as native Russian works: M. A. Engel'gardt, *Ch. Darvin* (St. Petersburg, 1894); M. A. Antonovich, *Ch. Darvin i ego teoriia* (St. Petersburg, 1896); Ernst Haeckel, "Transformizm i Darvinizm," *Mir Bozhii* (1900); N. K. Mikhailovskii, "Darvinizm i Nitssheanstvo," *Russkoe Bogatstvo* (February, 1898); K. A. Timiriazev, *Charl'z Darvin i ego uchenie* (6th ed., Moscow, 1908). A. Bers "Darvinizm i khristianskaia nravstvennost'," *Vestnik Evropy* (May, 1910).

[3] See Viktor Zhirmunskii, *Nemetskii romantizm i sovremennaia mistika* (St. Petersburg, 1914).

symbols in order the more subtly to express thought and feeling, more than a method that used one concept to convey the meaning of another. Symbolism to them meant also more than a school that championed and propagandized a literary style or method. In Russia symbolism connoted an idealistic philosophy, a *Weltanschauung*, inherent in a symbolist poet. Symbolism implied a revelation of ultimate reality through the physical phenomena of our world. In this aspect it harkened back to certain phases of Oriental philosophy, to Plato, to the mystics (especially Jakob Boehme), and to nineteenth-century idealism. Symbolism, therefore, implied also a way of life; a symbolist poet was to seek such a life as would afford him the greatest opportunity for gleaning visions of the ultimate. The poets, consequently, deemed it their duty to seek stimulation for their muse.

In literature this new period coincided with the end of the "golden age" of the Russian novel. The publication of Dostoyevsky's *The Brothers Karamazov* (1880) marked the end of an era. The older generation of writers had either died or retired. Dostoyevsky died in 1881; Turgenev in 1883; Goncharov produced no major novel after his *Ravine* (1869). Only Tolstoy remained, and even he announced his retirement from *belles lettres*.

Although in Russia the symbolist movement produced also prose and philosophical and critical essays, it featured principally the revival of poetry, and its writers regarded themselves first and foremost as poets, "bearers of rhythm." Here its origins can be traced directly to the Russian literature of the 1880's. With the older generation of novelists either dead or retired, the younger writers, the so-called "men of the 'eighties," proved temperamentally unsuited for works of heroic stature; they were a generation of short-story writers, second-rate poets, and third-rate historical novelists. Since Garshin and Korolenko belonged ideologically to the preceding decade, Anton Chekhov was almost the only writer of genuine talent to arise during the 1880's.

Of the older generation of writers, only the poets remained active in their particular literary sphere, except for Tolstoy. As political reaction took root, popular interest in poetry appeared to grow. Not only Pushkin, Baratynsky, and Tyutchev, but Fet-Shenshin, Apollon Maykov, Polonsky, and lesser lights returned into public favor, and such unexciting poets as Apukhtin and Nadson became the new favorites of Russian readers. Along with the rise of poetry an increasing interest in aesthetic doctrines and in the literature of the West became gradually noticeable, and with it a trend to free all literature, and particularly poetry, from subservience to the needs of society. It was a movement that favored the individual freedom of a writer, even to the extent of supporting an art-for-art's-sake philosophy. Yet the 1880's produced no literary school of their own. They merely marked the end of one period in Russian literature and sounded a few introductory notes that characterized the movement that was to follow. The 1880's were a decade that separated two literary eras.

The "men of the 'eighties" as a generation were temperamentally incapable either of protesting or of creating, but the generation that followed them rekindled the traditional search for truth that had characterized Russian letters. Consequently, the 1890's saw creative literature reborn among the younger intellectuals, who had struck out toward new horizons.

The 1890's thus became a decade of rebellion, of protest against the sordid Russian life, of ferment that permeated the activity of the intelligentsia. In the realm of the arts, the younger men and women felt so repelled by their surroundings that they strove turbulently to free themselves of all tradition and "to transvaluate all values."[4] This new trend produced a reaction toward individualism, reflected brilliantly on the one

---
[4] *Vengerov*, II, 9–136, *passim*.

8 *The Frenzied Poets*

hand in the literature of the early Gorky and Andreyev, and on the other in the works of the symbolist writers. The symbolist current, which nearly coincided with its Western prototype, also helped to activate a growing demand for foreign literature, music, and art. It thus came to herald a new "golden age" in Russian literature, and played a vital role in maturing the artistic taste of the Russian public.

2

THE EARLY PHASES OF THE SYMBOLIST MOVEMENT IN RUSSIA

IN RUSSIAN LITERATURE the intellectual trend to "transvaluate all values" began as an effort to establish the validity of certain aesthetic principles in the realm of lyrical poetry. In attempting to legitimize once more the poet's emotions as the sole province of the lyric, it strove to free poetry from subservience to the civic needs of society. Thus it represented a reaction against Nekrasov's dictum that:

> One has no need to be a poet,
> But be a citizen, one must

in favor of the equally well-known verse of Pushkin:

> We have been born for inspiration,
> Sweet melodies and prayers.

By and large the trend went against everything that the generation of the "fathers" had considered sacred.

The first bombshell fired by the "sons" burst in 1884, on the pages of the Kievan newspaper, *Dawn* (*Zarya*), which published two articles, one by I. I. Yasinsky (1850–1930) and the other by N. M. Minsky (N. M. Vilenkin, 1855–1937), two lesser-known writers. Both men protested not only against the lack of aesthetic appreciation in current criticism, but against the entire trend of thought in which the younger generation had been reared. The following passage illustrates how Yasinsky registered his protest.

10　The Frenzied Poets

There was a period in the life of our young intelligentsia when art was rejected, when beauty was regarded as a mere trifle, and answers to the "accursed questions" of the meaning of life, of truth, and of beauty were sought in textbooks on political economy... I must admit that life seemed frightfully dull... And I was not alone in feeling thus.[1]

Yasinsky's article further protested against the theory that "the aim of art" was "to teach," and insisted that its sole purpose should have been "to make people happy and... to delight them." In concluding his essay Yasinsky, himself a poet, expressed the belief that poetry plays an "all-important role in human affairs," and that a poet should, therefore, be regarded by his fellow men with the "highest esteem." Here he sounded one of the keynotes that the new movement was soon to treat as a cardinal truth. Here was a poet trying to assert himself as a superior being; here, too, was an artist rebelling against the minimizing effect that civilization had upon an individual.

In a subsequent issue of the *Dawn*, Minsky published a similar article which, however, went a step further in defending the "purity" of art and in expressing the importance of the individual. He stated his conviction that creative art was superior to the sciences inasmuch as a scientist could "only discover laws that already existed in nature," while an artist "created a new world of his own," never before known to man.[2] Minsky, therefore, reasoned that a poet should not permit any utilitarian considerations to influence him, and that the public could demand of poetry only aesthetic pleasure.

Minsky and Yasinsky in their demand for greater artistic freedom voiced the sentiments of the period; other writers and artists of the time expressed the same desire. Chekhov, too, protested against society's encroachment on the rights of an artist. In a letter to A. N. Pleshcheyev he wrote that his "holy

---
[1] From excerpts quoted in Ovsianiko-Kulikovskii, *Russkaia literatura XIX veka*, V, 73–74.
[2] N. Brodskii, ed., *Literaturnye manifesty* (Moscow, 1929), pp. 3–5.

of holies" was the "complete freedom of an individual" to write and think as he wished.³

Besides Minsky the 1880's produced another figure of significance in the early development of Russian modernism. He was A. L. Volynsky (pseudonym of Akim Lvovich Flekser, 1865–1926), whose critical articles began appearing in the St. Petersburg periodical *Northern Messenger* (*Sieverny Viestnik*) toward the close of the decade. He attacked the principles of social criticism that had become traditional in Russia since the days of Belinsky, Chernyshevsky, Dobrolyubov, and Pisarev, with a bitterness that attracted a number of enthusiastic followers of what became now known as "modernism," or "decadence," or the "new art."

By 1892 the general features of the new literary trend had become clear. They reflected the turmoil that was brewing in the intellectual life of the country. Consequently, they assumed the form of a struggle for greater individual freedom, and blended with that struggle a strain of pessimism and a mystical prophecy of a new era. In its appeal, the new movement presented a paradox. It attracted young men and women who firmly believed in individualism of a most extreme sort, and yet it banded these ultraindividualists into a closely knit group, all in the name of greater self-expression. During the early 1890's such young poets as Konstantin Balmont (1867–1941) and Zinaida Hippius (1867–1945) rose on the literary horizon, and such poets of traditional "civic lament and duty" as Minsky and Merezhkovsky embraced modernism.

In 1890 Minsky published his philosophical dissertation *In the Light of Conscience* (*Pri sviete sovesti*), which immediately stamped him as one of the leaders of the ultraindividualistic trends of the younger generation. Minsky's book emphasized as its chief principle that all life is "motivated exclusively by

---
³ Letter to A. N. Pleshcheev (October, 1889), *Pis'ma A. P. Chekhova*, ed. by M. Chekhov (Moscow, 1912), II, 407–408.

egoism,'"[4] and called for greater manifestation of individualism. In this work Minsky further developed the theses originally expressed in his article and, as a "new man," again sought to elevate himself above the "common herd." Despite the prestige that Minsky's book gave him in the eyes of the modernist young intelligentsia, he was incapable of assuming leadership in the modernistic movement and remained a fellow traveler.

The first cohesive force in Russian modernism was Lyubov Gurevich (1866–1941), a young woman of boundless energy and ambition, who was a passionate adherent of the "new art" and a particular admirer of A. L. Volynsky. In 1891 she had learned that the *Northern Messenger*, published by Mme. Yevreinov, was about to cease publication because of financial difficulties. Its discontinuance threatened to prevent Volynsky from publishing his writings. With a neophyte's fervor, therefore, Mlle. Gurevich initiated a campaign to raise the funds necessary to continue the periodical, so that Volynsky might remain "unhampered in writing his critical essays."[5] Like a number of other young people Mlle. Gurevich felt that the struggle for new cultural values was the most important issue in her life. Thanks to her efforts the periodical passed into the hands of a new publishing group, but was soon once more on the verge of bankruptcy. Convinced that she had a mission to fulfill, Mlle. Gurevich again came to the rescue and raised additional funds. Eventually she became the sole publisher and editor of the periodical, the mounting debts of which only further increased her determination to see her idea through to the end. Modernism for her had become a crusade. The *Northern Messenger* featured "belligerent" (*"boyevye"*) articles of Volynsky, who with ruthless abandon tore down the critical traditions of the past. True to the spirit of the younger generation, Mlle. Gurevich's periodical sought out everything in

---

[4] Quoted by Vladimir Solov'ev in his review of the book. *Vestnik Evropy* (March, 1890), 437–441.
[5] F. Fidler, ed., *Pervye literaturnye shagi* (St. Petersburg, 1911), pp. 191–192.

literature that was "audacious and bold, and that strove toward new horizons." Under her enthusiastic guidance, the magazine began slowly to raise its head, and within a few years increased its circulation from a few hundred to over 4,250 paid subscribers. Suddenly everything toppled. For a nonpolitical periodical, the blow came from a rather unexpected quarter—the censor, who, from mere personal animosity against the unfortunate Mlle. Gurevich, began systematically to persecute her venture. "One cannot imagine what took place," Lyubov Gurevich writes in her reminiscences. "The censor would often delete every other line of an article, without any regard to its meaning."[6] Within a short time the number of subscribers had dropped by one-fourth, and by 1898 the venture was obliged to go into bankruptcy, leaving its publisher more than 150,000 rubles in debt. Although the financial debacle of the *Northern Messenger* had "all but ruined [her] life," Lyubov Gurevich regarded her sacrifice for the modernist cause as "absolutely necessary and even inevitable."[7] The periodical she had guided accomplished one important thing: it laid the foundation for a unified modernist movement, and for the ultimate victory of symbolism in Russian poetry.

Perhaps more significant in the symbolist movement than Minsky, Volynsky, or Gurevich, was the figure of Dmitri Sergeyevich Merezhkovsky (1865–1941). Although his first book, a collection of mediocre poetry, had wholly conformed to the traditional civic themes, the content of his subsequent works showed a startling transformation. His second book of verse, *Symbols* (*Simvoly*, 1892), reflected the marked influence of two of the forerunners of Western symbolism, Charles Baudelaire and Edgar Allan Poe. In the following year he published a volume of prose essays that proved to be an important milepost in the self-expression of his literary generation.[8] His essay

[6] *Vengerov*, I, 258–259.   [7] Fidler, *op. cit.*, p. 196.
[8] R. V. Ivanov-Razumnik, *Istoriia russkoi obshchestvennoi mysli* (5th ed.; St. Petersburg, 1918), II.

14 The Frenzied Poets

On the Present Condition of Russian Literature and on the Causes of its Decline (*O prichinakh upadka* ...) found a hearty welcome among all supporters of modernism, not so much because it exposed the literary vices of the day, as because it uttered the secret thoughts of a generation aware that it was lost in the sea of life. It was the confession of a man who had just realized the tragic contradiction that had sprung from an organic necessity for faith and his own inability to believe—the contradiction that was the outgrowth of his newly discovered intellectual freedom to question and deny everything:

> There are no more barriers! We are free and alone ... The horror of it is incomparable. Never before has man felt in his heart such desire to believe, and never before has he felt himself utterly incapable of so doing.[9]

One may sense that one solution to such a plight might be mysticism. In Russia this led not only to symbolism as a philosophical outlook which proclaimed that a poet possessed the ability in moments of creative ecstasy to perceive the other, the "real" world, but also to the "God-seeking" movement that Merezhkovsky fostered. A realization of irreconcilable spiritual contradictions, as well as a sense of social insecurity and personal insignificance, resulted in an intellectual trend that was at once mystically hopeful, apocalyptic, hyperindividualistic, and decadently pessimistic. The younger poets were particularly fond of seeing themselves as prophets of a new dawn, as harbingers of a new spring, as higher men who sensed that humanity was on the threshold of a new cultural era, of a renaissance that should see all mankind transformed into a species of poets—and, therefore, into supermen.[10] These trends are illustrated in Merezhkovsky's early symbolist poetry.

---

[9] D. S. Merezhkovskii, *Sobranie sochinenii* (St. Petersburg, 1911), XV, 243 ff.
[10] Cf. *Nachalo veka*, pp. 107–116. See also Belyi's introduction to the periodical *Epopeia*, I (1922), 3–9.

Before the Dawn

Casting our eyes
Upon the paling East
We, children of sorrow and night,
Wait for our prophets to come.

We sense the unknowable
And, with hope in our hearts,
Dying we yearn
For the worlds uncreated.

Though our speeches are bold,
Doomed yet are we,
For we herald a Spring
That will come all too late.

Resurrection of the buried,
And the cocks' midnight crowing,
And the early morn's chill
These things are we.

Our laments are our hymns.
On behalf of New Beauty,
We break all commandments,
We transgress every limit.

We but lure the unsated,
We are mocked by the rabble;
We are embers on the altars
Profaned with ashes.

We're the path o'er the void,
We are children of night,
Who but wait for the sun's rays
Thus, like shadows, to perish.[11]

---

[11] Published in *Russkaia Mysl'* (September, 1894), 204. In reprinting the poem in his collected works, Merezhkovskii deleted the 5th and 6th stanzas; see his *Sobranie sochinenii*, XV, 7.

16 The Frenzied Poets

A striking parallel is obvious between this poem and Minsky's "Before the Dawn."

> Do not grieve that in darkness of night,
> People slumber a sleep of the dead,
> That the cock's silly crowing at times,
> Or the ominous growling of dogs,
> May disquiet the still of the night;
> 'Tis a dream that you dream before dawn.

As a direct contrast to these mystic notes, the debut of Valeri Bryusov in 1894 was intended to shock and scandalize the public. In February of that year a slender volume of some fifty pages appeared on the Russian book market. It was entitled *Russian Symbolists* (*Russkie simvolisty*) and was soon followed by two more books of identical title and format. Their editor and chief contributor was a twenty-year-old student of Moscow university, Valeri Bryusov. Since the books seemed deliberately to defy all standards of good taste in order to shock the public, they had an immediate *succès de scandale*. Bryusov and his companions sought to prove to the world that they were unquestionably children of the new generation, to whom "no more barriers" existed, and who had discarded all traditions of the past. Their first book featured translations from some of the better-known Western symbolists: Verlaine, Rimbaud, Mallarmé, Maeterlinck.[12] Yet Bryusov and his fellow translator A. L. Miropolsky (pseudonym of A. A. Lang, *ca.* 1872–1917) selected only the oddest, most "daring" verses of the French. Since the daily press was always on the alert for quaint items that might make good copy, Valeri Bryusov found his name spread immediately in the newspapers throughout the length and breadth of Russia; overnight he had become "famous." For a long time Bryusov and his companions remained fair game for the newspapers. And small wonder! In his efforts to prove that he had "transgressed all bounds" and had "permitted himself everything that had once been for-

---
[12] Máchal, *O symbolismu v polské a russké literatuře* (Praha, 1935), p. 104.

Early Phases 17

bidden," Bryusov did everything in his power to bewilder the placid "Philistines," an action which in itself, according to Arthur Symons, is a mark of the "middle class."[13] Bryusov wrote, for example:

> The corpse of a woman rotting and smelly
> A sickly steppe and a cast-iron sky ...
> Smirk resurrected, a long, long moment
> With reproachful guffaw confronts the eye.
>
> A diamond dream ... A palace lit on high ...
> And incense, tears, and dew below.
> The rotting smelly corpse is left aside
> Its eyes picked out by a carrion crow.
>   (signed) Z. Fuchs[14]

Other examples of this "symbolist" poetry remind one of paintings of our own contemporaries of the surrealist school:

> Corpses lighted by gas flames!
> A carmine ribbon on a scarlet bride!
> Oh! To the window let us go and kiss!
> Behold, how pale are the faces of the dead!
> Here children in a hospital are in mourning ...
> And these are oleanders preserved on ice ...
>
> For *Songs without Words* we find here a cover ...
> Through the windows, darling, we can see no moon!
> The flower in your lapel—that is our souls.[15]

The acme of such "arch-symbolist" nonsense Bryusov attained in the now famous one-line "poem,"

> O zakroy svoi blednye nogi!
> (Oh, cover thy pale legs!)

which he regarded at the time as "no more than a daring leap into the future."[16] When P. S. Kogan, a historian of Russian

---
[13] Arthur Symons, *Symbolism* (New York, 1919), p. 7.
[14] Quoted by Vladimir Solov'ev in *Vestnik Evropy* (January, 1895), 424.
[15] *Ibid.*
[16] Valerii Briusov, *Pis'ma k P. P. Pertsovu* (Moscow, 1927), p. 35.

18   The Frenzied Poets

literature, asked the young poet to explain the reason for the brevity of this poem, Bryusov remarked that poetry gained in intensity and suggestiveness in direct proportion to its brevity. Kogan then queried whether Bryusov's "poem" might not have gained in eloquence if reduced simply to the interjectory "oh!" Whereupon Bryusov, meditatively stroking his beard, answered, "You know, you may have something there!"

How well Bryusov and other self-styled "symbolists" had succeeded in "shocking the Philistines" may be seen from an anonymous review that appeared in one of the leading Russian periodicals of the time, *Russian Wealth* (*Russkoe Bogatstvo*):

> If, after reading a piece of poetry or prose, you involuntarily exclaim, "The devil knows what kind of stuff this is!" you will know that you have read a piece of symbolist writing.[17]

Similar outbursts from enraged "Philistines" greeted Bryusov's poetry everywhere. The majority of the better-known critics, however, simply ignored his efforts to arouse their wrath. An exception was the poet and philosopher, Vladimir Solovyov, who contributed critical articles to the *Messenger of Europe* (*Vestnik Evropy*) one of the leading liberal periodicals. Each of the three issues of *Russian Symbolists* he analyzed in a separate review, in which he blended satire with good-natured ridicule. He treated the endeavors of the young individualists as a huge joke, and finally crowned his third review with three parodies on the young poets. The most successful of them was:

> Vertical horizons
> Rise in chocolate skies,
> Like translucent wishes
> In a bay rum prize.
>
> Ghosts of fiery icebergs
> Flit in twilight bright;
> A Pegasus in hyacinth
> Harks not to my plight.

---
[17] Anonymous review in *Russkoe Bogatstvo* (August, 1894), 74.

> Inherent mandragora
> Rustles in the silt,
> And decadently unpolished
> Verse my ears doth wilt.[18]

When reviewing the first issue of *Russian Symbolists* Solovyov wrote that the booklet had "undoubted merit," for it "burdened readers with neither bulk nor content."[19] Concerning the book's coauthors he remarked that if Bryusov were "no older than fifteen" he might "someday become a poet," although "on the other hand he might never amount to much." Concerning Miropolsky, Solovyov had "nothing to say," for eight of the ten pages that contained his contribution were written in prose, and the "task of reading decadent prose was beyond" the reviewer. When the second book appeared, listing the names of ten contributors where only two had been before, Solovyov, tongue in cheek, expressed great amazement. Facetiously claiming a strictly scientific approach in his criticism, the noted philosopher tried to explain the rapid increase in the symbolist ranks. The only scientific theory that he could offer in explanation of the "procreational rapidity of the species ... that calls itself Russian symbolists" was that of "reproduction through *generatio aequivoca*."[20] He added regretfully, however, that he doubted whether "exact science would recognize" such an explanation. Solovyov's parodies concluded his review of the third issue of the series. In his essays, Solovyov underscored the weak points and excesses of which Bryusov and company had been guilty. Bryusov took the jibes good-naturedly and even seemed flattered by the attention that a man of Solovyov's standing had paid him. He wrote to P. P. Pertsov concerning these reviews: "I was simply delighted at the parodies. The weak points of symbolism [!] were correctly interpreted."[21] The entries in Bryusov's diary clearly show that he

---
[18] Vladimir Solov'ev, *Sobranie sochinenii* (2d ed.; St. Petersburg, 1911), VII, 169.
[19] *Vestnik Evropy* (August, 1894), 890–892.
[20] *Ibid.* (January, 1895), 421.   [21] Briusov, *op. cit.*, p. 45.

20 The Frenzied Poets

harbored no resentment against the philosopher. In 1900, he recorded that he had attended Solovyov's funeral and "kissed the dead man's hand." He added: "Thus was I destined to meet the critic of my first poems. And I had dreamed—and more than once—of long personal chats with him."[22]

Wishing to emulate Merezhkovsky, who had become a leader of the symbolist movement in St. Petersburg, Bryusov worked tirelessly to build a following in Moscow. The hostile reception that the critics and reviewers had given his first verses, and the ridicule that the daily press had heaped upon his sophomoric literary efforts, made Bryusov "virtually a literary outcast."[23] For five years after he had first appeared in print, no periodical would publish his poetry or prose. Yet this very ban spurred him on to fight for recognition and to gain a following of his own. He approached both tasks systematically and with dogged determination. He labored on his technique, sought contacts in the literary world, and cultivated particularly the friendship of young poets. No budding poet was too insignificant for Bryusov. His treatment of Alexander Brailovsky, a young high-school lad with only an average amount of poetic promise, illustrates this point. Bryusov met Brailovsky in the summer of 1896, while vacationing in southern Russia. Bryusov wrote in his diary that the thirteen-year-old boy "was naturally [!] a bitter opponent of [Bryusov's] 'symbolism.'"[24] For this reason Bryusov devoted "day after day" to this youthful acquaintance, whom he tried to convert to the new literary movement.[25] He even dedicated a poem to Brailovsky, in which he expressed his literary credo:

> O pallid youth, with the fiery glances!
> My own three commandments I give unto thee.
> Receive thou the first: "Do not live in the present;
> Only the future the bard's realm shall be."

---

[22] Briusov, *Dnevniki, 1890–1910* (Moscow, 1927), pp. 89–90.
[23] *Vengerov*, I, 410.
[24] Briusov, *Dnevniki*, p. 154.
[25] *Ibid.*, pp. 24–25, 154.

Remember the second: "Have compassion for no one;
Only thyself without bounds thou shalt love."
Keep thou the third: "Worship only the Muses:
Art for itself—without purpose or doubt."

O pallid youth, with a look of bewilderment!
Could I be sure my commandments you'll keep,
Mute I would fall as a warrior stricken
Knowing a poet will remember my sleep.[26]

To Bryusov the term "symbolism" connoted precisely these three elements. In his narrow worship of self rather than humanity, in his adoration of art rather than society, and in his striving to escape the present by turning to the future, Bryusov was a typical representative of the modernist mentality. The frankness with which he proclaimed his tenets reminds one of Minsky's *In the Light of Conscience.* Unlike Minsky, however, Bryusov possessed the personality and energy necessary for successful organization, and by 1900 he became the pivotal point of the Scorpio press (a publishing house sympathetic to modernism, established in Moscow by S. I. Polyakov), which was soon recognized as the leading outlet for Russian symbolism.

In the first half of the 1890's another star rose on the symbolist horizon. It was Konstantin Balmont, a lyric poet "by the grace of God." Although he had published his first book of verse in 1890, the amazing musical quality of his poetry did not become apparent until his second volume appeared, four years later. This won him not only the acclamation of the followers of the "new art," but also the recognition of many critics of the conservative camp. Although the older readers found Balmont's verses pleasing to the ear, not all of them were able to grasp the significance of his poetry. Tolstoy, a venerated representative of this older generation, on reading some of Balmont's verse is said to have exclaimed, "What charming

---
[26] Briusov, *Izbrannye proizvedeniia* (Moscow, 1926), I, 27.

nonsense!" remaining apparently deaf to the melody of the most musical of Russian poets.

Balmont was to Russian modernism what Verlaine was to its French counterpart. He elevated Russian poetry to hitherto unattained musical heights. Nor was this his only merit. Like many other symbolist poets, Balmont was well acquainted with Western modernist literature, which he translated for Russian readers. In his translations Balmont emphasized the poetry of the English-speaking peoples. He, more than anyone else, was responsible for popularizing in Russia Oscar Wilde, Walt Whitman, Edgar Allan Poe, and Shelley, to say nothing of Rosetti, Blake, Coleridge, and Tennyson. His translations of Poe are excellent on the whole, for Balmont was able to render much of Poe's musical charm into Russian.[27] His translation of *The Raven*, which he did in competition with Bryusov, is particularly deft; in fact, the Russian version of Poe's refrain "quoth the raven—'nevermore!' " (*"kárknul vóron—'nikogdá!' "*) sounds more sinister than the English original; sometimes, however, Balmont translates this line also with *"mólvil vóron—'nikogdá!' "* when a more melodious and less menacing note seemed appropriate. On the other hand, his translations of Shelley show unwarranted liberties with the original. Some wag from the daily press even dubbed him "Shelmont" for his efforts—a pun not only on the surnames of the two poets, but also on the word *shel'ma*, a Russian colloquialism for "rascal." Balmont did not limit himself to the English; his translations include verses from the classical Greeks, the Spanish, and one Italian (Giacomo Leopardi).

Balmont's influence on Russian poetry of the twentieth century has been very great. He showed the public and the poets alike the musical potentiality of Russian verse. The mellifluence, ease, and natural grace of his style soon conquered the

---

[27] Bal'mont's translations of the *Tales of Mystery and Imagination* appeared in print in 1895, and his *Collected Works of Poe* was published in four volumes, 1901–1912.

most stubborn critics of aestheticism in poetry. A typical example of his poetry, with its sonorous double and triple rhymes, is the following poem.

The Swan

Sleepy shores. The lake lies calm and mirrory.
Only there where dream the rushes tall
Someone's song reëchoes—and as wearily
    As the last sigh of a soul.

There a swan sobs his lament—a dying swan;
To his past he breathes a farewell sigh,
While above, afire from the setting sun,
    Flaming red appears the sky.

Why does his lament resound so tearfully?
And his breast throb with such pain?
At this eventide he wishes prayerfully
    To relive some hours again.

All that he recalls with pain or joyously,
All on which Love once her faith upreared,
Dimly, like a dream, slips by him, hopelessly
    Flaring once,—then disappears . . .

All that bears the stamp of the indelible
Into this last song the white swan pours,
As forgiveness for the unforgivable
    Of his lov'd lake he implores.

And when stars begin to glimmer distantly,
And the hazy fallow mists appear,
Softer, sadder comes the song—more poignantly,
    And the rushes swish austere.

For it is no longer now a living swan
Sobbing in this final hour of Death;
Faced by peace eternal, he, the pleading one,
    Glimpsed truth with his dying breath.[28]

---

[28] K. D. Bal'mont, *Polnoe sobranie stikhov* (4th ed.; Moscow, 1914) I, 61–62.

24 The Frenzied Poets

Yet Balmont's very strength, his lyricism, proved to be his most glaring weakness. For the sake of melody he sacrificed thought, content, and artistic restraint. In "The Swan," for example, by adding the last stanza, Balmont violates one of the first canons of symbolism: to be vague rather than obvious; to hint, rather than point. So long as the music of his lyrics was new, his poetry retained its charm; but when the novelty of his mellifluous verses eventually wore off, and his poetry brought nothing new in content, the public saw a nightingale, stripped of his feathers. To Balmont might well apply the famous verses of Igor Severyanin (pseudonym of Igor Lotaryov, 1887–1942), his most successful and ambitious imitator:

> I am a nightingale, and therefore,
> I fear, no sense I yield but song;
> I am so senselessly miraculous,
> That reason bows and comes along.

However, in the 1890's Balmont was a distinct asset to the movement. His knowledge of Western modernism, his individuality, his lack of emotional self-discipline, his romantic personality, secured for him a well-fitting niche among the Moscow symbolists, who believed that the eccentricities and excesses of their verses should be fused into their daily lives.[29] Bryusov and the other young symbolists claimed Balmont as "one of us." Balmont acknowledged the favor by readily admitting that he was a disciple of the "new art."

Gradually the symbolist movement gathered impetus. More and more of the better young poets began to align themselves with the new cause, and openly to acknowledge the epithets "decadent" and "symbolist." Fyodor Sologub (pseudonym of F. K. Teternikov), Zinaida Hippius-Merezhovsky, Alexander Dobrolyubov, Viktor Hoffman, Ivan Konevskoy (pseudonym of I. I. Oreus) admitted that a mutual bond existed between them and such avowed symbolists as Bryusov, Balmont, and Miropolsky.

---

[29] *Nekropol'*, pp. 7–25.

Of the entire "strange species ... who called themselves Russian symbolists," probably the most extreme in his philosophy of literature and life was Alexander Dobrolyubov. Like Balmont, Bryusov, and other budding symbolists, he tried to live a life that should be as bizarre as his writings. Dobrolyubov's strange behavior appealed to the other young eccentrics. On making his acquaintance Bryusov, for example, wrote that he was "charmed" by this youth of eighteen, who not only behaved oddly, but also "drank opium, and in general conducted himself like a real arch-symbolist."[30] Dobrolyubov's unconventional actions as much as his peculiar, unintelligible, and utterly unpoetic "verses," soon won him (and, incidentally, the modernist cause) a considerable following—particularly among impressionable high-school girls and young college women. Dobrolyubov lived in a small attic, the ceiling of which he had papered in black.[31] Scattered throughout his room were a "number of queer symbolic objects," which, on the authority of Dobrolyubov himself, were used in his black masses dedicated to the worship of Satan. In these surroundings Dobrolyubov received his friends and young admirers and held long discussions on various strange, often morbid subjects which he discussed in odd, obscure phrases. Before long the authorities discovered that a number of his young feminine followers had apparently taken too seriously his words on the "beauty of death," one of his favorite topics, and had committed suicide. Consequently, Dobrolyubov was obliged to leave Moscow university.[32] In the closing years of the nineteenth century, the period that marked the beginnings of the "God-seeking" movement (*Bogoistakelstvo*) among the Russian intelligentsia, Dobrolyubov suddenly turned mystic. Yet even here he preserved his individualism, for while the majority of the intelligentsia sought their god in the comfort of small

---

[30] Briusov, *Dnevniki*, pp. 17–18.   [31] *Vengerov*, I, 264 ff.
[32] *Ibid.*, 268; also Z. N. Gippius, "Filosofiia liubvi," *Mir Iskusstva* (May, 1901), 28–33.

circles and societies, Dobrolyubov accepted no such half measures. Following the tradition of the old Russian holy men, he encased his body in iron hoops and proceeded on foot to the Solovetsky Monastery in the far north of Russia. He did not, however, remain there long, but soon left the brotherhood and began wandering up and down the plains of Russia, preaching, in imitation of St. Francis, a gospel of love for "brother man," "brother beast," and even "brother thunder" and other "brother" elements of nature.[33] Eventually he founded an anarchist, pacifist, religious sect of his own. For his convictions he was exiled several times to Siberia. Finally he dropped out of sight.[34]

The end of the nineteenth century was distinguished by other events, more significant in the history of Russian literature and the evolution of symbolism than an individual "poet's" sudden turn to mysticism and away from literature. In 1898 the *Northern Messenger*, which for nearly a decade had provided a safe harbor for modernist prose and poetry, went bankrupt, as already noted. Despite the fact that the collapse of the *Northern Messenger* had left its publisher with a large debt, another modernist periodical immediately came into being. It was the lavishly printed *World of Art* (*Mir Iskusstva*, 1899–1904),[35] which was backed by the wealthy Moscow merchant Savva Mamontov (1852–1918) and the Princess Tenishev, two well-known patrons of the modern arts.

Whereas the *Northern Messenger* had given the greater part of its space to literature, the *World of Art* concentrated on raising its readers' appreciation of painting, sculpture, and architecture, particularly those of the modern schools, which were at that time little known in Russia. The leading spirit of the editorial staff was Sergei P. Dyagilev (*b.* 1872), the "Diaghileff" who later won fame abroad for his Russian Ballet. Dyagilev gathered about him a group of enthusiastic modern

---
[33] Gippius, *op. cit.*, p. 31. [34] Briusov, *Dnevniki*, pp. 149–150.
[35] P. P. Pertsov, *Literaturnye vospominaniia* (Leningrad, 1933), pp. 272–308.

painters and art critics, the most energetic among whom were the young painter-critic Alexander Benois (*b.* 1870) and another modernist painter, Leon S. Bakst (1866–1925). The profusely illustrated periodical which these men edited knit the modernist movement in Russian art into one cohesive force, and propagandized modern art so effectively that it soon won a comparatively large following. Even when in 1903 Mamontov and Princess Tenishev withdrew their financial support of the periodical, Dyagilev soon secured a new backer for his venture. The new Maecenas was none other than Tsar Nicholas II, who at that time was having his portrait painted by another member of the *World of Art* group, Valentin Serov (1861–1911). Nicholas continued his support of the periodical until 1904, when the Russo-Japanese war forced him to discontinue his aid. Although the editors soon received other offers of support, they decided to abandon their venture.

Though the *World of Art* was primarily concerned with the plastic arts, it was also willing to open its pages to the symbolist writers. Chiefly through the influence of D. V. Filosofov, a close friend of both Dyagilev and Merezhkovsky, it became the first periodical to accept from them not only poetry and fiction, which had been welcomed by the *Northern Messenger*, but even their critical and theoretical articles.

By the time the *World of Art* discontinued publication, symbolism had entered a new phase. Although it had crystallized as a trend in literature that stressed the use of symbols as a literary method, it had also split into several rival "schools." Because as a literary movement symbolism comprised poets who were above all else individualists, it harbored considerable differences of opinion as to the aims of symbolism and as to its interpretation. The growth of mutually opposed factions within the movement began to reveal itself even earlier, towards the end of the 1890's. Some of the symbolists declared that their interests lay in the problems of religion and

28   The Frenzied Poets

philosophy, while others appeared concerned solely with the aesthetic aspects of modernism.

The cleavage between the rival factions has often been represented as a geographical phenomenon. St. Petersburg had come to connote the "mystical" trend in Russian symbolism as exemplified by the Neo-Christian groups of philosophers and theologians who gathered at the Merezhovsky apartment, and by the "mystical anarchists" or "collective individualists" who met in Vyacheslav Ivanov's famous penthouse apartment, known as the "Tower," for early morning revels. Moscow, on the other hand, had been usually associated with the "aesthetic" and "decadent" trends, which Bryusov succeeded in uniting about the Scorpio publishing company. Although such a classification might simplify a general analysis of the symbolist movement, it fails to give an accurate picture. It ignores the fact that the spiritual father of the mystic trends in Russian modernist literature, Vladimir Sergeyevich Solovyov, was by birth and rearing a Muscovite himself, the son of a distinguished professor of Russian history at Moscow university. Another argument against the geographical classification is the fact that mere adherence to any one group did not preclude a writer from associating with other symbolist groups. Vyacheslav Ivanov, for example, was coleader (with Georgy Chulkov) of "mystical anarchism," a St. Petersburg faction of symbolism; yet the periodical that often published the work of that faction, the *Golden Fleece* (*Zolotoye Runo*), was published in Moscow, and even Ivanov himself published verses in the *Balance* (*Vesy*), a monthly publication that was inimical to the *Golden Fleece*. A factor that further complicates the picture is that Ivanov himself was born in Moscow, had graduated from Moscow university, and had at one time studied under Vladimir Solovyov. Boris Bugayev, a native of Moscow and a leading theoretician and critic of the *Balance*, associated himself not only with the "Scorpions" (the followers of Bryusov, and so called after the name of the publishing house) and the "Argonauts" (a Moscow group of modernists who were followers of Vladimir Solovyov), but also with the Merezhkovsky and the Ivanov groups in St. Petersburg.

The course of symbolism as a literary movement, which endured, roughly, until 1909, is rather well reflected by the periodicals that the rival factions supported. The *New Path* (*Novy Put'*, 1903–1904), *Questions of Life* (*Voprosy Zhizni*, 1905), *Divide* (*Pereval*, 1907) were publications of the "God seekers"; the *Balance* (*Vesy*, 1904–1909) was a monthly organ of the "Scorpions," sometimes also referred to as the "Moscow aesthetes"; the *Golden Fleece* (*Zolotoye Runo*, 1906–1909), a monthly, was published by the Ivanov-Chulkov group; *Northern Flowers* (*Sievernye Tsvety*, 1901–1904) was an annual miscellany, published by the Scorpio press; the *Gryphon* (*Grif*, 1903–1905) was a rival Moscow miscellany printed annually by the publishing house of the same name; *Torches* (*Fakely*, 1906–1907) was the miscellany of the "mystical anarchists"; and finally *Apollo* (*Apollon*, 1909–1917) was the organ of the "clarists" and, later, of the "acmeists."

A better and more complete picture of the movement may be obtained, however, from an analysis of the interrelations that existed between the dominant personalities of Russian symbolism. From the beginning of the twentieth century until the symbolist movement disintegrated, its outstanding personalities were Merezhkovsky, Hippius, Bryusov, Ivanov, Blok, and Andrey Biely. The personal biography of Andrey Biely links these personalities. It best reflects the interrelations of the various rival symbolist factions, and the turbulent course of the symbolist movement in Russia from 1902 to its close in 1909.

By tracing the personal development of Andrey Biely and his relations with the other leading Russian symbolists, we shall obtain a picture of the entire symbolist movement.

PART II

BORIS NIKOLAYEVICH BUGAYEV

3

CHILDHOOD

IF ONE CAN ASSUME that a man's childhood environment determines his character and molds his philosophical outlook, then Andrey Biely came by his personality and *Weltanschauung* quite naturally. "Andrey Biely" was born in Moscow on October 14 (old style), 1880,[1] as Boris Nikolayevich Bugayev. From his earliest childhood he felt that everything in his surroundings stressed the dualistic nature of existence. To begin with, since his parents had ever impressed him that they were *two* individuals rather than *one* family, the child came to realize how ill-suited a couple were his father and mother. In his reminiscences he records that it would have been difficult to find two people so unlike each other as his parents.[2]

Nikolay Vasilievich Bugayev, Biely's father, was professor of mathematics at Moscow university and a scholar of international reputation.[3] He had also achieved considerable distinction as an eccentric, as a man whose physical ugliness, intellectual brilliance, and unexpected behavior made him a near-legendary figure of Moscow intellectual circles.[4]

Alexandra Dmitrievna Bugayev (born Yegorov) was in almost every respect the complete antithesis of her illustrious husband. Whereas Professor Bugayev was physically unattractive, Mme. Bugayev, who was more than thirty years his junior, prided herself on being regarded as one of the most beautiful women in Moscow.[5] The popular Russian painter of

---
[1] *Vengerov,* III, 9.   [4] *Nekropol',* p. 63.
[2] *Na rubezhe,* p. 71.   [5] *Ibid.; Na rubezhe,* p. 78.
[3] V. G. Alekseev, *N. V. Bugaev* (Iur'ev, 1905).

the end of the nineteenth century, Konstantin Makovsky, is believed to have copied her features for his painting "The Bride at the Wedding Feast."[6] She was a typical social butterfly, a capricious, spoiled, self-willed little girl who refused to grow up and accept the responsibilities of a wife and mother. Since she had been reared in an atmosphere of adoration, she felt that her husband was neglecting her because of his mathematics. This bred resentment, which eventually developed into jealousy of all intellectual activity, the more so because her husband would often seek refuge from his home environment by fleeing to his university study. When the baby was born, the mother resolved that she would not lose a second member of her family to science,[7] and that the child, *her* child (*"Ty moy kot!"* "You're my cat!") should not be permitted to follow in his father's footsteps. Professor Bugayev's remark, made half in jest, that he "hoped that Boris would take after his mother in looks, but after himself in intellect,"[8] only strengthened her resolve.

Before Boris was three, he had become acutely conscious of the family conflict that raged over him. The struggle, not always silent, between his father and mother as to who should spiritually dominate his life produced in him an early division of loyalties to his parents, the "nightmare of scissors," which haunted Boris throughout childhood and early adolescence. The boy felt an instinctive affection for his father, yet felt that he owed allegiance to his mother, the more so since she had impressed upon him that he was *her* possession, *hers* to deal with as she pleased.[9] To her mind, there could be no split allegiance!

Nevertheless, Boris felt a strong natural kinship with his father since Professor Bugayev's intellect was an inexhaustible source of factual knowledge for the imaginative and curious child. Moreover, Boris sensed that he and his father were fellow

---

[6] *Na rubezhe*, p. 78.
[7] *Na rubezhe*, pp. 163 ff.; cf. also *Kotik Letaev*, *passim*.
[8] *Nekropol'*, pp. 64–65.   [9] *Na rubezhe*, p. 181.

sufferers subjected to his mother's frequent displays of temper and hysterics. To him the eccentricities of his father's behavior often appeared as a vicarious rebellion against his surroundings. Subconsciously recognizing a common bond between himself and his father, Boris longed to emulate him. For his mother Boris felt an unaccountable, vague compassion; it was in the nature of an uncontrollable longing to protect and comfort a beautiful, sensitive, aesthetically appealing yet often unhappy, neurotic young woman. Boris felt a vague guilt toward his mother; that in admitting inwardly an affinity with his father, he was denying his mother her due as her "cat" (*kot*). His sense of guilt toward his mother further increased as he realized that he was the prime cause of her unhappiness, and that were it not for him, his parents might be free to separate.[10] His mother sensed Boris' natural inclination toward his father, and reacted accordingly.

Determined to have no "second mathematician" in the family, Mme. Bugayev resolved to retard the intellectual development of her "kitten" (*kotik*, diminutive for *kot*).[11] The mere thought that Professor Bugayev might succeed in influencing his son, would send her into hysterics. Fearing that the child might develop into a scientist if left to associate with his father, she would become unstrung and would threaten to leave her husband and take the boy with her. Professor Bugayev's booming, emphatic "never!" would then touch off the battle between the "gladiator and the lioness," while the trembling child, torn in his loyalties, would crouch huddled up in a corner of the living room and "await the end of the world."[12]

Thus, early in life, Boris began to distinguish between the security of his calm and serene nursery, where he was left happily alone; and the terror of the "other world," that of his father and mother, and of people in general, the "outer" world

[10] *Ibid.*, p. 72.
[11] *Ibid.*, p. 73.
[12] *Ibid.*, p. 79.

of bickering and strife, that filled him with dread and abhorrence, and even with a sense of guilt. He recalls the shock that this outer world invariably produced on him:

> As a child I would thrust my way into the environment of the outer world—our apartment, and, frightened by it, I would crawl back into my hole—the nursery.[13]

The parents' conflicting personalities made the boy's development extremely difficult. At every turn his mother would try to arouse a feeling of shame and guilt in the child for being like his father. Any sign of native intellect on his part would evoke from his beautiful mother a venomous "Ugh! A second bulgy-headed mathematician!" In an effort to circumvent such censure the boy developed a dual personality. He appeased his mother by habitually hiding behind a cloak of feigned stupidity, which he rarely shed, unless alone with his father.[14] Friends of the family, for the most part members of the Moscow academic circle, were often amazed by the child's apparent imbecility. On visiting the Bugayevs they would tactlessly voice their surprise within earshot of the boy: "My, isn't that Bugayev youngster a little idiot, though!"[15] The sensitive child naturally resented such remarks. In revenge for such humiliations, Boris would then exploit his mask. Hiding under his guise of idiocy, he would naïvely remark to the offender: "Look, Professor Blank, you have a big wart on the end of your nose!" And the "little idiot" soon became known as the "ill-bred little idiot."[16] Small wonder that a child reared under such conditions should acquire a thorough dislike of all professors, and of everything that they, as a group, represented. Boris' retaliation thus often reminded him of his father, whose pranks he regarded as tokens of inward rebellion against the mother's authority. Since, however, rebellious acts invariably

---
[13] *Ibid.*, p. 163.
[14] *Ibid.*, p. 115.
[15] *Ibid.*; cf. also *Vengerov*, III, 9–10.
[16] *Na rubezhe*, p. 115.

brought censure and a reiteration of social canons ("you must be like everyone else"),[17] the standards and ideals of the academic circle, as well as everything that it held venerable, eventually became odious to him. Everything about his home environment seemed obnoxious. Its atmosphere stifled him. Ultimately it bred open rebellion and, meanwhile, it suggested to the child various avenues of escape.

Fortunately for the boy's intellectual development, his mother engaged a nurse for him. Nurses are in the habit of telling fairy tales to their charges, and—like Pushkin's famous Arina Rodionovna—Boris' nurse was no exception. She introduced him to a new world, a world of mystery and imagination, a world of thrills and horrors, a world that provided Boris with the escape for which he longed. He soon realized that in the world of his own imagination he knew no outer restraint. He was master there! He could play being bogey man, and none would restrain him, because no bogey man actually existed.[18] Yet he dared not play being a real person like his aunt Maria (M. I. Lyaskovskaya), whom everyone in the household feared, and who, therefore, was an actual bogey. Therefore, the boy made it a habit of vanishing into this world of make-believe. No sooner, however, had his mother discovered that her son had found through imaginative play a method of stimulating his mind, than she put an end to the fairy tales and replaced the offending nurse with an "unimaginative, sober-minded German girl."[19] But servants rarely stayed long with the Bugayev household and the German girl too, fortunately for the child, was soon discharged.

At the age of three, the boy was placed under the tutelage of his first governess. Boris Bugayev carried a fond memory all his life of his Raisa Ivanovna. In his autobiographical tale *Kitten Letayev* (*Kotik Letayev*), he exclaims of her, "that

[17] *Ibid.*, p. 41.
[18] *Ibid.*, p. 164.
[19] *Ibid.*, p. 174.

dear!"[20] and in his memoirs, written a few years before his death, he records that "everywhere, constantly, next to me was the dear, gay, fairy-like Raisa Ivanovna."[21] She was the first human being who gave him real companionship. Unlike his parents, who, Boris felt, regarded him as little more than a source of quarrel, Raisa Ivanovna immediately became the boy's elder playmate. She came to symbolize the security that the boy lacked in his abnormal home surroundings. She made him feel quite at ease with her, as though there were "something cozy" about her personality. She would play with him, read to him, and keep him amused and interested. And she brought to him a new world—that of poetry. Often she would read to him verses of the German romanticists—Uhland, Heine, Eichendorff:[22]

> In the evenings Raisa Ivanovna would read to me of boats, swans.... I would not understand a thing and yet it all seemed wonderful.[23]

Thus Boris soon came to associate the rhythm and melody of poetry with the sense of security that Raisa Ivanovna gave him. Although he could not grasp the thread of the the narrative, he was deeply moved by the music of poetry.[24] This sudden awareness of poetry was further augmented by an appreciation also of music itself. At twilight as the child would lie in his bed, in the secure isolation of his nursery, he would hear his mother playing the piano. Her favorite selections, the sonatas of Beethoven, the nocturnes of Chopin, and the Lieder of Schumann and Schubert,[25] excited the small boy's imagination and aesthetic response, and filled him with an unaccountable inner satisfaction.

---

[20] *Kotik Letaev*, p. 99.   [21] *Na rubezhe*, p. 183.
[22] The German romantics appealed also to Alexander Blok. (See Fidler, *Pervye literaturnye shagi*, p. 85.) Blok, however, became acquainted with them through the Russian translations of Zhukovskii.
[23] *Na rubezhe*, pp. 174–175.   [25] *Na rubezhe*, p. 177.
[24] *Vengerov*, III, 10–11.

Childhood 39

Music and poetry helped Boris to resurrect his earlier glimpses of his fairy world. Thus, long before he read Schopenhauer, he felt that the real, the acceptable world was the world of music, which was "a product of his imagination."[26] Forbidden to acquire factual knowledge, his mind now found fancy-created new worlds that provided him with an escape from his home environment. Continuous flight from reality into a world of imagination, however, overstimulated the child's intellect and brought with it nightmares, as well as escape. Before long the high-strung boy was on the verge of a nervous collapse. As a consequence Raisa Ivanovna had to go the way of her predecessors, and with her went the poetry and the fairy tales, which the family physician, Dr. Rodionov (a representative of the physical sciences and, therefore, of a positivist philosophy), declared had been injurious to Boris' health.[27]

The horror of reality returned. One governess followed another. The fairy tales were gone; all that remained of Boris' dream world was music, the sonatas and nocturnes that his mother played.[28] The boy returned to his disguise of idiocy.

By the time Boris was six, even his mother was convinced that her Kitten had been sufficiently retarded mentally, and decided to try her hand at educating him. As one may readily imagine she had no aptitude whatever as a teacher and, when lesson after lesson proved a complete failure, Mme. Bugayev's hysterical scenes became more a matter of routine than ever before.[29] She refused to believe that the failure lay with herself. Since she continually screamed of his stupidity, Boris, convinced that his adored mother could not possibly be wrong, began to develop a serious inferiority complex. He felt that he must be "astonishingly stupid"—too stupid ever to learn anything, far less complete his schooling.[30]

[26] Ibid., p. 182.
[27] Ibid.
[28] Ibid., p. 203.
[29] Ibid., p. 204.
[30] Ibid., p. 212.

The Frenzied Poets

Not until the boy was eight, did his mother even partially remove her quarantine on his father and at last permit Professor Bugayev to give his son lessons in arithmetic and grammar. Although the elder Bugayev was a scholar and teacher of vast experience, he failed to realize that the boy needed most of all security and companionship. Despite the fact that lessons with his father progressed more satisfactorily than they had with his mother, Boris, who had become allergic to learning, made little progress.[31] He might well have fallen in a psychopathological condition had fate not sent him another friend in his new governess, Belle Radin.[32]

Mlle. Radin quickly sensed what the boy was experiencing, and adopted toward him an attitude of a sympathetic friend and equal, rather than that of a governess. She realized that Boris was not the little idiot he pretended to be, and that the mask of a fool had become a habit with him. Patiently she began to draw him out of himself. Under her encouragement Boris gradually began to emerge from his shell. Heretofore he had always been without playmates. Boys of his own age had refused to play with an eight-year-old who still wore curls—for his mother insisted that his forehead ("the bulging forehead of a second mathematician!") must be hidden.

But with the advent of the new governess the situation changed. Wherever Boris' governess went, she won friends not only for herself, but for him as well. Best of all, however, was the fact that now the parents did not interfere with Mlle. Radin's methods of rearing the child.[33] Like two of her predecessors, the boy's first nurse and Raisa Ivanovna, Mlle. Radin encouraged him to develop his imagination. But she discarded fairy tales and introduced him to such red-blooded authors as Jules Verne, Mayne Reade, and James Fenimore Cooper, whom they read together in French.[34] Boris regarded his new governess as a savior, and under her guidance began to advance

[31] *Ibid.*, p. 214.
[32] *Ibid.*, p. 73.
[33] *Ibid.*, pp. 216–217.
[34] *Ibid.*, pp. 213–214.

intellectually as well as spiritually. Although he could not immediately shed his inhibitions and complexes, he now developed far more normally than hitherto. Boris always remembered Mlle. Radin's four-year stay—until his second year in the gymnasium—as a slow "emancipation" from the bonds of his home environment.[85]

Meanwhile, Professor and Mme. Bugayev renewed their feud over the boy. Now they began to quarrel over the choice of a gymnasium for him. His mother had her mind set on the fashionable Polivanov school, while his father insisted that the boy attend the First State Gymnasium, the school from which he himself had graduated with a gold medal and a straight "A" record (for the entire eight-year curriculum).[86] For once it was fortunate for Boris that Mme. Bugayev's whim prevailed, and in September, 1891, Boris Bugayev was enrolled as a pupil of Lev Ivanovich Polivanov.[87]

Polivanov proved an inspiring teacher, and under his encouragement the former "little idiot" quickly became the outstanding pupil in his class.[88] But Boris' triumph was short-lived. After a successful first year his interest in studying began to wane, and eventually he relapsed into his former state of "idiocy."[89] An important reason for the apparent intellectual relapse was that the boy had lost the encouraging support of Mlle. Radin. When Boris entered the second grade, his parents decided that the governess had fulfilled her mission and discharged her, and when she was gone the boy returned into the former state of insecurity and inferiority. Nor were all his teachers as inspiring and sympathetic as Polivanov. His Latin teacher, for example, was particularly indifferent to the boy's progress. The teacher's lack of enthusiasm brought a corresponding decline of interest in Boris, at first toward Latin, then

[85] *Ibid.*, pp. 225–226.
[86] *Ibid.*
[87] *Ibid.*, p. 260; *Vengerov*, III, 10.
[88] *Na rubezhe*, p. 307.
[89] *Ibid.*, pp. 308, ff.

toward other subjects as well. Professor Bugayev, unable to understand his son's apparent delinquency, began once more to chide Boris for his stupidity. The boy's self-confidence, which Mlle. Radin had taken such care to build up, soon vanished, and a number of years had to pass before Boris began once more to feel sure of himself.[40]

Despite young Bugayev's apparent lack of interest in his studies, the Polivanov school had a great influence on the boy's mental development. It gave his natural bent for knowledge an opportunity to develop unhampered. At home, on the other hand, the atmosphere was quite different. His parents completely failed to understand the youth's wants. The example of his father's achievements in the world of science had filled Boris with a desire to read the works of such men as Darwin and Bacon; of various zoölogists, botanists, and meteorologists. Although many such books could be found in his father's study, none of them was offered to him. Like many other hypersensitive children, Boris could not, or would not, bring himself to ask for them, and his conscience prevented him from reading them "on the sly."[41] Then one day new horizons unexpectedly emerged before him. He discovered a new interest which soon overshadowed everything else. It led him to commit an act which to him seemed a horrible crime, *The Crime of Nicholas Letayev*, as he eventually recorded it in an autobiographical novelette.[42]

"One miserable autumn day" Boris strayed off his usual route to school and found himself standing in front of the Ostrovsky Library.[43] He suddenly decided that he might just as well come a "couple of stupid hours late to school" and spend

---
[40] *Ibid.*
[41] *Ibid.*, p. 327.
[42] The incident is described in *Na rubezhe*, pp. 329–334, and is the central theme of Belyi's *Prestuplenie Nikolaia Letaeva*, later renamed *Kreshchenyi kitaets*. Khodasevich in *Nekropol'*, interpreting Belyi's fiction in the light of the Oedipus complex, states that the plot originally called for parricide, a supposition which Belyi refutes indirectly in his memoirs.
[43] *Na rubezhe*, p. 330.

that time in looking over the library's catalogue. The first titles that he chanced upon were some dramas of Ibsen. He took out "The Warrior's Barrow," opened its pages, "and—was lost." Instead of staying the intended two hours, he stayed six reading Ibsen. The following day he simply had to return to the library to finish another Ibsen drama; no sooner was that accomplished, than he plunged into Dostoyevsky's *Crime and Punishment;* then came the *Idiot.* Fifty successive days his reading orgy continued. Boris' experience of these fifty days was "like being born completely anew."[44] During that time the youth, who had hitherto known practically nothing of literature, read "Ibsen, Hauptmann, Sudermann, all of Dostoevsky, all of Turgenev, Goncharov, Goethe's *Faust,* Hegel's *Aesthetics,* ... Fet, Polonsky, Pushkin, Nekrasov, Nadson ... the complete set of the *Northern Messenger;* he discovered Sologub ... Bunin ... Hippius."[45] The writings of these authors, plus the works of Schopenhauer, Belinsky, and Ruskin, which he read later, laid the foundation for his philosophy of life: the *Weltanschauung* of a symbolist.[46] Then came the day of reckoning; at the end of fifty days he was discovered. He felt as though within him "Cain had killed Abel—the purity of (his) conscience." Soon Professor Bugayev and Polivanov were holding a "long conference." While the boy suffered mental anguish, his fate was being decided, and he was genuinely surprised to learn that he had been pardoned.[47]

The boy's "crime" practically determined the course of his future. Problems of the natural sciences, which had once so keenly attracted him, now suddenly lost their lure. Problems of aesthetics, modernism, and romantic philosophy now became paramount. Art had displaced science.

Soon another event of great importance to Boris Bugayev's future took place. In 1893 the family of M. S. Solovyov moved into the same apartment house in which the Bugayevs lived.

---

[44] *Ibid.*
[45] *Ibid.,* p. 331.
[46] *Na rubezhe,* p. 331.
[47] *Ibid.,* p. 332.

Mikhail Sergeyevich Solovyov was the brother of the mystic poet-philosopher Vladimir Solovyov whom Boris had often seen at his parents' afternoon and evening teas, but whom he really came to know only at the home of Mikhail and his wife, the charming Olga Mikhailovna. The advent of the Solovyovs opened a new chapter in Boris Bugayev's life.

Mikhail Solovyov became a second father for Boris, and his wife replaced Mlle. Radin. She became the woman to whom Boris would now turn for sympathy and security.

4

BORIS BUGAYEV AND THE SOLOVYOVS

IN HIS MEMOIRS Boris Bugayev refuses openly to acknowledge that his mother played the dominant role in forming his character; nevertheless, anyone reading the chapters describing his childhood will readily see that she played the leading part in shaping his life and his mental outlook. Boris intimately associated the world that lay outside his person with the personality of his mother. Early in life he learned that this outer material world was the real one, as contrasted with his own, inner world of make-believe. Yet the insecurity and tension that he felt emanating from that outer world, the world of his mother, filled him with apprehension, and aroused a desire to flee from its reality, and thus to escape from his mother. The attitude of neurotic, capricious Mme. Bugayev toward her son prompted him to turn to other women for comfort, security, and appreciation. The boy found such solace first with Raisa Ivanovna, then Mlle. Radin, and later Olga Mikhailovna Solovyov. In his relations with these women, he found nourishment that his ego craved, and which he missed in his associations with his mother. Even as a man, Boris Bugayev sought similar companionship from women, beginning with Zinaida Hippius and her sisters, and continuing with Margarita Morozov and Asya Turgenev, each of whom became something like a substitute mother to him. Furthermore, he found welcome support from them in his effort to reject the reality of the oppressive outer world, and with it, of course, his mother.

46 The Frenzied Poets

Boris Bugayev regarded three persons as his early "companions in life": Professor Bugayev, his father; Lev Ivanovich Polivanov, his teacher; and Mikhail Sergeyevich Solovyov, his friend. These three men, if we may trust Bugayev's own statement, molded his life and left their imprint on it.[1] His antagonism toward his mother apparently reached such proportions that he excluded not only her but all members of her sex from the category of "life companion," an obvious fallacy in view of the major part that women played in his life.

For him each of the three men was a "mold of a different sort" that determined the contours in which his character was destined to emerge. Professor Bugayev was a "convex mold" that aggressively impressed its many protrusions on the "soft wax of Boris' personality." As a human being, Professor Bugayev "completely enthralled his son";[2] his every mannerism, every eccentricity etched itself indelibly on the boy's impressionable mind. His father was unlike the placid, run-o'-the-mill average human being. Since the boy from early childhood had developed an inclination toward the unusual, unconventional, and bizarre, Professor Bugayev's idiosyncrasies so appealed to Boris that eventually he imitated his father's mannerisms. In speaking, for example, Boris Bugayev never remained still, but, like his father, accompanied each word with small gestures of his hands, facial contortions, and Zarathustra-like pirouettes. So strong was the impression that his father made on him, that, in many of Boris Bugayev's prose works, one of the central characters is an eccentric individual with but slightly disguised traits of the elder Bugayev; Professors Letayev and Korobkin, and to a lesser extent (chiefly in manner of speech) the elder Ableukhov,[3] reflect the personality of Professor Bugayev. But even though Professor Bugayev unconsciously attracted the boy, he was essentially a "convex mold" that pro-

---
[1] *Na rubezhe*, p. 361 ff.   [2] *Nekropol'*, pp. 66–68.
[3] Cf. Professor Letaev in *Kotik Letaev* and *Kreshchenyi kitaets*; Professor Korobkin in *Moskva* and *Maski*; and to a certain extent Senator Ableukhov in *Petersburg*.

duced "concave" impressions on his son's will. The boy responded antagonistically, and the resulting print was "negative, rather than positive." Although Professor Bugayev did not encroach upon Boris' freedom in larger matters, he did "unbearably interfere in the trifles," and this officiousness, however well-intended, invariably aroused opposition rather than coöperation in his son. Thus, Professor Bugayev prevailed upon his son to matriculate in the College of Natural Sciences, yet, because he tried to direct Boris into mathematics, the young man fled into geography. When the father came to the boy "with a volume of Spencer," the son "plunged into art." Each time his father attempted to force Boris into any direction, the youth reacted negatively, often even against his own natural inclination.[4]

Boris' second guide was Lev Ivanovich Polivanov. He was at once "convex" and "concave." His "convexity" lay in his active instruction, in his lectures and classroom work, when he guided his pupils' minds into certain channels. His "concavity" lay in his gift of listening to his pupils during his conferences with them, and in drawing ideas out of them.

Mikhail Sergeyevich Solovyov was Boris' "third companion" in life. He was "entirely concave," and was the "plaster of Paris cast" that brought out all the positive contours in the boy's character. Solovyov, therefore, played an outstanding role in the youth's development, and herein the Solovyov family aided him greatly.

The name Solovyov has left an enviable record in the annals of Russian culture. Sergey Mikhailovich Solovyov (1820–1879) was the first Russian historian of international stature. No less than four of his children were active in the fields of literature and philosophy. Vsevolod Sergeyevich (1849–1903) was a popular writer of historical novels. Poliksena Sergeyevna (1867–1924) was a poet who, under the pseudo-

[4] *Na rubezhe*, p. 362.

nym Allegro, also achieved national recognition. The historian's most illustrious offspring was the poet and mystic philosopher, Vladimir Sergeyevich (1853–1900), who has already been mentioned; he was not only the spiritual father of the twentieth-century Russian symbolist movement, but the founder of twentieth-century Russian religious philosophy. Finally, Mikhail Sergeyevich (1862–1903), who became young Bugayev's closest friend, collaborated with his brother in translating and editing the *Dialogues* of Plato.

A few months after Mlle. Radin had left the Bugayev household, new tenants moved into the apartment below the one which the Bugayevs occupied.[5] One day while playing at the entrance of the house, Boris noticed a "short, respectable-looking gentleman" getting out of a sleigh; he was in his middle thirties, and his most distinguishing features were a "long, pale nose, and a golden goatee." The door that swallowed the stranger bore a new shiny brass plate, which informed the curious Boris that his new neighbor was Mikhail Sergeyevich Solovyov. Before long Boris began encountering an "odd, yet ... cozy-looking" lady at the door of the Solovyov apartment. "The huge brown hat ... that hid most of her long, weather-beaten face and tight-set mouth" interested him immensely. His mother told him that the strange lady, Mme. Solovyov, was a painter and writer. Boris soon discovered also that the Solovyovs had a son, Sergey, who was several years his junior. Whereas the older Solovyovs appealed to Boris and piqued his curiosity, their son impressed Boris unfavorably because of the hauteur, dignity, and aloofness with which he conducted himself in church.

Boris' actual acquaintance with the new neighbors came through Mme. Bugayev. One day the Solovyovs called on their neighbors. Olga Mikhailovna Solovyov explained that she wished to paint a portrait of the beautiful Mme. Bugayev. The

[5] *Ibid.*, p. 354 ff.

request flattered Mme. Bugayev, who quickly assented and, thereafter, began visiting the Solovyov flat for daily sittings. Naturally, the new neighbors impressed Boris' mother very favorably. Each day she would return singing new praises of them. "Olga Mikhailovna is *so* interesting!" and "little Seryozha is simply adorable!" "Oh, Kitten," she would exclaim, "if you would only get acquainted with them!" One day Mme. Bugayev invited Seryozha to call on them, much to the dismay of Boris, who considered anyone of Seryozha's age a mere child (he was eight, almost five years younger than Boris). The meeting, however, proved unexpectedly pleasant, for Seryozha established himself as a precocious child who had, moreover, tastes similar to those of Boris.[6]

Within a few days Boris returned the call. M. and Mme. Solovyov shook hands with him in greeting, and their gesture was devoid of the air of condescension that Boris encountered at home, among the professorial acquaintances of his parents. Everyone enjoyed the visit, and before long Boris became one of the family.

At home he had had no companions. The professors and their wives who dropped in occasionally, paid homage to his parents; in their presence the boy would sit mute, his activities confined to listening to their conversation. He was well aware that his parents regarded him as a small child. At the Solovyovs', however, Boris was pleasantly astonished to find himself not only treated as an equal but actually lionized. He was made to feel important. He discovered that at the Solovyovs' everyone was eager to talk and listen to him, and to hear his opinions on various subjects. The Solovyov flat, therefore, soon became more than an escape from home. It became his "window to life."[7]

Boris liked the atmosphere at the Solovyovs'. Here was one corner where for the first time he was not belittled. On the

[6] *Ibid.*, p. 358; also *Epopeia*, I, 127.   [7] *Nachalo veka*, p. 13.

contrary, he had little attentions bestowed upon him, and was generally made to feel important. The Solovyovs' drawing room, as pleasing as the hosts themselves, soon became the center of Boris' intellectual and social life.[8] In it he soon spent all his free hours in interminable conversations with his newly discovered foster family. The Solovyovs seemed to "draw out his spiritual power." Each member of the family appealed to Boris in his own peculiar manner, which predicated the relations that he soon established with each. In Seryozha he found "a kindred spirit"; Olga Mikhailovna "stimulated his imagination"; and his "will shaped itself under the lucid . . . vision of Mikhail Sergeyevich's mind." Boris Bugayev believed that during the next seven years Mikhail Solovyov "more than anyone else transformed him from a 'little idiot' into a man of the world." Moreover, quite unlike Professor Bugayev, Solovyov "accomplished this transformation without ever exerting any force" on the youth with the result that Boris' "personality developed directly in line with Mikhail Sergeyevich's retreat." Tactfully and patiently Mikhail encouraged Boris' intellectual powers, and by listening calmly stimulated him to express his own views on all manner of subjects. "Directly along the path of Mikhail Sergeyevich's withdrawal" Boris strode toward new horizons. While the elder man sat listening, Boris would try to unravel before him his "philosophy of aesthetics, preach Schopenhauer and Kant, and plague him with the complex correlations between philosophy and the natural sciences," which he forever sought to reconcile. Probably the greatest achievement of Mikhail Solovyov was in converting the Bugayev boy to the idealistic philosophy of Vladimir Solovyov, after which "Wundt, Haeckel, Hegel, Helmholtz, Hertwig, and others faded into the background."[9] Thus Boris' earlier interest in the materialism of the physical sciences developed into an interest in the idealism of metaphysical thought. To a certain

---

[8] *Ibid.*, p. 117; *Epopeia*, I, 137–146.
[9] *Na rubezhe*, p. 361.

degree, the change symbolized a victory of the inner world of his imagination over the outer world of physical reality.

At the Solovyovs', Boris began also to develop his literary talents, and, under their encouragement, to express himself in writing. Boris found that, while at home his father ridiculed his first poetic efforts, at his foster home his friends gave generous words of praise and assurance. The calm nods of approval from Mikhail Solovyov, and his wife's more vociferous support eventually convinced him that he did possess some literary talent. Since in the eyes of Boris and Seryozha, Mikhail Solovyov was the ultimate authority in literary criticism, Boris accepted his verdicts without qualification and naturally rejoiced to find that his own work possessed literary merit.

Thanks to the Solovyovs, Boris decided that his future lay in some form of artistic endeavor, but until 1901 he wavered, uncertain in what direction he could best apply his artistic talent: whether to music, philosophy, poetry, imaginative prosé, or literary criticism, with the last two appearing least likely because he had little faith in himself as a littérateur. Then, in the spring of 1901, he read his first "symphony," a modernistic tale in poetic prose, to Mikhail Solovyov. The older man exploded in enthusiastic praise. "Boris," he exclaimed, "you are a writer!" The young man needed no more encouragement—he took his mentor at his word. His future was determined.

After Boris Bugayev had decided that literature would be his field, the question of a suitable pseudonym arose. Out of consideration for his father, then dean of the faculty of sciences at Moscow university, Boris Bugayev could not publish his "decadent," that is, unconventional and modernistic, writings under his own name. To the average man, a writer in the *style moderne* was engaged in a scandalous profession.[10]

Just as Mikhail Solovyov had decided Boris' choice of

[10] *Nachalo veka*, pp. 119–120.

52   The Frenzied Poets

career, he also determined the pen name that the young man selected—"Andrey Biely" ("Andrew the White"). Young Bugayev, true to his young and impulsive romantic nature, had first chosen "Boris Burevoy" ("Boris the Stormy") as his *nom de plume*. Mikhail Solovyov pointed out, however, that some punster might interpret the surname "Burevoy" as meaning *"Bori-voy"* ("Boris' wail") and suggested in its stead "Andrey Biely." Although in connotation the pseudonym by Solovyov was almost diametrically opposite to that which Boris Bugayev had originally selected, the young man accepted Andrey Biely without a murmur of dissent.[11]

The Solovyov family directly influenced also the mental outlook of their protégé. Whereas at home the scientific background of his father encouraged Boris to accept a materialistic concept of reality, the Solovyovs stimulated an idealistic view. The personality of Mikhail Solovyov's brother, Vladimir, played a particularly significant role in young Bugayev's spiritual development.

Boris was a mere child when he first met Vladimir Solovyov, for the philosopher used to be a frequent visitor at Madame Bugayev's Sunday afternoon teas. The air of mystery which seemed to accompany the prematurely aged man had always intrigued the small boy. There was something bizarre about this man. He was a near giant in stature, yet his long, emaciated arms betrayed a lack of physical strength; his thin spindly legs seemed disproportionately long when compared to the rest of his body; the spiritual depths reflected in his grey eyes were contradicted by the sensuous line of his large mouth. "His beautifully molded head, crowned with a shock of long grey hair and bordered by a long beard,"[12] suggested a prophet from the Bible. Yet his actions, as he would slyly dip his long fingers into a tray of chocolates, were often those of a mischievous

---
[11] *Na rubezhe*, pp. 486–487; *Nachalo veka*, p. 28.
[12] *Arabeski*, pp. 388–389.

schoolboy; and his laughter sounded like the "cackle of a demon." The duality of the philosopher's personality struck a responsive chord in the heart of Boris, who was already developing a dual nature of his own.

The eccentricities of Vladimir Solovyov's character naturally appealed to the boy, who liked anything that was out of the ordinary. At the same time, however, Solovyov perplexed the youngster. Boris was never quite certain in which of the two Vladimir Solovyovs he should believe: "Goddie" (*"Bozhenka"*) Solovyov, the character suggested by his Biblical mien; or "Bogey" (*"Buka"*) Solovyov, the personality revealed by his demoniacal laughter. He was never quite certain which of the two Solovyovs was the real one: the "helpless child . . . with the shaggy gray mane of a lion," or the "sly demon . . . with the disconcerting cackle, 'heh-heh-heh!' "

Both sides of Solovyov's nature are represented in his poetry. The struggle between the sensuous artist and the ascetic mystic is revealed in his works. Although most of his verse is striking in its spiritual intimacy, occasionally some elements arise in it that seem utterly incompatible with the general tenor of his works. Thus, alongside his serious poetry one finds humorous verse that colors his correspondence and reflects his "demoniacal" side. At times it sounds even a Rabelaisian note.

Vladimir Solovyov's humor manifested itself in his parodies on the literary atrocities of Bryusov and his Russian symbolists.[13] Another aspect of his humor, which is nearly always directed against himself and usually ridicules his own poor health (from which he suffered most of his life), appears in his ironical poems. Whenever he felt particularly depressed, either physically or spiritually, Solovyov was wont to pen a humorous jingle and send it to some friend. One such verse is contained in his letter to M. M. Stasyulevich, dated July 26, 1896.

---
[13] See chapter ii.

54 The Frenzied Poets

> Dear Mikhail Matveyevich,
> I'm writing from my cot.
> I'm doubled up from ailments,
> And full of sundry rot.[14]

Another is his own epitaph, which he sent to V. L. Velichko (September 12, 1892).

> Vladímir Solovyóv lies in this lonely spot—
> Once a philosopher—now bones is all he's got.
> Though amiable to most—to some unkind he'd been.
> Yet having loved insanely, he fell in this ravine.
> Poor man! He lost his body, he lost his soul and togs:
> The soul went to the devil, the corpse went to the dogs.
> O passerby, pray heed this terrible example!
> Eschew erotic peril! Religious faith is ample![15]

A touch of vulgarity and profanity is revealed in the following grotesque Easter greeting, sent from Cairo to Stasyulevich (April 14, 1898).

> Hristos voskrese! [Christ is arisen!]
> Here we are in Odessa...
> The wind freshens,
> And the thermometer
> Approaches zero.
> Yonder flies a flock of gulls,
> A wave looms large.
> There is friend Ernest
> Vomiting overboard
> At the sea devil.
> A fog surrounds us.
> Closer to the Bosphorus,
> The swells are lower
> And the mercury is higher...
> Yonder also are toys:
> Barracks and cannons—
> The journey is ended.[16]

---

[14] Vladimir Solov'ev, *Pis'ma* (Moscow, 1908), I, 136.
[15] *Ibid.*, p. 198.
[16] *Ibid.*, p. 144.

Bugayev and the Solovyovs

Despite the Rabelaisian element in his lighter verses, Vladimir Solovyov's humor, like his "demoniacal laughter," perhaps expresses hysteria, rather than healthy ribaldry. His humor appears to be motivated by a grim effort to escape reality. Certainly in his serious lyrics Solovyov reveals his own emotional experiences and also strives to fathom the other world—the world not of the seeming, but of ultimate realities.

Vladimir Solovyov became the most persuasive disseminator of Platonic idealism in *fin-de-siècle* Russia. His famous poem, "Friend Beloved" reveals the cardinal tenets of his philosophy. Since it echoed the ideas that many of the Russian intellectuals wished to believe in, it became the rallying poem for those who would reject the final reality of the material world:

> Friend Beloved, do you not see
> That the world that round us lies
> Is mere shadow, mere reflection
> Of what's hidden from our eyes?
>
> Friend Beloved, do you not hear
> That the grating sound of life
> Can be but distorted echoes
> Of the chords above the strife?
>
> Friend Beloved, do you not sense
> That in this world naught is real
> Save what heart to heart in greeting
> Only mutely can reveal.[17]

Again, in "The Moment" the mystic mood of Solovyov's poetry reveals itself.

The Moment

> Once more oppressive shadows overcast the sky
> With dreams that one has lived, and souls one has forgot.
> In awe the spirit bows before an unknown future
> While tears stream towards an irrevocable naught.

---

[17] Solov'ev, *Stikhotvoreniia* (6th ed.; Moscow, 1915), p. 111.

56 *The Frenzied Poets*

What has gone by and will return evokes no tears;
The moment that has perished fills one with regret.
It's gone fore'er—and slow the heavy-footed years
Are doomed eternity's fleet moment to beset.

Or is this but deceit, and is the past just shadows
Of dreams that one has lived, and souls one has forgot?
In awe the spirit bows before the unknown future
While tears stream towards an irrevocable naught.[18]

At times it is difficult to believe that the same man who wrote the jingles quoted earlier could have written "The Moment" or the tragic "White Bells Again," destined to be his swan song.

White Bells Again

During the stormy,
   Hot summer days,
Gracefully white,
   Ever unchanged.

Phantoms of Spring
   Scorched though you be!
Here are you, dreams
   Of eternity.

Evil, forgotten,
   Lies sinking in blood;
Purified rises
   The sun of love.

Daring young schemes
   In an aching heart.
Angels, white angels,
   Risen about.

Graceful, ethereal,
   Ever unphased
During these sultry
   Burdensome days.[19]

---

[18] *Ibid.*, p. 152.
[19] *Ibid.*, p. 213.

In his spiritual development, Vladimir Solovyov traversed a rocky path that led him through the chasms of unbelief to the heights of religious faith, and thereby resembles to some extent Dostoyevsky's Ivan Karamazov, whose prototype Solovyov is believed to be. After a sheltered childhood, spent in the serene pious atmosphere of his home, Solovyov as a precocious youth of fourteen suddenly lost faith in God. With almost fanatic abandon he plunged into a study of the natural sciences, embraced a positivist philosophy and militant atheism (under the influence of which he even destroyed the ikons in his room). For some five years he professed that only a materialist philosophy could assure progress and happiness for humanity. Then, just as suddenly, he experienced a complete change of heart, and he became once and for all a staunch champion of a devoutly religious idealism. At the core of his outlook was the concept that the ultimate aim of the universe lay in establishing a personal relationship between God and his highest creation, man. In this process man would achieve, through "perfect love," God-manhood and immortality, and Hagia Sophia (the Wisdom of God; the divine Wisdom), would be the vehicle to bring man this love.

Consequently, Solovyov did not limit himself to propagandizing the Platonic concept of the universe, but also sired on Russian soil the cult of the divine Sophia, the divine revelation and the bearer of perfect beauty and harmony, the eternal woman-soul of the universe, whom Goethe depicted as *das ewig Weibliche* in the second part of Faust. This cult of Sophia claimed even such prominent thinkers as Sergey Bulgakov (1871–1943).

According to Solovyov,[20] Sophia is the companion of God. As such she is the image of the perfect woman-soul. Because God would share his joy with every human, Sophia's image is

---

[20] Solov'ev, "Smysl liubvi," *Sobranie sochinenii* (2d ed.; St. Petersburg, 1911) VII, 3–57; see also Nicolas Zernov, *Three Russian Prophets* (London, 1944), pp. 116–151.

accessible to every living being. The eternal woman-soul, a living, spiritual entity herself, carries out the divine will by reflecting her image in mortals. Each person loves an ideal of the other world. In life each individual loves that, essentially human, being who might best reflect Sophia's image as each individual intuitively conceives it.

To Solovyov, personally, Sophia meant even more than this. Not only did he find the mundane reflection in more than one woman (two of whom coincidentally, bore the name "Sophia": Sophia Petrovna Hitrovo and Sophia Mikhailovna Martynov), but the divine hypostasis, the real Sophia, had appeared before him on three separate occasions. Solovyov described these meetings in his narrative poem "Three Meetings" (*Tri svidan'ya*).[21] Her vision first came to him when he was a boy of nine. She appeared before him a second time, about a dozen years later, at the British Museum, where he was engaged in research for his book, *La Russie et l'église universelle* (published in 1875). Here she directed him to journey to the Arabian desert. Complying with her order, Solovyov immediately dropped all his work, somehow scraped together the money, and set out for Arabia. In his poem "Three Meetings" dedicated to record his three meetings with his muse, Solovyov manages to laugh at himself as he recalls that while dressed in a "silk top hat and dress coat," and waiting for her to appear in the desert he was shot at by a group of Bedouins who had "mistaken him for the devil!" Whereupon, bound hand and foot, he was escorted to the rim of the desert and released on the promise that he would never again come near this oasis. There, at night, Sophia appeared before him, filled his soul "with azure joy," and vanished for the third and last time.

Solovyov's cult of Sophia bore some strange fruit, such as the affair of Anna Schmidt. Under the pseudonym of A. Timshevsky, Anna Schmidt wrote articles on mysticism and

---

[21] Solov'ev, *Stikhotvoreniia*, pp. 191–210.

religion for a Nizhni-Novgorod newspaper. Boris Bugayev described her[22] as a curious combination of a "little girl," "a dwarf," and an "old, old woman," with the "wrinkled brown face of a baked apple." For years she had been a great admirer of Vladimir Solovyov and on reading his poem "Three Meetings" suddenly became convinced that she herself was none other than the radiant Sophia, and that those meetings had taken place actually at her behest. Shortly before Solovyov died, Anna Schmidt wrote him a letter, in which she hinted that she knew much more about his muse than she could have known through mere coincidence, and that she had written an autobiographical work and an essay dealing with the woman-soul of the universe. Even though she had confused him with his eldest brother Vsevolod (who had dabbled in the occult arts), Solovyov answered her that he should like to become better acquainted with her writings "and most of all with you, yourself." They continued to correspond, and Solovyov learned that Mme. Schmidt had experienced certain visions (not unlike his own of Sophia). He was not fully convinced, for her visions affected "only the intellect" and not the spirit, as he pointed out to her. Finally she revealed to him that she was the actual incarnation of divine Sophia, come to earth to unite with the reincarnated Christ—Vladimir Solovyov. Alarmed at her statements, the philosopher hastened to deny her interpretation of his identity. "Your confession," he wrote her, "makes me profoundly compassionate and prompts me sorrowfully to intercede on your behalf with the Almighty." In conclusion, he begged her "never to return to this subject again," and promised that he would "burn her factual heretical confession not only as a precaution, but also to signify that the affair was only ashes." Eventually, he consented to see the woman in order that he might personally undeceive her. After their meeting he wrote her: "Our meeting has produced no unfavorable im-

[22] *Nachalo veka*, pp. 121–128.

pression; in other words, everything is as it had been before."[23] Shortly afterwards, Vladimir Solovyov died. Mme. Schmidt, however, refused to be discouraged. After his death, she paid several visits to his brother Mikhail and other disciples of the philosopher, all of whom she tried with doubtful success to convince of her true identity. She died in 1905.

An interesting commentary on the mentality of certain strata of the Russian intelligentsia is the fact that the Solovyovs as well as others took this woman quite seriously. In 1916, S. N. Bulgakov published her *Notes,* including her "Third Testament," which he called an amazing document. Mikhail and his family had to reject the claims she made concerning her own and Vladimir Solovyov's identities; certain doubts apparently arose in their minds. Alexander Blok received a letter from her in which she still hinted rather broadly that she was none other than the incarnated woman-soul. Blok, as late as 1904, gravely had to assure Mme. Schmidt that his poems dedicated to the Lady Beautiful were not addressed to her. In May of 1904, he wrote concerning her to his mother:

> Anna Nikolayevna Schmidt has again written [begging me], for Heaven's sake to arrange a meeting... Fortunately, she already knows from Seryozha Solovyov that my verses are *not* addressed to her... Seryozha says that *she is right in many respects,* but he does not believe in her.[24]

The romantic aura that was attached to Solovyov's personality and poetry made him a symbol to those who, consciously or otherwise, sought to justify a mental outlook based on intuition rather than reason. Through his poetry, Solovyov became the common bond that united the so-called "second generation" of Russian symbolists, the outstanding exponents among whom were Vyacheslav Ivanov, Alexander Blok, and Boris Bugayev.

[23] Vl. Solov'ev, *Pis'ma* (St. Petersburg, 1922) pp. 8–13.
[24] Aleksandr Blok, *Pis'ma k rodnym* (Leningrad, 1928), I, 121.

These three men all shared in varying degrees his Platonic concept that this world was merely the shadow of the real world. For these three men, symbolism in Russia was no mere literary style, nor even a literary school, but a philosophic view of life that permeated their writings. Solovyov's poetry left its imprint on the work of each of them.

Of the three, Vyacheslav Ivanov was least dependent on Vladimir Solovyov. Ivanov's contact with the philosopher was confined to attending several series of Solovyov's lectures in Russia. During the last years of the philosopher's life, when Solovyov's influence reached its zenith, Ivanov was studying abroad, where he remained until 1904. Furthermore, Ivanov's verse shows a predilection for classical antiquity, a motif that is foreign to Solovyov's lyrics. Nevertheless, Ivanov shares with Solovyov the themes of mystic love and the belief that this world is only a reflection, an echo of the more real world. Solovyov had expressed both these notions in his verse:

> Death, just as Time, may still reign o'er the earth;
> Call them your masters not.
> Everything fades, as it whirls in the dark,
> Love alone ne'er is forgot.[25]

Alexander Blok has a greater right than Ivanov to call himself a disciple of Solovyov. This is true even though Blok met Solovyov but once[26] and was unfamiliar with his poetry until after he had entered the university. Yet when Blok finally became acquainted with the philosopher's poetry, he was startled to discover that it contained the very ideas for which he had long been trying to find words. In one of his early letters to his lifelong friend Yevgeni Ivanov, Blok wrote that Solovyov's poetry had been like a "sacred revelation" to him.[27] Most of Blok's subsequent lyrical poetry may be interpreted as a re-

---

[25] Cf. Solov'ev, *Stikhotvoreniia*, p. 94.
[26] Blok, "Rytsar'-monakh," *Sobranie sochinenii* (Berlin, 1922), VII, 179–186.
[27] Blok, *Pis'ma k E. P. Ivanovu* (Leningrad, 1936), p. 25.

62 The Frenzied Poets

flection of the Solovyovan cult of Sophia. To be sure, Blok's muse is rather the shadow of Solovyov's companion, and like all shadows, her contours depend upon the position of the sun in the firmament. Her silhouette often becomes distorted, and varies from that of the Lady Beautiful to that of the Unknown Demi-mondaine; and yet the shadow is ever cast by the same figure. Throughout his life, Blok remained a true Solovyovan symbolist. He felt intuitively the reality of another world. To him Vladimir Solovyov was both prophet and teacher. In a letter to his father (October 29, 1904), Blok acknowledged his indebtedness to Solovyov, whom he had quoted rather freely in various epigraphs to his poems: "...Vladimir Solovyov's place in the epigraphs is only too appropriate. If anything, I am too greatly indebted to him..."[28] And in a letter to his mother, written in July, 1917, Blok quoted poetry for the last time. The lines

> Oh no ! With thistles I, and thorn
> Smothered the crops that sprang in heaven
> With the chaff of yearnings all earth-born.
> ... (I forget the rest)[29]

were from Vladimir Solovyov.

Boris Bugayev had a far greater opportunity than either Ivanov or Blok to become a faithful disciple of Solovyov. The latter two poets had practically no personal contact with the philosopher. Bugayev, on the other hand, even as a small boy, used to see the mystic at home. Later when Mikhail Solovyov's family moved into the same apartment house, Boris began to meet Vladimir Sergeyevich there as well.

Not until their last talk together, a few weeks before the philosopher's death, did the young man grasp the full meaning of Solovyov's innermost ideas.[30] Nevertheless, since Vladimir

---
[28] Blok, *Pis'ma k rodnym*, I, 129–130.
[29] *Ibid.*, II, 394.
[30] *Arabeski*, p. 394.

Solovyov's philosophy of the duality of existence coincided with Bugayev's own inner needs for rejecting the reality of this world, it became an integral part of Bugayev's own views. Nor was this dualism the sole element of Solovyov's philosophy that appealed to Bugayev. Solovyov's visions of Sophia as the eternal woman-soul of the universe, his apocalyptical premonitions, his belief in the Messianic destiny of Russia—all these ideas Bugayev accepted and incorporated into his works.

Another element in which Bugayev resembles Solovyov is the touch of light humor, which time and again recurs to brighten Bugayev's writings; perhaps an outstanding counterpart to Solovyov's poem "Three Meetings" may be seen in Bugayev's narrative in verse *First Meeting* (*Pervoe svidanie*, 1921). Bugayev's fondness for self-criticism is another token of his debt to Solovyov. Here, however, a difference between the two poets should be noted. Solovyov nearly always laughs at his discomforts. Boris Bugayev, as Andrey Biely, on the other hand, cries out in anguish and despair. His self-mockery recalls to mind the psychopathic self-torture and self-abasement that abound in the hysterical scenes of Dostoyevsky's novels.

Of the three followers, Boris Bugayev, a graduate of the faculty of natural sciences, was the least capable of accepting blindly any philosophical arguments based on an intuitive approach.[31] Yet Bugayev found the ideas of Vladimir Solovyov so attractive that during the better part of his life, he sought proof that could "scientifically" uphold Soloyov's philosophy. Throughout his literary works Andrey Biely is haunted by one spectre: how to depict the shadowy substance of man's mundane existence, and how to prove to his own satisfaction that man in this world is indeed only a shadow. In this respect Biely remained a true symbolist to the end of his days; and he owed an inestimable debt of Vladimir Solovyov.

---

[31] See chapter v.

Soon after Vladimir Solovyov died in August, 1900, the direct influence of the Solovyov family on Boris Bugayev began to wane. The Mikhail Solovyovs, nevertheless, had safely launched their protégé on his literary career. Once the Solovyovs had decided that young Bugayev's future lay in literature, they bent all their efforts to secure his success. For this purpose they used their influence to introduce Boris to the most influential figures of Russian modernism. They soon acquainted him not only with such local Muscovite celebrities as Valeri Bryusov, but with such St. Petersburg luminaries as Dmitri Merezhkovsky and his wife, Zinaida Hippius. The Solovyovs were also responsible for Boris' mystical and fateful friendship with Alexander Blok, the most famous Russian poet of the symbolist movement. More than this, Mikhail Solovyov was the man who persuaded Bryusov to include Bugayev's *Dramatic Symphony* among the Scorpio publications, and to expedite matters he even paid for the printing himself. Thus the Solovyov apartment may truly be regarded as a springboard from which Boris Bugayev as Andrey Biely plunged into the literary sea.

5

BORIS BUGAYEV AS MAN AND ARTIST

ALEXANDER BLOK, the most widely known of the Russian symbolists, once described Andrey Biely as the "least physical" of Russian poets. Another Russian literary figure, the poet Marina Tsvetayeva,[1] also identified Biely with the spiritual world rather than the physical. D. S. Mirsky summed up these views by comparing Biely to Ariel, but "to an undisciplined and erratic Ariel."[2] And, indeed, so undisciplined and erratic was this twentieth-century Russian Ariel that he often seemed hysterical, and at times even deranged. Plagued ceaselessly by the "accursed questions," Bugayev-Biely spent his entire existence in a frenzied search for the meaning of life, for some definite proof that God and an afterlife exist. His scientific training did not allow him to believe in anything that he could not empirically prove. Therefore, Bugayev-Biely suffered throughout his life, burdened by a dualism innate in all "moderns," children of a lost generation, who vacillate in anguish between irrational faith and scientific skepticism and who are unable to embrace either wholeheartedly. In this, Boris Bugayev was a true product of his environment, time, and experiences.

Bugayev's personality vividly reflected the conflicting influences that shaped his essentially dualistic character. His mother's personality determined his emotional instability as

[1] Marina Tsvetaeva, "Plennyi dukh," *Sovremennyia Zapiski*, LV (1934), 198–255.
[2] D. S. Mirsky, *Contemporary Russian Literature*, p. 226.

well as his hysterical and capricious temperament; his mother was responsible for his predisposition to intuitive judgment and to music—a factor that determined his striving to express himself vaguely and lyrically, through intangible melody and rhythm, rather than explicitly, through concrete words. Paradoxically, this lyrical nature of Boris Bugayev existed side by side with a scientific nature, which he owed to his father, from whom he inherited a critical intellect and an avid thirst for knowledge. For this reason he loved mathematical precision and scientific systemization, just as much as he did chaos and intuitive perception. Thus, his home surroundings encouraged the boy's character to follow two contradictory paths.

Bugayev's friendship with the Solovyovs developed still further the dualism of his nature. At home, his father strove to inspire his son with a critically scientific attitude toward knowledge, while the Solovyovs encouraged a mystical trend of thought. The two incompatible trends were bound to produce a clash within Bugayev. Unfortunately for him, he was so thoroughly conditioned to both outlooks that he could discard neither, although he realized the weak points of each. The split within young Bugayev was further widened by the use of the new name, Andrey Biely, which he had received at the Solovyovs', and which seemed to endow him with another personality. To the conflict between the scientific critic and the intuitive mystic within him was added the clash between Boris Bugayev, a brilliant, charming, and retiring cultured individual, and Andrey Biely, an equally brilliant, yet often quarrelsome, egocentric genius. In private life, the personality of Bugayev prevailed, but in his life within the intellectual Bohemia, the character of Andrey Biely came to the fore.

Until the autumn of 1899, when Bugayev entered the university, the Solovyov apartment was the sole social and intellectual center of his life. Because Mikhail Solovyov had the faculty of drawing out of him the half-formulated ideas that floated in his mind, and helped him shape them, the youth became accustomed to "bring all his impressions to the Solovyovs'."[3] Mikhail Solovyov, sitting and listening to Bugayev expand upon his ideas, helped him to express them in an articulate manner. For this reason, the Solovyov home appeared indispensable to the young man's life.

In 1899, yielding to his father's wishes, Bugayev matriculated in the College of Sciences of Moscow university. Nevertheless, the mere fact that he had agreed to study natural sciences by no means signified that he had surrendered to his father. The young man had resolved also to complete the curricula of the historico-phililogical (liberal arts) faculty; and his matriculation at the university as a student of geography did not imply that he had relinquished his interest in the arts. Yet, once he had undertaken a serious study of geography, he remained faithful to his decision; in 1903 he completed the prescribed curricula, which included courses in chemistry, physics, and mathematics, as well as in geography.

Boris Bugayev's scientific training had far-reaching effects on his life. It intensified his craving to understand everything, and this desire to gain knowledge through understanding clashed with his predisposition for perceiving through intuition. Although his studies in modern science had undermined any implicit trust in intuition, they also proved to him that science itself could provide no absolute knowledge. The realization that absolute knowledge was impossible brought with it a sense of frustration, futility, and uprootedness.

Although he realized that his search for an infallible all-explaining philosophy could bear no fruit, Bugayev would not despair. On the contrary, he continued his search with unabating fervor, which only increased with confirmed and unavoidable failure. In this respect he was a typical representative of the modernist mentality, with its frantic search for a soul, for

[3] *Nachalo veka*, p. 117.

68   The Frenzied Poets

religion, for the meaning of life, truth, and beauty. Thus the new trends in art and literature appealed to him with increasing poignancy.

At the university, despite his scientific curriculum, Bugayev's interest in modernism found added support among his fellow science students. An unexpectedly large number of his colleagues seemed to share his interests in the new trends of thought and culture. These young men soon formed the nucleus of an informal circle that at the turn of the century began to meet at the home of V. V. Vladimirov, one of Bugayev's gymnasium comrades. Vladimirov was a young mathematician and painter "with ideas," who had studied the various theories of art as well as those of Darwin and Ostwald.[4] Another member of the group was A. S. Petrovsky, a chemist who likewise could not confine his interests to scientific methodology, but who also developed ideas of his own on poetry and aesthetics.

By 1901 the original trio of Vladimirov, Petrovsky, and Bugayev had expanded to include other budding chemists, physicists, mathematicians, and sociologists—men of scientific training of all varieties, who, despite their positivistic background, radiated an atmosphere of seeking new ideas and new methods of expressing their feelings. Perhaps because they had no actual, definite organization, their circle grew rapidly. They were not bound by any specific program; their only demand was that each of their members should be interested in the modern trends of culture. Yet, even though they were absorbed in the study of Baudelaire, Verlaine, Mallarmé, Maeterlinck, Verhaeren, Nietzsche, and Stefan George, this group of young Russians prided themselves on being independent of Paris, Brussels, or Berlin, the recognized centers of Western modernism. They were all young, full of a spontaneous exuberance, and often permitted a blend of "Rabelais with Edgar Allen Poe"[5] to characterize their meetings. In jest these

[4] *Ibid.*, pp. 21–22.   [5] *Ibid.*, p. 19.

young people decided that the search for their goal resembled the quest for the Golden Fleece. They, therefore, adopted the name of "Argonauts." Having no formal organization (even as late as 1907 these "seafarers" had no "harbor" of their own) their loose movement, nevertheless, could claim a number of cells among the cultural centers of Moscow: at the Astrovs', at the "House of Song" (the d'Alheims'), among the "Scorpions," in the Religious-Philosophical Society, in the Society of Free Aesthetics. All of these "were islands among which the Argo sailed,"[6] propagandizing the "new art" in music, painting, and literature.

At their gatherings the Argonauts would argue about problems of culture and aesthetics, would read poetry of their favorite writers (not necessarily modernist), V. V. Vladimirov's sister Anna would sing, and the whole company would spend a jolly evening. They pretended that aboard their imaginary ship they journeyed during these evenings "to the land of symbolism."[7]

Despite its mask of frivolity, Argonautism was essentially a serious cultural phenomenon. All its adherents felt that a common bond united them; that they were impelled by a search for new values and by a vague sense that mankind stood on the threshold of a new era, that they were facing an intellectual and spiritual renaissance. None of them could say what, precisely, was the substance of this new current. But they could sense it in the writings of such Western modernists as Nietzsche, Ibsen, Verlaine, Rimbaud, and Mallarmé. To these authors the Argonauts added the spiritual and philosophical poetry of Tyutchev, Fet, Baratynsky, and Vladimir Solovyov. Believing that the millennium was at hand and a complete revaluation of old values inevitable, they sought a new guide, a new gospel that might point the way. Dissatisfied with science, because it could reveal no ultimate, transcendent truths, they hoped that

[6] *Ibid.*, p. 25.   [7] *Ibid.*, pp. 23–26.

somehow intuition might provide them with the key to infallible knowledge. At the same time they denied that this material world was the sole, true, and real world. They preferred to trust Vladimir Solovyov's concept that beyond the grasp of man's intellect there existed another, more real world, and that what man knew was only the shadow and the echo of this more real existence. They therefore chose to accept Schopenhauer's view that an artist, prophet, or philosopher, in a fit of ecstatic frenzy or passive contemplation could intuitively perceive what lay beyond an ordinary man's power to grasp. The new life and the cultural revolution that they prophesied was to see the entire human species raised to the level of artists. Man was thus to become a Nietzschean superman. The new life, they believed, would be transfused with art, and each individual's existence would become so filled with moments of ecstasy that his visions of eternity would continually coincide with his experiences. Under such conditions life was to be no longer a drab, commonplace, and debasing existence, but a colorful, exotic, creative process. Thus in their *Weltanschauung* the Argonauts were typical symbolists, although few of their number were actually poets or artists. The greatest poet among them unquestionably was Boris Bugayev. He was the prophet and the poet who spoke for them.

The year 1900 loomed alarming for many mystically inclined Russian intellectuals. The apocalyptic prophecies of Vladimir Solovyov seemed on the verge of fulfillment. His *Three Conversations* (*Tri razgovora*) predicting as they did a menace from the Orient that would presage the appearance of Antichrist, gathered credence as turmoil spread over China. Trouble seemed to be brewing also at home. Even the very men whom modernists in Russia idolized seemed to perish one by one. In 1900, Ruskin and Nietzsche died insane; Oscar Wilde died in disgrace; and finally, Vladimir Solovyov himself, whom some regarded as reincarnated Christ, died and failed to arise from the dead as many of his followers expected. A vague sense of alarm, inexplicable, subtle, and insidious, filled the air; the world was obviously in its final hour.

Nevertheless, the year passed without catastrophe, and with the arrival of the twentieth century Bugayev found new horizons stretching before his eyes. The year 1901 appeared to him as his "year of dawn."[8] It marked his coming of age; it brought Mikhail Solovyov's complete recognition of Bugayev's talents as a writer and, with it, authorship; it also gave him a number of new friends in the literary world as well as at the university. In addition, that year marked the beginning of a real companionship between him and his father, who now proved willing to recognize his son as a mature individual.

The newly discovered horizons led Boris Bugayev to pursue his search for an all-embracing truth beyond the drawing room of the Solovyovs. He felt that, because of his university associations and his contacts with the literary world, he was beginning to outgrow the Solovyovs' narrow family circle. He felt an ever-impelling urge to expand intellectually beyond the confines of their parlor.

Olga Solovyov felt offended, and quite understandably ascribed Boris' yearning for new associations to ingratitude. Consequently her relations with Boris, although still outwardly cordial, lost their original spontaneity. Bugayev therefore sought all the more the companionship of the Argonauts, with the result that soon the Vladimirov apartment became his "center, number two." The Solovyov family, nevertheless, continued to play an important part in his development in the literary world, and his early writings unmistakably bear their stamp.

Bugayev's earliest literary work was essentially lyrical. It comprises his first three *Symphonies* and his first book of verse, *Gold in Azure* (1904). The novelty and freshness of Andrey

---
[8] *Epopeia*, I, 131.

Biely's writings astonished readers who were sympathetic to modernism, and who, from the very first, recognized in Andrey Biely a radical innovator in Russian literature. His readers felt his lines vibrating with the voice of a truly "new man," who had discarded the language of his fathers, because it could not adequately convey the inner experiences of a radically changed mode of life and thought.

His first published work, the *Dramatic Symphony*, introduced a new literary genre. The *Symphony* was a lyrical tale, written in poetic prose that was heavily in debt to such diverse sources as Gogol's lyrical passages, Nietzsche's *Also sprach Zarathustra*, and the prophecies of the Revelations of St. John. It emphasized not so much the thread of narration as the rhythm and music of language, which it blended with colorful imagery, often repeated as a refrain. The *Symphony* sought to create a mood rather than tell a story, and consequently appealed to the senses more than to the intellect. The new genre was admirably suited to convey the young author's urgent, constantly repeated message that our everyday existence and our everyday world are not real, but "dreams, only dreams." This is the message that underlies Biely's imaginative writings, all of which strive to show the irreality of our existence. In order further to stress the irreality of the physical world, Biely time and again resorts to satire in depicting scenes from life. Here he again appears as a disciple of Gogol. The apocalyptic theme present in the first three *Symphonies* harmonizes with the troubled expectancy of the mystically inclined Russian intellectuals, who at the turn of the century felt that the end of their world was imminent and that the new world would bring with it at least a new species of mankind, if not actually the millennium.

Biely's *Symphonies* were as radical a departure from Russian literary tradition as had once been Pushkin's *Ruslan and Ludmilla* or *Boris Godunov*. In many respects, Biely's work represents a transition from nineteenth-century Russian literature to a new stage. It is at once the last link in the chain that began with Pushkin, and the first link of something new. Characteristically, the writer's first book of poetry, *Gold in Azure*, broke away from the nearly century-old verse traditions of the Pushkin period.

Although in some respects Biely's poetry resembles his *Symphonies*, on the whole it is more autobiographical and personal. His *Symphonies* are prophetic visions that reveal themselves to a poet in the throes of creative ecstasy. His verses, on the other hand, record not only the poet's dreams but the flow of the moods and events of his life. Biely's poetry is as much a lyrical diary as are the verses of Alexander Blok, and his first three collections, *Gold in Azure* (1904), *Ashes* (1909), and *The Urn* (1909), record a rapturous flight toward the sun, a flight that ended in disaster, despair, and resignation.

Although in their ethereal and mystical moods his verses undeniably reflect the influence of Fet, Tyutchev, and especially Vladimir Solovyov, much in them is quite unlike anything that Russian readers had met before. *Gold in Azure* astonished the readers by its freshness and novelty.

Biely was the first modern Russian poet to break away completely from the fetters of traditional metric-tonic Russian versification. His remarkable sense of rhythm enabled him to disregard set metrical patterns and to introduce the pause as a metrical element. He applied to literary versification the rhythmic principles of the folk poetry and thus brought the written forms closer to the natural rhythm of the language.

The breadth of Biely's genius prompted him to enter yet another field of literature: that of literary theory, which he examined from the point of view of symbolism. In his theoretical articles he attempted to formulate a concrete definition of symbolism, its meaning and aims. The more important articles of his earlier period are "Forms of Art" (1902), "Criticism and Symbolism" (1904), and "Symbolism as a Concept of the Universe" (1904). In these articles Biely is still very vague in defining symbolism, and more concrete in illustrating it. Music, in its Schopenhauerian interpretation, is the keynote of these articles, and it parallels the lyricism of Biely's prose.

In his earliest verse, Biely appears as a Solovyovan prophet, whose trumpet sounds a note of apocalyptic expectancy. In foretelling the end of time and the coming millennium, he is one of the chosen few who can "foretell,"[9] who "know"[10] that "sacred days"[11] are at hand, who recognize the "sorrow ('*skorb*'), such as was not from the beginning of the creation which God created unto this time (Mark XIII, 19)."[12] He senses that everything is radiantly prepared for the great day, that the air itself is "luminous to the point of pain."[13] He rejoices as he awaits from hour to hour the advent of the millennium.

The imagery and language strike the reader by their originality. The lines are saturated with the vivid colors of a brilliant sunset, blended with the solitary melancholy of its pastel afterglow. The poet's consciousness throbs with the belief that he is one with the limitless universe. The slumbering trees, the sighing breeze, the fragments of clouds that dot the evening sky—all speak to him with the voice of eternity, which now caresses and fills him with rapture,[14] now fills him with anticipation and then with alarm.[15] Strange creatures populate the landscape; the fauns, giants, hunchbacks, and wizards that are resurrected from antiquity, classical mythology, and Germanic folklore, add to the "neoprimitivism" of the scenes.[16] Typical of his mood are such phrases as "the hot sun—a ring of gold"; "eternity's streaming waterfall"; the "golden amber hour."[17]

---

[9] Andrei Belyi, *Zoloto v lazuri* (Moscow, 1904), p. 225.
[10] *Ibid.*, p. 226.
[11] *Ibid.*, p. 251.
[12] *Ibid.*, p. 226.
[13] *Ibid.*, p. 22.
[14] *Ibid.*, pp. 5, 15, 17, 20, 29.
[15] *Ibid.*, p. 23.
[16] *Ibid.*, pp. 140–182.
[17] *Ibid.*, pp. 16–19.

The sun's ancient contour
golden, and flaming,
orange and winelike
o'er crimson streams[18]

Crimson pillars of beryllium
softly stream amidst emeralds . . .[19]

Biely seems never at a loss for words. If the Russian language lacks a word that he wants, Biely coins it, especially if it be an adjective with an exotic connotation; such are modifiers as "ambering" (*yantareyushchi*). The hour of sunset is Biely's favorite time of this period. With barbaric abandon he depicts it as a riot of color; the west is aflame, and the sky directly overhead is a clear, lucid azure. "Ruby-colored clouds" appear "scattered like beads" in a rapturous "azure of the sky."[20] His sky is studded with "rubies and gold,"[21] while an Argonaut's "Golden Fleece," the "vanishing, flaming shield of the sun" slips quickly away beyond the horizon.

Characteristic of the major mood of the book is "In the Hills," one of his best-known poems, written in characteristically Bielyan lines of varied length.

In the Hills

Bridal crowns on the hills,
I'm elated. I'm young.
With a freshening chill
Are my hills o'erhung.

Here, up my cliff,
Wends a hunchback his way,
Pineapples in hand
from his underground plot to display.

---

[18] *Ibid.*, p. 21.
[19] *Ibid.*, p. 156.
[20] *Ibid.*, pp. 3–6.
[21] *Ibid.*, p. 21.

In magenta-hued robes he danced
as he lauded the azure-blue dust.
With his beard he swept up
silvering blizzards in gusts.

In a rumbling bass voice
He cried out loud and low.
High into the sky
a pineapple he let go.

And describing an arc,
o'er the hill, over forest and dell,
the pineapple glowed
as it fell,

and colored the dew
with its pillars of gold.
Below, people said:
"Lo, the sun disk behold!"

Gold fountains of fire
rang as they fell from the blue
bathing the cliffs
in vermilion crystals
of dew.

Filling my goblet with wine
I quietly stole up from the holm
And suddenly drenched the old man
With a torrent of foam.

Despite the apparent optimism of these poems, an opposite mood is also found in *Gold in Azure*. It is a mood of doubt and irony that borders on despair, hysteria, and cynicism. The poems written during 1903, especially during the month of August after his father's death, illustrate this side of Andrey Biely.

The year 1903 was an important transitional period in Bugayev's life. It ended the joyous, carefree mood that he had expressed in his first literary works and marked the beginning of nearly a decade of spiritual depression that often bordered on despair. On January 16, 1903, came the first shock: the death of Mikhail Sergeyevich Solovyov, followed by the suicide of Olga Mikhailovna, who after spending her last spark of nervous energy at the bedside of her husband, put a bullet through her head.[22] Meanwhile, the elder Bugayev's health had been sinking rapidly, and he died shortly after Boris had graduated from the university. With these three deaths and an early love affair[23] (with a young poet, Nina Petrovsky), from which he eventually fled, ended the first period of Bugayev's literary career.

Up to this time the notes of melancholy and loneliness were isolated in Biely's poetry, as in "Melancholy" (1901).[24] For example, there are few lines such as "Wretched and poor in the wasteland I wander weeping . . . . So cold and so frightened am I" (1901);[25] and only occasionally did he hear the "lazily swaying rustle of oats" voice the doubts buried in his own dual nature:

> The weary world falls peacefully asleep—
> ahead meanwhile
> since long ago none waits for spring;
> and you shall die
> for naught exists—and naught will ever be—
> you shall grow still;
> the world will vanish; God will forsake it then.
> What do you will?[26]

Now, however, these *motifs* loom increasingly large and their specter soon overshadows everything else.

Biely feels that through his prophecies he has betrayed those near him. He therefore openly accuses himself of being a "false

[22] *Zhivyia litsa*, I, 6–9; also *Nachalo veka*, pp. 199–203.
[23] See his poem "Legenda" in *Zoloto v lazuri*, p. 154.
[24] *Zoloto v lazura*, p. 169.
[25] *Ibid.*, p. 165.
[26] *Ibid.*, p. 13.

78 The Frenzied Poets

prophet," a "pseudo-Christ,"[27] "a fool." In a typically Dostoyevskyan mood, he insists on openly shrilling his sins, heaping ashes on his head, and, as his hysteria mounts, in exposing the false prophet as a madman and in placing him behind bars, with the mob hastening "by kicks the sobbing madman's departure."[28] He addresses his other self:

> O! My Tsar!
> You are pitiful so in your fright
> as before
> you have hid 'midst violets white.[29]

Time and again he prays "fatigued with doubt,"[30] which, "like the moon, has risen once again." In despair he cries:

> Where, O! great God
> Art Thou!...
> Reveal Thyself, O! sacred child ...
> Answer, great God! ...
> [But] No answer issues forth ...[31]

The pessimistic mood, which was distinctly shaped by the personal events in Bugayev's life, intensified as time went on. Another factor in his personal life that filled him with a feeling of futility, guilt, and remorse was his fateful and frenetic love affair with Lyubov Dmitrievna Blok, wife of Alexander Blok, whom he regarded as his "spiritual brother." (The affair is discussed later in detail.) Sociohistorical events further heightened his growing dejection. The disastrous Russo-Japanese War (1904–1905), the unsuccessful revolution of 1905–1906, the ensuing political reaction and the air of apathy and demoralization that subsequently enveloped much of the intelligentsia, completed the transformation of his former rapture into a mood of hysteria and despair.

---

[27] *Ibid.*, p. 18.
[28] *Ibid.*, p. 19.
[29] *Ibid.*, p. 33.
[30] *Ibid.*, p. 35.
[31] *Ibid.*, p. 27.

Although Biely's first book of verse, *Gold in Azure*, is dominated by an apocalyptic fervor and by an impulse to reach the clean, clear azure of the sky, his second collection of poems, *Ashes* (1904–1908) depicts an abrupt descent to earth. The prophetic motifs of Vladimir Solovyov now yield to the civic despondency of Nekrasov, coupled with the despairing abandon of Dostoyevsky. During the period 1904–1907, Biely completed *The Goblet of Blizzards*, his fourth and last *Symphony*, which was the shriek of a soul in agony. Biely himself termed it a "psychological document on the state of a contemporary mind."[32] Escape became imperative. To continue along the same path would have been to agree that "nothing matters."[33] Biely's muse consequently undergoes a transformation. No longer does he seek eternity; he is now troubled by a spectre of a new "beloved"—Russia. His vision of her is no idealization of reality. She appears to him as the land "where horror lurks under each shadow" and

> Where pestilence, warfare, and illness
> Have etched their infernal design . . .

In the volume, *Ashes*, Biely cremates his early raptures and holds a wake, which in such poems as "Joy in Russia" amazes the reader by its rhythmic abandon and the despondency that underlies the mood. More and more, now, Biely turns to regular forms in his Nekrasovlike lament of Russia.

In seeking to escape the pain of his despondency, Biely concentrated again on philosophical studies. But now his former enthusiasm for Schopenhauer and Nietzsche gave way to a systematic reading of the Neo-Kantian philosophers Cohen, Natorp, and particularly Rickert, in whose ethics Biely sought the answer to the tormenting question: what is the purpose and the meaning of life? Early in 1909, toward the end of this period, Biely published his third book of verse, *The Urn*, which

---
[32] Belyi, *Kubok metelei* (Moscow, 1908), p. 4.
[33] Cf. *Arabeski, Simvolizm*.

was to symbolize the vessel in which the poet collected the "ashes of his scorched raptures."[34] *The Urn* is as purely subjective as his previous works and clearly reflects an effort to find peace in philosophical meditation.

After 1904, Biely's essays also began to reflect the man's rising hysteria, frenzy, and despair. To begin with, most of the articles written during the period 1906-1908 treat the polemical campaign that was then absorbing his attention. Biely, who had always regarded creative art as something in the nature of a sacred rite, became indignant when a new trend, "mystical anarchism," began to profane it. The spleen which the circumstances of his personal life had aroused in him found an outlet in his invectives against the mystical anarchists and others whom he suspected of undermining the future of symbolism. Although Biely's attacks lacked the light satirical touch that lent Pushkin's polemical writings their devastating effectiveness, they are unsurpassed for sheer rhetoric of furious indignation.

Biely's purely theoretical articles of this period reflect his own disillusion with all the fond hopes of his youth. No longer does he regard symbolism as the *Weltanschauung* of the immediate future, of "tomorrow."[35] He now sees it as an achievement only of the distant future, toward which all culture must slowly and painfully evolve. Therefore, he comes to the decision that any attempt to "define the contours of symbolism" can produce only a "temporary, working hypothesis," by means of which an all-inclusive methodological foundation of art might be gradually built.[36]

His search for an infallible methodology of art, led Biely to attempt a system of aesthetics based on scientific investigation. To this end he organized the Rhythmics Society (*Ritmicheskii*

---

[34] Belyi *Stikhotvoreniia* (Berlin, 1923), p. 213.
[35] *Nachalo veka*, p. 329; cf. "Emblematika smysla," *Simvolizm*, pp. 49-143, 483, 506.
[36] *Omut*, pp. 212-213; cf. "Smysl iskusstva," *Simvolizm*, pp. 195-230.

Bugayev as Man and Artist 81

kruzhok) in 1909.[37] Since he believed that form and content were mutually interdependent,[38] and both were predetermined by a poet's vision of the ultimate reality, Biely concluded that by analyzing any one component of art, it would be possible eventually to determine the very essence of art itself. For this reason the Rhythmics Society set as its aim a systematic study of the formal elements of Russian verse.[39] In 1910 Biely published the results of a few aspects of his investigations.[40] He approached the problem of style statistically. His first experiments in this field laid the foundation for the Russian formalist school of criticism, which claimed a number of significant literary figures.

The year 1908, in which Biely published his last *Symphony* and completed his two books of verse, *Ashes* and *The Urn*, terminated the lyrical period of his career. The year 1909 ended his attempts to define symbolism as a *Weltanschauung* and led him to scientific analysis of the formal elements of art.

At about the same time Biely entered upon still another stage in his literary development, by beginning his first novel. He started his *Silver Dove* (*Serebryany Golub'*) in 1908, and the first installment appeared in the April, 1909, issue of the *Balance*. Although in technique the novel resembles the *Symphonies*, it differs from them in that it emphasizes narrative rather than mood. While the *Silver Dove*, like the *Symphonies*, deals with the theme of doom, it differs from the *Symphonies* in that it holds no promise for the future. Its hero, Daryalski, an intellectual (who has many points in common with Biely), in seeking spiritual rebirth involuntarily turns to the Russian people but, like Biely, finds in Russia an image of chaos rather

---
[37] *Omut*, pp. 392-396.
[38] *Simvolizm*, pp. 175-194, and *passim*.
[39] The system which Belyi devised to analyze poetry is described in detail by Henry Lanz, *The Physical Basis of Rime* (Stanford University Press, 1931) ; see also such books as B. V. Tomashevskii's *Russkoe stikhoslozhenie* (Petrograd, 1923), and V. Zhirmunskii's *Vvedenie v metriku* (Leningrad, 1925).
[40] *Simvolizm*, pp. 231-285; 562-627.

than a reflection of logos. Fatefully he is drawn into the whirlpool of the dark powers and eventually falls their prey. The *Silver Dove* reflects the influence not only of the eschatological writings of Vladimir Solovyov, but also of the tales of Gogol, and, despite its occasional lapses into the trivial, produces a powerful effect.

The period 1906–1909 Biely called a journey through a "spiritual morass" of life.[41] It was his journey through the "years of political reaction in Russia, through bitter personal experiences, through disillusion in love, through . . . the moral decay of the intelligentsia . . . which sought to escape its environment in the stifling narcotics of eroticism." Even complete preoccupation with philosophical studies failed to alleviate his depressed mood. Biely realized that for him philosophy produced only introspective irony. He became convinced that he had to leave Russia. The economic straits in which he found himself after his father's death only further increased his despair. With his mother controlling what money had been left, Biely was obliged to rely increasingly upon his literary talents for subsistence. Because his reading public was limited, Biely was scarcely able to provide for himself. Realizing to what extent he was dependent on his mother, he all the more resented his situation.

In his desire to escape the grim reality of life in Russia, Biely found a providential companion, the charming "Asya" (Anna Alexeyevna) Turgenev, a niece of the famous novelist. Owing to financial stress, her life at home was not a happy one. A budding artist, she wanted an opportunity to continue her studies abroad. They saw themselves as kindred souls, as stepchildren of fate. Both considered themselves broken by life; both were artists by nature: he, a poet, she, a painter; both were penniless; the future in Russia seemed to hold nothing for either. They therefore resolved to join their lots and to

[41] *Omut*, pp. 399–405.

Bugayev as Man and Artist 83

escape together into a new life "beyond the stifling environment which they found around them." Biely therefore decided to alter his path radically and to break with modernism. The advent of Asya Turgenev marked the beginning of a new period in Biely's life and works.

Once Biely and his fiancée had agreed on their future, the problem of financing their "escape" arose. Biely appealed for advance royalties on his future writings to his old friend and fellow Argonaut, who owned the publishing house of Musaget (*Mous-agetes* = "leader of the muses," i.e., Apollo). Medtner allowed him an advance of 3,000 rubles. Their traveling expenses thus assured, Biely and Asya decided upon a journey to Italy, Tunis, Egypt, and the Holy Land. Since Asya Turgenev "despised conventions" and "had sworn never to agree to a marriage by the church" (as required by Russian law), the young couple dispensed with the religious ceremony. On November 27, 1910, they left Moscow.

For the next decade and more Asya was the factor that dominated Biely's life. First of all, she soon estranged him from his former environment. Many of the followers of that exotic individual, "Andrey Biely," regarded his new attachment as a renunciation of his sacred duty as a poet;[42] no being as ethereal and romantic as Andrey Biely had the moral right, they argued, to submit to the passions of mortals. His followers resented Asya's success and the revelation that their idol was mere man. Nor was this resentment limited to Biely's admirers. When his mother learned that the young couple planned to depart without an official ceremony, she denounced Asya as a scheming interloper.[43] Other friends, on hearing of his plans, also were shocked and felt that Asya Turgenev was wholly to blame for corrupting "their Boris Nikolayevich."[44] Medtner, a staunch advocate of Germanic culture, was disappointed because the

---
[42] Tsvetaeva, *op. cit.*, pp. 210–212.
[43] *Literaturnoe Nasledstvo*, pp. 443–452.
[44] *Omut*, pp. 342–348. *Literaturnoe Nasledstvo*, pp. 442–445.

couple was going to Italy, rather than Germany. He tried to persuade Biely to reconsider his itinerary, but failed, and an estrangement between the former comrades followed. A few old friends, M. O. Gershenzon and N. A. Berdyayev among them, remained faithful and understanding.

The young couple left Moscow in November, 1910. Within the next six months they visited Venice, Naples, the ruins of Pompeii, Palermo, Tunis, Carthage, Port Said, Cairo, the pyramids, the Sphinx, and Jerusalem. Finally shortly after Easter, 1911, they returned to Russia by way of Constantinople and Odessa. The journey made an ineradicable impression on both of them. Drinking in all the historical sights, they felt themselves dwarfed by the events of the past. Man seemed insignificant and helpless, indeed, at the hands of fate and the blind elements. The impact of Africa was especially strong. Already here, in Biely's descriptions of the white cubes, rhombi, and parallelepipeds that dotted their landscape, are presaged the geometrical designs of the novel *Petersburg*, which Biely created within another year. Africa already foreshadows Petersburg, the city that has no physical dimension beyond that of a point on a map, the city that is but a phantom: a powerful, evil, metaphysical force. The Sphinx, the pyramids, the sultry African night, filled Biely and his Asya with the foreboding of a catastrophe threatening mankind and its civilization.[45] The pages of Biely's *Travel Notes* abound in premonitions that were soon to find a more concrete expression in his cycle of *Crises*, essays analyzing European culture and civilization. The couple returned to Russia convinced more than ever before of the existence of another world. It was as though on the Dark Continent they had come face to face with mystery. By the time they reached Moscow they were quite ready for theosophy, anthroposophy, or any other system of philosophy that dealt with the occult.

---

[45] B. Kuz'min in his prefatory note to Belyi's "Reminiscences" in the *Literaturnoe Nasledstvo* also marks the resemblance between them and *Petersburg*.

Bugayev as Man and Artist 85

In the fall of 1911, Biely began his second novel. Originally he had planned it as a sequel to the *Silver Dove*, as a second part of a trilogy *Orient and Occident*. But he became so engrossed in his plot that the book soon became an entirely independent work, and his original plan for a trilogy was abandoned. The book remained unnamed for several months, until Vyacheslav Ivanov christened it *Petersburg*. The novel again deals with an intellectual, this time with one Nikolay Apollonovich Ableukhov, whose search for truth involves him in the revolutionary movement, until one day he discovers that he is obliged to assassinate his own father, Senator Ableukhov. As important as the hero is the evil spirit that lurks in the background: Petersburg, the city of the mists. Biely's picture of the city is the crowning vision of the evil power that Pushkin, Gogol, and Dostoyevski had recorded in such works as *Bronze Horseman*, *Nevsky Prospect*, and *White Nights*. Some critics, notably Ivanov-Razmunik,[46] regard *Petersburg* not only as Biely's prose masterpiece, but also as the masterpiece of his generation. The novel's planned acoustic effects, its deliberate impression of chaos, and its ponderous rhythmical majesty leave its readers at once bewildered, oppressed, and somewhat awestruck. *Petersburg* is truly the apogee of an era that stressed individualism in literature. Despite the outstanding merits of his novel, Biely could find no publisher for it. Because of the polemic campaign which he had waged on behalf of symbolism against all other literary trends that did not coincide with his own views, Biely discovered that he had become a *persona non grata* in all editorial offices of Russia. No periodical was willing to publish his works. For a year or so, Biely strove to find a place in Russian literature, but to no avail.

Meanwhile Asya insisted on going to Brussels, where an old friend of her family had been teaching her engraving. Biely once more was obliged to raise funds for a second "escape"

[46] Ivanov-Razumnik, *Vershiny* (Petrograd, 1922).

86 The Frenzied Poets

from Russia. In March, 1912, through the generosity of Alexander Blok, Biely and Asya were able to start for Brussels.

More important than these events was the influence that Asya's own inclination toward mysticism had on Biely's state of mind. More than ever before he felt that mankind faced a grave, unknown crisis as it stood "on the watershed" of a new era, and experienced a fresh thirst for "infallible" knowledge. Strongly influenced by Asya's interest in the occult, he undertook to study theosophy and soon turned to "anthroposophy," a philosophical current resembling somewhat theosophy, with which it was at one time connected in the person of Dr. Rudolf Steiner, its founder and chief interpreter.

Anthroposophy appealed to Biely as a science that professed itself capable of explaining the realm of the spirit. It asserted that it could infallibly reconcile all the differences existing between science and mysticism. As a rational system of metaphysics it claimed that it was an irrefutable source of knowledge, both physical and transphysical.

The main tenet of anthroposophy is that the cosmic spirit is the primary source and cause of the material universe, and that matter is a coagulated form of spirit.[47] Beyond the material world, which alone is accessible to an average individual's conception, lie other worlds of spirit, which he cannot grasp with his perceptional organs. The intellect can discern only a part of the truth. The other (and greater) part of reality, although beyond the reach of man's ordinary mechanism, may be perceived through a special cognitive power concealed within his spirit. By developing this latent power, man can develop the organs that will enable him to perceive the transphysical world and even hold intercourse with it. But in order to develop these organs man must first approach spiritual perfection, which alone can release his coagulated spirit from the physical into an ethereal state. When the human ego reaches the maximum

[47] See Rudolf Steiner, *The Philosophy of Spiritual Activity* (London-New York, 1939); cf. V. Gol'denberg, *Antroposofskoe dvizhenie i ego prorok* (Berlin, 1922).

of perfection it passes into a purely spiritual form of existence. The eventual aim of mankind is to achieve an "optimum of dematerialization" in order that man (and with him, cosmos) may "dissolve in an all-embracing force of love." Since anthroposophy seemed to answer the "damning questions" that disturbed him, Biely clutched at its teachings.

In 1914 Biely, urged by Asya, joined the Steiner anthroposophical colony at Dornach near Basel, Switzerland. There he became absorbed with the building of the anthroposophical temple, the "Johannesbau" (later rechristened the "Goetheanum," and destroyed by fire in 1922), and seemed to be wholly converted to the principles of his new religion. Nevertheless, not even anthroposophy satisfied his spiritual demands. When it had failed to soothe the yearning for mystery that filled Biely's typically Russian spirit, he began to fall away from it. By 1916, disillusioned with the life at Dornach, he began longing for Russia, where he would not be constantly bombarded by the "chatter of foreign words."[48] The thought that he was doomed to live indefinitely "among half-crazy 'occult' old maids," and to watch his Asya engaged in handicraft day after day "pounding her hammer on hard wood" was "driving him insane."

When in 1916 he became subject to military service, Biely seized upon this as an excuse to leave Dornach. Even though he felt out of sympathy with wars of any kind, he preferred to return to Russia that summer rather than remain longer among the anthroposophists.[49] Asya remained at Dornach, possibly having discovered, as rumor had it, a "new interest in life."[50]

Although Biely must have sensed that his dream of peace with Asya had ended, he was loath to relinquish it, and for the better part of the next seven years his restless spirit swayed between hope and disillusion.

---
[48] *Perepiska*, p. 302.
[49] V. Lidin, ed., *Pisateli* (Moscow, 1928), p. 46.
[50] *Nekropol'*, pp. 89–93.

88 The Frenzied Poets

During his stay abroad with Asya, Biely wrote little. His poetry consisted chiefly of the fairy-tale cycle *The Princess and her Knights* (*Korolevna i rytsari*), apparently written specially for Asya.[51] His prose took the form of meditations concerning the series of "crises" that faced mankind and civilization.[52] This series unmistakably reflects the influence of World War I on Biely's train of thought. Late in 1915 he began his brilliant autobiographical tale, *Kitten Letayev*, which he completed after going back to Russia. The life of Biely after his return to Russia in 1916 falls outside the scope of the present study, and can be treated here only in the briefest fashion.

Back in Russia in 1916, Biely once more plunged into writing. The intellectual ferment, the brewing revolution, the excitement of the war, as well as his own restlessness, stimulated him to great activity.

Finding that his own presentiments of an impending crisis were reflected in the doctrines of R. V. Ivanov-Razumnik (one of the leaders of the left-wing Social Revolutionaries), Biely allied himself with the "Scythian" movement that Ivanov-Razumnik had sponsored. The Scythians were a mystical-religious group of revolutionaries who believed that Russia would be the Messiah destined to lead the world to a new historical era. When the Bolshevik revolution came in November, 1917, the Scythians welcomed it as a mystical manifestation that carried with it a "purifying power of destructive cataclysms."[53] They hoped that the revolution would destroy the old world and all its values, so that a new mankind could be born. To Biely the November revolution had been a mystically revealed climax to his own cycle of "crises." Although his sympathies lay with the Socialist Revolutionary party, rather than with the Social Democrats, he, like other Scythian "maximalists," welcomed the new order since it represented a new

---

[51] See his *Korolevna i rytsari* (Petrograd, 1919).
[52] See his *Na perevale* (Moscow-Petrograd-Berlin, 1923).
[53] Mirsky, *op. cit.*, p. 242.

manifestation of the nearness of "the end." This action made Biely, like Blok and Yesenin, a "traitor" in the eyes of most of his literary colleagues. Alexander Blok records in his notebook an incident at a literary meeting where the crowd shouted "traitors!" at Biely and Yesenin.[54]

After the revolution of 1917, Biely began to take an active part in a number of new cultural organizations. In addition to the Scythians, he associated himself with the Moscow *Proletkult, TeoNKP* (Theoretical Section of the Commissariat of Education), and The Palace of Fine Arts; and early in 1919 he organized the *Volfila* (Free Philosophical Association) the purpose of which was to acquaint the masses with the social and philosophical "problems of artistic culture."[55]

During the early years of the revolution Biely, like most Russians, shared with the country "want and illness."[56] Like many other writers he tried to go abroad to escape the miserable living conditions. The urge to leave the country was further strengthened by a desire to clarify his relations with Asya.[57] Each application for a visa was denied, and each succeeding denial increased his desire to leave Russia.

In August, 1921, Blok died and Gumilyov was executed. Biely's desire to leave became almost a mania. At one of the meetings dedicated to the memory of the late Alexander Blok, Biely suddenly began to scream demands that he be permitted to go abroad. "I have no room of my own! I am a writer of the Russian land, and I have not even a stone whereon to bow my head!" In one room next to his someone "keeps sawing," in another room someone "keeps hammering with an ax!"

I cannot write! This is a disgrace! I must stand in line to get my ration of fish! I want to write! But I also want to eat! I am no spirit! To you I am no spirit! I want to have herring on a clean plate, on a

[54] A. Blok, *Zapisnye knizhki* (Leningrad, 1930), p. 198.
[55] *Perepiska*, p. lix.
[56] *Nekropol'*, pp. 85–86.
[57] *Ibid.*, p. 87.

small plate, and I do not want to have to wash it! I deserve what I ask! For I have worked since childhood! And right here in this hall I see loafers, parasites who have two and three rooms each... And I am a proletarian: A *Lumpenprolet!* Because I am in rags! Because they have done away with Blok, they want to do away with me! I'll not permit it! I will scream until I am heard! A-a-a-a-![58]

Biely's act so impressed his friends that within a short while, thanks to their efforts and particularly to those of P. S. Kogan, he was on his way to Berlin, where he was to meet Asya.

Here he lived through the last chapter of his affair with Asya Turgenev. Perhaps wishing to repay him for refusing to remain in Dornach, she now openly flaunted her attachment for Alexander Kusikov, a lesser poet of the "imagist" school. With a trace of bitterness Biely noted that "somehow, she had—changed."[59]

Stung to the core "not so much by jealousy, as by the shame," that she could have preferred Kusikov to him, Biely took to drinking. He apparently desired to show the world how far he had fallen. He began to spend hours in a certain beer garden, where he paid especial attention to the proprietor's daughter, Marie. Half seriously, half in mockery, he treated Mariechen as the incarnation of Vladimir Solovyov's divine Sophia. Marie's father, with an eye toward business, prevailed upon her to encourage Biely's attentions. The sight of a famous poet making a fool of himself amused the customers, who would therefore frequently buy him drinks and induce him to dance before them. Quite conscious of his degradation, yet eager to torture himself still further, Biely would oblige his jeering audience.[60]

By the spring of 1923 Biely began to show signs of weariness. But although his anthroposophical friends in Russia begged him to return to Moscow, he stayed in Berlin. He ap-

---

[58] Tsvetaeva, *op. cit.*, p. 219.
[59] Belyi, *Zapiski chudaka* (Moscow, 1922), II, 232.
[60] M. A. Osorgin in an unpublished letter to the author.

peared determined to drain the last drop of his bitter cup. Finally in the fall of 1923, feeling that he could endure such life no longer, he suddenly returned to his native land.

Asya returned to the anthroposophical colony in Dornach to study engraving, and has remained there.

During the period 1916–1923 Biely's narrative genius came to the fore, while his lyrical talent declined noticeably. His shorter poems of this period are filled with anthroposophical abstractions, which irritate most uninitiated readers. His two books of poetry, *The Star (Zvezda,* 1921) and *The Berlin Songbook (Berlinsky pesennik,* 1922), are markedly inferior to his first three volumes of verse.

The revolution inspired Biely, like Blok, to write a longer poem. Biely's *Christ Is Arisen (Hristos voskres,* 1918), like Blok's *The Twelve (Dvenadtsat,* 1918), interprets the revolution in the light of a religious revelation; but unlike Blok's masterpiece, Biely's poem is undeniably one of his weaker efforts.

In contrast with this poetry, Biely's one narrative autobiographical poem, *First Meeting,* charms its readers by its freshness and its light satire on early twentieth-century Moscow. The poem presents a curious blending of Pushkin and Vladimir Solovyov. In mood the *First Meeting* resembles the lighter passages of *Eugene Onegin,* and in rhythm it reminds one of the effortless ease of Pushkin's verse, probably as the result of Biely's prosodic researches. Its theme—Biely's first meeting with his beloved, in whom he sees incarnated Sophia—is definitely Solovyovan. The influence of Vladimir Solovyov is also reflected in the constant play on words throughout the poem. Such lines as *"Grafínya tólstaya, Tolstáya,"* ("the stout Countess Tolstoy") remind one of Solovyov's *"sogben ot neduga dugoy"* ("bent double from my malady"). The *First Meeting* unquestionably ranks among the finest longer poems of the past one hundred years.

Biely's prose of these years consists of works that are autobiographical in varying degrees. They began as fiction and eventually developed into genuine memoirs, a genre in which Biely has no peer in Russian literature. The best-known fictional works of this period include his novelette *Kitten Letayev* (1916), in which Biely attempts to give an anthroposophical interpretation of his existence from the prenatal period through childhood. *Kitten Letayev* has a sequel in *The Crime of Nicholas Letayev (Prestuplenie Nikolaya Letayeva)*, known also as *The Baptized Chinese (Kreshchony kitayets,* 1920), which continues the recollections through adolescence. One other autobiographical novel, *Memoirs of an Eccentric (Zapiski chudaka,* 1922) deserves attention. It relates the journey of a poet, Leonid the Icy (Leonid Ledyanoy)—obviously an ironical reinterpretation of Biely's originally planned pseudonym Boris Burevoy—to Dornach, his life there, and his return to Russia during the war. These *Memoirs* are written in a metrical prose so regular that it is likely to annoy a reader. All these semiautobiographical works reflect a desire in Biely to write a genuine autobiography.

The death of Alexander Blok (August 8, 1921), a man whose life Biely believed was fatefully linked with his own, gave him the opportunity that he sought. Almost immediately he published his series *Reminiscences of Blok*. The original series of essays soon grew in scope and volume, and became the 800-page *Epopée* that dealt fully as much with Biely's own life as it did with that of Blok. Its success led to a third version, *The Turn of the Century (Nachalo veka)*, fragments of which appeared in the Russian emigré press during 1922 and 1923.[61] In the last years of his life Biely wrote the fourth and last (unfortunately incomplete) version of these reminiscences. This new version now became an extensive series (over 800,000 words): *On the Border of Two Centuries (Na rubezhe*

---
[61] See *Sovremennyia Zapiski* for 1922.

Bugayev as Man and Artist 93

dvukh stoleti, 1929); *The Turn of the Century* (*Nachalo veka*, 1933); and *Between Two Revolutions* (*Mezhdu dvukh revolyutsi*, 2 parts, 1934 and 1937). Here Biely gives a pungent satire of Russian metropolitan intellectual circles of the symbolist period.

After returning to Russia in 1923, Biely continued writing at his former rapid pace. He produced three more novels: *The Moscow Eccentric* (*Moskovski chudak*, 1925), *Moscow under the Blow* (*Moskva pod udarom*, 1925), and *Masks* (*Maski*, 1931). They were parts of a new tetralogy that he failed to complete. Although in style these volumes continue the tradition of Biely's other prose works, they are on the whole of lesser value. During this period he tried to adapt his *Petersburg* to the stage and attempted to combine *The Moscow Eccentric* and *Moscow under the Blow* and rewrite the novels into a play. He completely rewrote also the verses of *Ashes*, published in 1929. He recorded his travels to the south of Russia in two books, *Wind from the Caucasus* (*Veter s Kavkaza*, 1929) and *Armenia*. His literary researches resulted in two works, *Rhythm as Dialectics and Pushkin's "The Bronze Horseman"* (*Ritm kak dialektika i "Medny vsadnik" Pushkina*, 1929) and *The Art of Gogol* (*Masterstvo Gogolya*, 1934). Yet the most imposing work of Biely's last years is his *Memoirs*, which have already been mentioned. In them he proves himself not only a master satirist, a true pupil of Gogol and Dostoyevsky, but also an artist. These recollections are marked by the fresh imagery and the lyrical feeling of a true symbolist poet.

Little is known of Biely's personal life after his return to Russia in 1923. His social life seems to have been very modest, although his friends, judging by his correspondence,[62] were numerous. In 1924 he married another former devotee of anthroposophy, Klavdia Nikolayevna Vasilieva. Although quite disillusioned with the German and Swiss anthroposo-

[62] See *Literaturnoe Nasledstvo*, pp. 634–636.

94 The Frenzied Poets

phists, among whom he had lived, he continued to be interested in the philosophy itself.[63]

During his later years Biely seemed greatly concerned with proving to himself as well as to his Soviet readers that he had a rightful place in the new order, that spiritually he belonged to the new Russia. In his lifetime Biely failed in this, and to an objective observer Biely seems to regard the new Russia as an alien land. His literary colleagues appear to him not as "we," but as "they," to whom he was obliged to justify his works and even his existence. Consequently, he concluded his volume *The Turn of the Century* with the plea: "Whether I shall continue these memoirs rests not with me, but with the readers."[64] Because the young critics of the new generation rebuffed him, Biely lost his self-confidence, his belief in his own usefulness to Russia and to Russian literature. On January 8, 1934, he died of arterial sclerosis.[65] In death his young contemporaries proved more charitable than they had been during his lifetime. In its obituary the newspaper *Pravda* wrote that "A. Biely, one of the most significant symbolists ... died a Soviet [!] writer."[66]

Biely's literary output is large. Besides revisions of his poetry and other works (which he often rewrote completely), he published more than fifty volumes and over three hundred essays. The one central impression that they create is that of a brilliant, restless, undisciplined, and frantic spirit that tries vainly to find his peace in the conflict of ideologies popular in his time. The grandiose literary plans that Biely periodically conceived—his trilogies, tetralogies, his memoirs—reflect his tremendous nervous energy and his boundless imagination. Yet, precisely these qualities prevented his completing one task before undertaking another, so that his several major schemes remained unfinished.

[63] Boris Zaitsev, "Vstrechi s Andreem Belym," *Russkiia Zapiski* (July, 1938), 78–93.
[64] *Nachalo veka*, p. 481. [66] *Ibid.*
[65] *Pravda*, January 9, 1934.

Biely is not and never was a "popular" writer. By nature he is too subjective and esoteric to appeal to a wide public. Only the writers and the elite among modernist readers could truly appreciate him. Nevertheless, owing to his brilliance and imagination he influenced Russian literature to a very great degree. For two decades and more, after the symbolist movement had begun to retreat, Russian poets from Mayakovsky to Aseyev reflect Biely's stimulus. The Russian prose of the 1920's also bears the indelible stamp of Biely's craftsmanship. Even in the field of literary scholarship, the formalist school undeniably had its roots in Biely's volume *Symbolism* (1910).

Throughout his life most critics belittled Biely's significance. Only the modernists praised his earliest works; the others either ignored or ridiculed his "ultradecadent" efforts. Even after his literary talents had gained general recognition no publisher wanted his writings, because Biely's polemics of 1906–1909 had made him many enemies. For years he was an outcast, obliged to remain outside the literary pale. Although the Bolshevik revolution of 1917 completely changed the Russian literary scene, the new order soon created a new obstacle for Biely's recognition. It was the officially accepted materialistic concept of life, a philosophy that was alien, even hostile, to Biely's spiritual nature. This barrier remained throughout his lifetime. Only after his death did his peculiar, misfit genius begin to reap its due, for Biely was the most original and probably the most influential writer born of the symbolist movement in Russia.

PART III

ANDREY BIELY AND "LA MÊLÉE SYMBOLISTE"

6

ANDREY BIELY AND VALERI BRYUSOV

ANDREY BIELY'S RELATIONS with Valeri Bryusov (1873–1924), like his relations with Blok and other symbolists, were by no means smooth. At one time or another in his career, Biely was at odds with practically every one of his literary friends. Nor did he quarrel with them only on literary grounds. Purely personal elements such as jealousy or ambition frequently appeared as determining factors in his feuds. And since Biely's works were closely associated with his personal life, his personal quarrels often affected his work, as well as his actions. His relations with Bryusov, like those with Blok, influenced his life and with it his literary creations.

Bryusov was the "little Napoleon" of Russian symbolism. Finding that the role of "leader" appealed to him, he deliberately imitated the Corsican conqueror. For that reason he particularly cherished the portrait that M. A. Vrubel (1856–1910), an outstanding modernist painter and sculptor, painted of him in 1905, at a time when Vrubel was confined to a sanatorium for the mentally afflicted. It depicts Valeri Bryusov standing in his favorite pose, with his arms crossed over his chest;[1] his broad face is stern; the high Mongolian cheek bones and the short, black, spade-like beard lend it an air of severity. Yet his black beady eyes suggest a feline slyness and belie a carefully studied solemn pose, calculated to impress his public. The portrait is a remarkable piece of interpretation: Bryusov, the poseur, shines through Bryusov, the leader.

[1] *Zolotoe Runo* (July, 1906).

The Frenzied Poets

Valeri Bryusov was a self-made poet, unlike Andrey Biely and Alexander Blok, poets by the grace of God. Bryusov approached poetry as a craft which could be learned and rationally applied. Of inspiration he once wrote:

> On, faithful ox, imagination,
> Come willingly, else we shall clash.
> I'm here; and hard my flagellation:
> Like me you'll toil or feel my lash.
>
> Think not at all of morning dew,
> Forget about nocturnal rest!
> Plod on along—alone we two,
> My ox and I, plod on abreast.[2]

Biely appropriately characterized him as a "poet of marble and bronze."[3] His carefully chiseled lines, although frequently erotic in content, lack an inspired glow and remain cold and stony.

Early in life, while still in his teens, Bryusov came to the conclusion that he was a poet. An ardent individualist, he became intrigued by the innovations that the French symbolists had brought into poetry; and in symbolism he envisaged a stepping stone to his own success and glory. Before long Bryusov had decided what his course of action was to be, and in March, 1893, he wrote in his diary:

> Talent, even genius, honestly applied, will bring only slow success at best. That is not enough for me. I must find something else... I must discover a guiding star that may lead me through the fog. And I see it. It is decadence. Yes! Whatever else may be said of it—that it is false, that it is funny—it is at least going forward, it is developing, and the future will belong to it. All the more so if it finds a worthy leader. And that leader shall be I! Yes, I![4]

Once he had decided upon his destination, Bryusov saw himself confronted with two main tasks. The first was to be-

---

[2] Valerii Briusov, *Stikhotvoreniia* (Moscow, 1939), p. 127.
[3] A. Belyi, "Poet mramora i bronzy," *Arabeski*, pp. 453–457.
[4] Briusov, *Dnevniki*, p. 12.

come so versed in the theories of poetry and symbolism as to win undisputed leadership among the younger poets. The second was to obtain a maximum amount of publicity in a minimum period of time.

Bryusov immediately began a planned campaign. First he plunged into a serious study of the symbolist movement in France and Belgium. As early as 1892 he translated one of Maeterlinck's plays.[5] At high school he busied himself distributing verses of the French symbolists among the students and teachers.[6] Eagerly he welcomed every opportunity to forego his school work in order to spend his time at poetic studies. Thus in December, 1892, he recorded gleefully in his notebook that because of the severe frost he had not gone to school, but spent the whole morning translating Verlaine, explaining in brackets that Verlaine was a symbolist poet.[7] By August, 1894, he had completed the translation of *Romances sans paroles*. Once more he recorded his achievement in his diary:

> At last something has been accomplished. The work to which I have devoted myself will not make my name famous, but it will be a valuable contribution to Russian literature. It is the translation of Verlaine's "Songs without Words."[8]

By this time Bryusov had also undertaken his second assignment, to acquaint the Russian reading public with his name. He solved this problem with success and dispatch. As a youth of twenty he became nationally known practically overnight, by publishing his three pamphlets, *Russian Symbolists*,[9] which delivered a resounding "smack on the face of public taste."

Although the "shocked Philistine" press reacted with expected indignation and heaped such epithets as "insane," "hooligan," and "half-broken-down boulevardier" on Bryusov and his collaborators, Bryusov seemed happy. His "success"

[5] *Ibid.*, p. 9.
[6] *Ibid.*, pp. 10–13.
[7] *Ibid.*, p. 10.
[8] *Ibid.*, p. 18.
[9] See chapter ii.

surpassed his own expectations. With pride reminiscent of Mitya Kuldarov, hero of Chekov's story, *Joy*, Bryusov recorded in his diary the progress that he had made:

> At the beginning of this notebook no one knew me. Today, the "News of the Day" [*Novosti dnya*] referred to me simply as "Bryusov," confident that the name was familiar to its readers.[10]

With the notoriety that the *Russian Symbolists* brought him, Bryusov found himself forced to confine his literary interests to purely passive pursuits. Since no Russian editor would consider publishing the verses of a literary hooligan, Bryusov began to study literature with great energy, and embarked upon a patient struggle to establish his respectability.[11] Occasionally, he would publish (at his own expense) a small book of verse more in keeping with accepted literary traditions, such as *Chefs d'oeuvre* (1895), *Me eum esse* (1897), *Tertia vigilia* (1900). Most of his time, however, he studied the classics of Russian poetry: Pushkin, Tyutchev, Lermontov, Fet. Occasionally he published translations of the better-known French symbolists, but was careful to keep within the bounds of good taste. Recognition as a serious poet and scholar came gradually. Not until 1898 did he find himself acceptable to editors, and then, strangely enough, it was the *Russian Archives* (*Russky Arkhiv*), a serious scholarly publication with a conservative background, that invited him to contribute critical and research articles on Russian poets. P. I. Bartenev, the editor of the journal, who offered him this opportunity, found that his appraisal of the young man's ability was sound, and Bryusov eventually emerged as an accepted authority on Pushkin and other notable figures of Russian literature. His serious study of nineteenth-century Russian verse helped him to develop a genuine appreciation of the classical (in the sense of Pushkinian) tradition of Russian poetry, and greatly influenced

---
[10] Briusov, *Dnevniki*, p. 20 (December 14, 1894).
[11] *Vengerov*, I, 111–112.

his own verse technique. For inspiration in content, however, Bryusov turned toward the West.

On the threshold of the twentieth century Bryusov suddenly discovered Verhaeren, whose urban themes and sense of a new pulse of life instantly appealed to the young Russian poet. Bryusov now became a poet of the city, its noises, its vices, its crowds. Verhaeren saw the city as an octopus stretching out its grasping tentacles, sucking the life blood of humanity. Bryusov, as the following poem shows, envisaged it as a dragon.

To the City

You proudly reign above the vale,
Your lights would pierce the very sky,
Round you, like lines of picket-rail,
Funnels of many a factory lie.

You are of steel, of brick, of glass
Enmeshed within a wiry net.
You charm the time to make it pass,
It never fails your keen magnet!

As wingless dragon waits its prey,
Across the years your watch you keep.
And through your veins (those pipes men lay)
Gas courses, even waters creep.

Your belly's never satiate—
Although you rob, age after age;
Malice complains within your gate
And poverty groans e'er with rage.

You stubborn monster, monster sly,
You have built palaces for looks;
Raised festive temples too, hard by,
For women, paintings, and for books.

But, O Unbridled, you call forth
The hordes to storm your temples high;
And madness, need, and pride of birth
You send each other to defy.

104 The Frenzied Poets

> At night while in the crystal halls
> Debauchery and laughter meet,
> And poison of sweet hours enthralls,
> Foaming in goblets, deadly neat,
>
> You bend the spines of surly slaves,
> So that the whirling swift machine
> May forge the sharpness of its blades
> Of steel's ecstatic lightsome sheen.
>
> Shrewd serpent with the crafty gaze!
> All in a burst of rage so blind
> You've lifted up, by your own ways
> The knife whose poison you shall find.[12]

Bryusov was not a symbolist of the same type as Vladimir Solovyov, Vyacheslav Ivanov, Alexander Blok, or Andrey Biely. Despite his essay "Keys of Mysteries," which he published in the *Balance* shortly after its creation, Bryusov found metaphysics and mysticism alien to his rationalistic and positivistic intellect. This essay, proclaiming that a poet, being a superior creature, held keys to mysteries that lay beyond the confines of our material world, appears to be mere lip service, paid in a moment of enthusiasm. Nor could he accept symbolism as a technique that required a poet merely to suggest, rather than state explicitly what he had to say; Bryusov was too much a classicist for that. To him symbolism was a literary method, to convey moods, emotions, experiences, and sensations.[13] For this reason symbolism to him was also a way of life. To obtain material for his art, Bryusov endeavored to live his life in such a manner as to experience a maximum of emotional sensations.[14]

By 1900, thanks to the prestige gained as a collaborator on the *Russian Archives*, Bryusov realized his ambition and became a recognized leader among the adherents of the "new

---
[12] Briusov, *Izbrannye proizvedeniia*, II, 86–87.
[13] Briusov's statement in *Apollon* (July–August, 1910), 31–35.
[14] *Nekropol'*, pp. 26–60.

art." Thus, despite his own positivistic inclinations, he played for a number of years the dominant role in Russian symbolism, a movement that basically professed an idealist philosophy. He owed his position as much to his organizing ability and business acumen as to his literary talent. Already at the turn of the century Bryusov began uniting a group of writers about the editorial offices of the Scorpio press. He used every opportunity for attracting to this publishing house, of which he was virtual manager, authors who sympathized with modernism. Contact between Bryusov and Andrey Biely became inevitable.

Biely's relationship with the Solovyovs paved the way for a meeting with Bryusov. Shortly after Biely had written his *Dramatic Symphony*, Mikhail Solovyov offered the manuscript to Bryusov, praised its author to the skies, and argued persuasively that the Scorpio press should publish it immediately. To insure its publication, Solovyov even provided the cost of printing.

When Bryusov learned that a new star, Andrey Biely, had risen on the symbolist firmament, he hastened to secure an alliance with Mikhail Solovyov's protégé. The two poets had attended the same school and had known each other by sight for a number of years, but did not become formally acquainted until December, 1901, at the home of the Solovyovs.

In the presence of such a celebrated "decadent" poet as Bryusov, Boris Bugayev tried to act the part of "Andrey Biely" and show himself to best advantage. Bryusov evidently was not particularly impressed. He recorded their meeting: "Boris Nikolayevich Bugayev (author of the *Symphonies*, and the son of Professor Bugayev) ... tried to say very decadent things...."[15]

Within a year, however, Bryusov had revised his estimate of the author of the *Symphonies*, for in his diaries he now recorded that "Bugayev [was] probably the most interesting

---
[15] Briusov, *Dnevniki*, p. 110.

106 The Frenzied Poets

man in Russia."[16] Biely apparently improved on closer acquaintance, and within a few months Bryusov acknowledged that his new friend was "a very great poet and *the most* interesting man in Russia."[17]

Nor was Bryusov the only man who held Biely in such esteem.[18] Vladimir Pyast, one of the lesser twentieth-century poets, writes that "Andrey Biely was the object of rapture," wherever he went.[19] And well he might have been, for at the turn of the century Biely was "very young, golden-haired, and charming to the nth degree."[20]

Andrey Biely was the darling of Russian literary circles. No sooner had he embarked upon his literary career than he became a legendary figure. Compared to the other poets, philosophers, and theoreticians of symbolism who lectured publicly on the subject, Andrey Biely was a mere youth. Yet despite his tender years, the erstwhile "idiot" displayed an erudition that amazed most of his learned colleagues, to say nothing of the average man in the audience, who was left gaping from sheer incomprehension and astonishment after every one of Biely's discourses. The young man's learning, coupled with countless little mannerisms, many of which he had acquired from his father, set him distinctly apart from every one else. Biely possessed another characteristic: he was the embodiment of mercurial motion. "Boris Bugayev never walked," writes Zinaida Hippius, who once was his close friend, "he danced."[21] Another contemporary of Biely, Vladislav Hodasevich, characterized the poet's movements: "He was constantly prancing about," "making half-turns," "pirouettes," "half-squats" as in his terpsichorean gyrations[22] he apparently attempted to imi-

---
[16] *Ibid.*, p. 121.
[17] *Ibid.*, p. 122.
[18] Cf. the reminiscences of Khodasevich, Tsvetaeva, Piast, Zaitsev, and Gippius; and Osorgin's letters to the author.
[19] Vladimir Piast, *Vstrechi* (Moscow, 1929), p. 20.
[20] *Nekropol'*, p. 15.
[21] *Zhivyia litsa*, I, 45.
[22] *Nekropol'*, pp. 7–99.

tate Nietzsche's Zarathustra. At any symbolist gathering he was the one person who caught the spectators' eye.

Now that Bryusov had acquired respectability, the conservative press pounced upon Biely as the prototype of the "decadent poet," and abusively guffawed at his prose and verse, which amazed readers by their freshness, "novelty, daring ... and flashes of genius."[23] Everyone in general "was entranced by him ... and in his presence everything seemed to change instantly." Even in a room full of other glamorous celebrities, when Biely entered all attention immediately became focused on the slight, narrow-shouldered young man, whose very entry "seemed to illuminate the room."[24]

Biely's eyes made a particularly strong impression. Olga Forsh in her novelette *The Raven* (*Voron*) describes that impression by referring to him as the "sapphire youth"; Zaytsev writes that they were the color of "enameled porcelain";[25] and in her brilliant memoirs of Biely, Marina Tsvetayeva relates how a female admirer of Biely once phoned him in order to ascertain the exact shade of his eyes.[26] Pyast recalls a scene in which Biely "squatted by the fireplace and began to stir the dying coals.... With melancholy, slightly surprised, slightly frightened eyes, he gazed at the embers as they would flare up and die down again ...."[27]

In his lighter moments Biely would entertain the gathering by sitting down on the rug, and "very cutely and humorously crossing his eyes."[28] Although "it seemed that everyone was a little in love with him,"[29] Biely appealed particularly to the opposite sex. He was "all softness, sweetness, and affection,"

[23] *Ibid.*, pp. 15–16.
[24] Piast, *op. cit.*, pp. 22–23.
[25] Boris Zaitsev, "Vstrechi s A. Belym," *Russkiia Zapiski* (July, 1938), 79.
[26] M. Tsvetaeva, "Plennyi dukh," pp. 202–205.
[27] Piast, *op. cit.*, p. 23.
[28] *Zhivyia litsa*, I, 45—an "accusation" that he indignantly denied in his memoirs.
[29] *Nekropol'*, p. 80.

108 The Frenzied Poets

and friends naturally felt inclined to call him "Borya,"[30] the affectionate diminutive for Boris.

Biely-Bugayev was the romantic figure, the Prince Charming, the "glamor boy" of the Moscow symbolists, and the mere mention of his name quickened the pulses of high-school girls. In her late teens, Marietta Shaginyan, daughter of a university professor and a poet herself, spent "half a wintry night" waiting in the snow for a glimpse of her idol.[31]

Bryusov's personality was the studied opposite of that of Biely. Where Biely appealed to the hearts of his public, Bryusov appealed to the imagination. Biely was ever charming, Bryusov sullen. Biely was disarming, Bryusov "demoniacal." Both certainly were "characters."

In 1903 Bryusov persuaded S. A. Polyakov, owner of the publishing house of Scorpio and patron of the modern arts, to establish a periodical for the new literature. He argued that because the *World of Art* devoted itself principally to the graphic arts, and the *New Path* concerned itself mainly with religious and philosophical trends, modernist literature had no organ of expression. Thus the *Balance* came into existence. Polyakov, himself a translator of Ibsen and Hamsun, became the nominal editor and publisher, but the actual manager of the enterprise was Bryusov. The *Balance* did not confine itself to featuring the works of the Russian symbolists, but included such foreign modernist celebrities as Rémy de Gourmont, René Ghil, Jean Moréas, Emile Verhaeren, Oscar Wilde, Aubrey Beardsley, Maurice Maeterlinck, Nietzsche, and Papini.

Once he had secured the *Balance*, Bryusov began to enlist the aid of various symbolist writers and made certain that Andrey Biely should be a member of the editorial staff of the magazine.

---
[30] *Zhivyia litsa*, I, 21.
[31] *Nekropol'*, p. 80.

After Mikhail Solovyov died, Bryusov for a short while took his place in guiding and advising Biely on matters pertaining to the latter's literary career. Thus, we see Bryusov explaining to Biely how the Scorpio publishing house had arrived at the figure of "100 to 150 rubles" that they offered the young poet for his book of verse.[32] Similarly we see Bryusov discouraging Biely from seeking to make a livelihood in literature. In a letter dated July 6, 1903, Biely stated that because of his father's death he was obliged to earn his living, and that he planned "to write for the newspapers." Bryusov replied:

> You know that you are not "literature" in the sense of Verlaine's "et tout le reste est littérature".... *Scribere ut edas,* as you yourself well know is painful. ... As for me, I may publish even "Lord knows" where, just as I may kiss every woman I see ... just as I may reach the very last boundary of shame. You cannot do that. And of course herein lies your immeasurable superiority over all of us. Everything touches you to the very bottom of your soul. We have temporal words, which we forget. You possess only eternal words, words for eternity, for ever. No, you can not become a littérateur.[33]

Biely appreciated Bryusov's guidance and regarded him with something akin to reverence. Bryusov appeared to him both as a teacher and a wizard. In one of several poems that he dedicated to Bryusov, Biely wrote of him:

> While temporal torrents burst their cage
> That tear my mantle in their rage,
> I call to men, and prophets seek
> Who of celestial myst'ries shriek.
>
> I walk ahead; brisk is my pace,
> And lo! a cliff; I see your face
> Bewreathed with stars, a stubborn sage
> With knowing smile and knowing gaze.[34]

Soon, however, the two personalities clashed dramatically.

[32] Briusov's letters to Belyi, *Literaturnyi Kritik* (October–November, 1939), 236.
[33] *Ibid.,* pp. 236–237.
[34] N. Ashukin, ed., *Valerii Briusov* (Moscow, 1929), p. 179.

110   The Frenzied Poets

Two accounts of the affair exist, one by Biely,[35] the other by Vladislav Hodasevich,[36] a younger poet, who was for a while a close friend of Biely, but bitterly quarreled with him later. The drama between the two romantic figures of symbolism arose on commonplace ground, the familiar triangle, or, since the lady in question was a married woman, a quadrangle. Biely in his memoirs discreetly veils her identity under the initial N. On the other hand, Hodasevich, to whom Biely during his stay in Berlin (1921–1923) had confided many facts of his private life, including the entire episode with the Bloks,[37] disclosed all details of the affair. Of the two versions, Biely's account must receive more weight, for it appears as a primary source of information, while Hodasevich's redaction is often based on hearsay. Several critics,[38] moreover, have doubted the objectivity of Hodasevich's revelations, which were possibly motivated by a desire for revenge, because Biely had insulted him in public.[39]

The lady was Nina Ivanovna Petrovsky, wife of Sergey Sokolov (who wrote under the pseudonym Krechetov), by profession a lawyer, by avocation a poet and translator. He was also head of the publishing house Gryphon, another modernist enterprise and rival of the Scorpio. The story clarifies certain elements of the symbolist movement and incidentally provided Bryusov with the material for a novel; it is therefore narrated here in some detail.

Nina Petrovsky was only a minor poet, yet she was a typical representative of the age of symbolism. In a period when an artist or a poet strove to fuse art with life, to "weave his personal biography into his creations," Nina Petrovsky, like the others, sought from life the emotional material that she might

---

[35] *Nachalo veka*, pp. 276–287, 467–477; *Omut*, pp. 336–342.
[36] *Nekropol'*, pp. 5–99.
[37] K. Mochul'skii, *Aleksandr Blok* (Paris, 1949), p. 143.
[38] Osorgin, Adamovich, Aldanov.
[39] Osorgin's letter to the author.

transform into her art.[40] Since love opened to a symbolist poet a direct route to an inexhaustible source of emotional experiences, the symbolist poets in their "search for the greatest possible emotional stimulus, often turned to the tender passion."[41] Nina Petrovsky, though not beautiful, was young, reasonably intelligent, somewhat sentimental, and possessed the important asset of being able to fit into her surroundings. Thanks to these qualities, she became the object of adoration and love of the poets.

One of Nina's first affairs was with the dashing and (in his own estimation) irresistible poet, Konstantin Balmont, whose amorous adventures were the gossip of the literary circles of Russia. She gladly served as his inspiration and muse, but after her passion for Balmont had died, Nina felt remorse. She was seized by an urge to display her contrition publicly, robed herself in a long black gown, and adorned her penitent figure with a large black cross and a string of prayer beads.[42] To her friends and acquaintances she turned with a mute plea for sympathy. The charming young Andrey Biely was among them.

Laboring under the delusion that he "possessed the wisdom necessary to mend broken hearts," Biely offered her his moral support and sympathy.[43] In an effort to assuage her spiritual pain, he began to expound his philosophy of life to her. Nina proved an admirable listener, and the result was that he succumbed to a "feeling of compassion ... for the sad, tender, receptive girl."

Nina was so encouraged by his attentions that she fell in love with him.[44] The hysterical era had apparently unbalanced her nervous system, as it had that of many other "children of the lost generation." Balmont in his autobiography states that many of his friends committed suicide and that his brother

---

[40] *Nekropol'*, p. 8.
[41] *Ibid.*, pp. 13–14.
[42] *Ibid.*, p. 14.
[43] *Nachalo veka*, p. 276.
[44] *Nekropol'*, p. 16.

went insane.⁴⁵ She, at any rate, came to rely increasingly on Biely's "understanding." But the more she clung to him for support, the more repellent became her attentions to her young "savior." When Biely began to tire of his role of a young Orpheus leading an hysterical Eurydice out of Hades, Nina, noticing the change in his attitude, became desperate.

Meanwhile Bryusov also had developed a liking for the young lady and secretly began to shower her with attentions, even though he was at odds with her husband, whose publishing house loomed as a rival for his own, Scorpio. Wanting to bring Biely back into her fold, Nina began searching for somebody who might help her. Her quest stopped at Bryusov, who was not only regarded as a romantically "demoniacal" figure, but was actually an amateur exponent of the black arts—hypnotism, demonology, magic, and spiritualism.⁴⁶

Bryusov dabbled in occultism probably not so much because he believed in it, but because he wished to make a "decadent" gesture. Nina decided to join him in his experiments, and Bryusov may even have practiced hypnotism on his neurotic pupil.⁴⁷ It is quite likely that Bryusov was jealous of his protégé's success in literature and with Nina, and, therefore, excited her already active imagination in the hope of alienating her from Biely.

Nina began to suffer from hallucinations and nightmares which she ascribed to the dark powers at Bryusov's command. Consequently, she began to plague Biely to rescue her from "the evil forces." For a period, the more she raved, the more he considered it his duty to rescue her. But in the end, Biely, himself on the verge of hysteria, was unable to endure the strain of the frenetic affair and fled to Nizhni Novgorod, where he took refuge with his friend Emili Medtner,⁴⁸ a brother of the composer Nikolay Medtner.

---
⁴⁵ *Vengerov*, I, 58–59.
⁴⁶ *Nekropol'*, p. 18.
⁴⁷ *Nachalo veka*, p. 281.
⁴⁸ *Ibid.*, p. 280.

Biely and Bryusov 113

Such is Biely's description of the affair. Hodasevich, on the other hand, interprets it from a Freudian psychopathological point of view.

Women excited Andrey Biely far more than one may be led to believe. Here his double nature stood out especially clearly.... He would invariably pursue the same tactics. He would fascinate a woman by ... appearing to her in an aura of mystic charm that seemed to preclude any thought of sensual longing. Then he would suddenly reveal his real desires. If the woman, astonished by the suddenness of the attack, and sometimes even offended, refused to yield, Biely would become infuriated. On the other hand, each time that he gained his objective, he felt himself besmirched, and would again become infuriated. Occasionally, like the bashful Joseph, he would affect a last-minute escape, just before his "fall." In such instances he would become doubly indignant; both because he had been tempted, and because he had not been led astray far enough.[49]

Hodasevich insists that Biely "fled from Nina, lest her too earthly love should soil his immaculate robe." He fled from her also "in order that he might shine even more radiantly before another, whose name appeared to designate her as the incarnation of Sophia, the Woman Clothed with the Sun"—Lyubov Dmitrievna Blok.[50] Interesting as Hodasevich's interpretation is, Biely's poetry indicates that his affair with Nina Petrovsky ended several months before he met Lyubov Blok.

Eventually Biely severed connections with Nina Petrovsky. Convinced that black magic had been of no avail, she turned to more concrete measures. She appeared at one of Biely's lectures with a revolver in her handbag, apparently determined to avenge her pride with blood. According to Biely's version, however, she was so captivated by the lecture that after it was ended she aimed her pistol at Bryusov, the evil spirit who had been haunting her. Bryusov quickly wrested the revolver away from her, and here the incident ended.[51] According to Hodase-

[49] *Nekropol'*, pp. 68–69.
[50] *Ibid.*, pp. 16–17.
[51] *Nachalo veka*, pp. 285–286.

vich, Nina aimed point blank at Biely, pulled the trigger, and the gun misfired. Probability certainly supports Biely's version; revolvers do not misfire frequently. The unfortunate Nina turned to morphine and finally died a suicide in 1928.[52]

In the fall of 1903, while the relations between Nina and Biely were still good, Sergey Sokolov, who apparently ignored his wife's eccentric behavior, invited both Bryusov and Biely to submit their manuscripts for a pending edition of the Gryphon miscellany. Biely obliged with several poems. Bryusov, fearful lest by aiding a rival organization he might hurt his own publication, not only informed the Gryphon that he could not contribute to its miscellany, but also pleaded with Biely to withdraw his manuscripts, and the younger man complied with the request.[53]

In the meantime, Bryusov became so absorbed in his amorous intrigue with Mme. Sokolov that he permitted his business instinct to be temporarily beclouded by his jealousy of his younger, albeit unsuspecting, rival. He allowed himself to forget that Biely remained a valuable ally for the *Balance* and changed in his attitude toward his protégé. Whereas formerly the two men used to enjoy "long talks together ... about Christ ... and used to joke about centaurs and their habits,"[54] now Bryusov ceased playing the genial, solicitous colleague and became inexplicably curt, morose, and inhospitable. When Biely, perhaps from spite, for he was aware that the relations between Bryusov and Sokolov had been strained, recalled all his manuscripts from the Scorpio and offered them to the Gryphon, Bryusov lost his temper and said a "number of very unpleasant things" to the young man. Bryusov soon received a letter from his erstwhile colleague stating that he would no longer participate in the *Balance*. Realizing that the loss of such a collaborator as Biely might harm the success of his pub-

[52] *Ibid.*, p. 278; *Nekropol'*, pp. 7 ff.
[53] *Nachalo veka*, p. 283.
[54] Briusov, *Dnevniki*, pp. 134–135.

lication, the businessman in Bryusov prevailed, and he wrote his rival the following conciliatory letter:

My dear Boris Nikolaevich,
   Your letter "to the publishing house" with your refusal to participate in it has amazed me. I had believed that ... the bonds that existed between us were too strong to snap after a ten-minute exchange of recriminations.... You heard only the insulting words. To me you can never become an abstract Andrey Biely, and I know of no one ... whom I should prefer having as my friend rather than yourself....
   The affair goes beyond just you and me.... To be sure, neither the Scorpio nor the "Balance" would disintegrate with your departure. Many others will join us, for about us already has formed the vortex that sucks in all those who float near by. But with your departure the Scorpio will be deprived of all that is inherent in you: *your* faith, *your* vision, *your* youth.... If you value not only your poetry and images and books, but also the power that they have over people, and the triumph of all that you believe in, then in leaving the Scorpio you are committing a crime....
   In conclusion, a word about myself. If I said anything insulting to you either yesterday or today, forgive me. I did not say it with the intent of insulting you, but in order to express what is in me. I shall never be ashamed to beg your forgiveness, and shall never consider it degrading.... I shall not cease loving you, no matter what sort of man you may become, what you may do, or what you may reply to this letter. I cannot help reproaching you, but I shall feel boundlessly sad and depressed if you remain a stranger to me, if we are obliged to continue our work without you.
   I have faith that you will reply,

Yours,
Valeri Bryusov.[55]

Within a short while Bryusov personally called on Biely and the two men were "touchingly reconciled."

However "touching" the reconciliation may have been, it was not complete and was, in fact, only a truce that lasted for about a year. Yet it moved Biely to dedicate several poems to Bryusov. The best of these is a brilliant sketch of the Scorpio's

---
[55] *Literaturnyi kritik* (Oct.–Nov., 1939), 238–239.

116 The Frenzied Poets

mastermind in which the staccato strokes of Biely's brush do justice to Bryusov's crisp personality.

> Sad your mien. Your dress coat buttoned,
> Serious, lithe, severe, straight-laced,
>
> You are bowed o'er heaps of writings
> Toiling for the coming days.
>
> There, you run: your pace is easy,
> Cane a-twirl—prepared to strike.
>
> As you leap, your black beard dances,
> Power and passion show alike.[56]

Meanwhile, Bryusov, constantly worried because the *Balance* was less successful than he had hoped for, thought that the periodical was "perishing." His relations with the hysterical Nina added to his worries. He thought also that Biely showed insufficient concern over the fate of his magazine. As the year 1904 progressed, Bryusov became more irritable toward Biely. With feeling he wrote in his diary that although Biely had signed the constitution of the *Balance* (giving it an option on his works) he disclaimed knowing what was in it.[57]

When in January, 1905, Biely went to St. Petersburg to see the Bloks and the Merezhkovskys, Bryusov became indignant, for Biely's action seemingly showed him quite indifferent to the critical state of affairs in the Scorpio office. When early in the spring of 1905 Biely returned to Moscow, Bryusov, "badly out of sorts," appeared in Biely's apartment and tossed upon the table some proofs for him to read. Suddenly, "like the pop of a champagne cork," Bryusov addressed a curse and a "very foul accusation" against D. S. Merezhkovsky, at whose home Biely had stayed during his visit in St. Petersburg. Then, just as suddenly as he had entered, Bryusov walked out.[58]

---
[56] A. Belyi, *Stikhotvoreniia* (Moscow, 1940), pp. 157–158.
[57] Briusov, *Dnevniki*, p. 135.
[58] *Nachalo veka*, p. 469.

As soon as Biely's wits returned to him, he felt obliged to avenge the honor of his recent host. He indignantly wrote Bryusov that he "forgave him his words, since he [Bryusov] was a well-known scandal monger." Biely had not long to wait for a reply; it was a challenge to a duel! "Suspecting Nina's hysterical hand in the mess," Biely accepted the challenge, although he added that he saw no actual cause for it.

Then the two natures in Bryusov clashed again. Once more the practical man emerged as the victor. Bryusov appeared at the apartment of Sergey Solovyov (who was to serve as one of Biely's seconds), "moved, mellow, and melancholy ... and sat down to write a placating letter which he asked Seryozha to deliver" to Biely.

Their next meetings took place at the editorial offices. Here Bryusov "cooed" to Biely:

Yes, it is well to die young. If you only would die young, Boris Nikolayevich. Before ... you have outlived your talent.... Just now would be about the right time![59]

When Biely, taken a little aback, replied that he should like to live "at least another couple of years," Bryusov magnanimously agreed, "Well, all right, have your couple of years." With this, the affair of Nina Petrovsky ended.

True to the symbolist canon that prescribed the "fusing of life with their art," Bryusov used the affair of Biely, Nina, and himself as the main theme of a novel. This was his prose masterpiece, *Fiery Angel*, which appeared in the *Balance* during the years 1907–1908.

According to his widow, Bryusov had spent a number of years in collecting the material for his novel, which he originally intended to call "The Witch." The novel itself was written hurriedly, in installments, which had to appear monthly in his periodical. Long before he began writing his tale, Bryusov had plunged into a study of medieval superstition with all the

---
[59] *Ibid.*, p. 470.

"passion of a zealot."[60] Throughout his affair with Nina Petrovsky, he continued his investigation of the life and customs of fifteenth-century Germany and displayed an especial interest in witchcraft. His papers contain numerous notations gathered primarily from his reading.

Germany of the fifteenth and sixteenth centuries, which combined a naïve medieval faith in magic with the nascent skepticism and humor of an Erasmus, became the background for his novel. In it Bryusov portrays himself as the hero, the narrator Rupprecht, and describes the difficulties that one faces in "fussing with witches." Nina Petrovsky was the model for his portrait of the witch, Renata, who is in love with Count Heinrich. Count Heinrich, whom she saw as Madiel, "the fiery angel," was drawn from Biely, and the basis for the narrative of what occurred between Count Heinrich and Renata was founded on the "tall tales" that Nina Petrovsky would tell Bryusov about his rival. Many of Count Heinrich's speeches Bryusov had actually heard Biely utter, frequently prompting Biely to use the very words that Bryusov wanted to hear. For the locale of the story Bryusov took twentieth-century Moscow, as the hysterical young woman imagined it, and then transplanted the resulting picture into fifteenth-century Germany. Bryusov's erudition and narrative talent enabled him to master his task so well that a German reviewer doubted that the *Fiery Angel*, which he read in an authorized German version, was actually composed in modern times and not a translation of an earlier original.[61] At the end of the novel, Rupprecht and Count Heinrich part on a friendly note. In real life, however, the feud outlived the love affair.

After the would-be duelists had become reconciled, their relationship entered a second truce. The men, working together in the editorial offices, met at frequent intervals, and with other

---

[60] *Ibid.*, p. 284. Also *Nekropol'*, pp. 18–19, where Khodasevich gives the origins of the *Fiery Angel*.

[61] Aiaks [A. Izmailov], "U V. Briusova," *Birzhevyia vedomosti*, March 23, 1910, quoted by Ashukin, *op. cit.*, p. 230.

members of the staff collaborated in determining the official policy of the *Balance*.[62] By 1907 a serious schism had occurred in the ranks of the symbolists, among whom several new factions had arisen to threaten the supremacy of the Bryusov group.

Fearing to lose his own position as leader, Bryusov convinced his colleagues that the rival groups were actually undermining the ideals for which symbolism stood. Although the Scorpions may have felt that Bryusov's interest in the welfare of symbolism was prompted by personal ambition, they accepted him as their leader, because the matter seemed urgent enough to "permit no vacillation" and because Bryusov was "a necessary man." Yet, perhaps because Bryusov's interpretation of symbolism[63] did not correspond to that of many of his colleagues, they decided against placing him in charge of matters pertaining to symbolist theories, and instead chose Biely as the chief theoretician of the *Balance*. Thereafter Bryusov left all these matters to Biely and gradually began to lose interest in the periodical. The relations between the men remained those of impersonal collaboration. In the February, 1909, number of the *Balance*, Bryusov felt obliged to warn his readers and critics that he disclaimed all "responsibility for articles appearing in the *Balance* other than those bearing his own signature."

Thus, by 1909, Bryusov had quite lost his enthusiasm for the *Balance*, and began to submit most of his articles to *Russian Thought (Russkaya mysl)*, an established and traditionally reputable periodical. Shortly afterwards he received an offer to join its editorial staff. To Bryusov this meant that he, a former "decadent" and "literary sportsman," had at last received nation-wide recognition. His ambition was crowned. Inasmuch

---
[62] *Omut*, p. 204.
[63] *Apollon* (September, 1910), 31–34. Here Briusov insisted that symbolism was "only art," and that, Belyi, Blok, and Ivanov to the contrary, it was not and had no intention of being a metaphysical philosophy.

120 The Frenzied Poets

as symbolism had served its purpose, and the *Balance* was no longer necessary to him, he withdrew from the organization. With his friend Bryusov gone from its editorial staff, Polyakov, the "angel" of the enterprise, probably felt that the costly periodical could be discontinued.

In its issue of December, 1909, the *Balance* published a valedictory editorial which proclaimed that:

> ... the two missions of the *Balance* [fostering new ideas and the culture of young talent] had created "the symbolist movement" in Russia, had organized it, and had transformed it from an object of universal rejection and repudiation into an all-penetrating cultural phenomenon that no one rejects any longer....
>
> So long as the problem that the *Balance* had posed remained unsolved, the periodical was not afraid to march forward. With time its external enemies did not increase but decreased. Its road led from complete rejection to an almost universal recognition, to the triumph of the ideas that it held dear. We believe and proclaim that in this triumph lies the basic reason for the discontinuance of the periodical....
>
> Through the victory of the ideas of symbolism: namely, that the new art contains the best forces of the spiritual life of the earth and as such is the revelation, through which mankind might some day attain the ultimate truth ... the periodical has become unnecessary, for it has attained its goal and *eo ipso* the means have become superfluous.[64]

The editorial spoke the truth; symbolism had won general recognition, and therefore the *Balance* was no longer needed, since the symbolists now had other periodicals open to them.

The symbolist movement, as a loose literary school, had originated from a yearning for a greater individualism in literature, and issued from the writers themselves. It had achieved unity because established critical opinion rejected its principles, which were contrary to the traditional dictates of social utilitarianism. In order to obtain a hearing for its cause, symbolism was obliged to pool the artistic resources of its individual adherents. And if symbolism was to become acceptable

---
[64] *Vesy* (December, 1909), 189–190.

to the broad reading public, each adherent, regardless of how individualistic he might have been, was obliged to submit to a "party program." When finally by 1909 the collective goal had been attained and its leading writers had gained national recognition as poets, no further organization and discipline was necessary. Balmont, Blok, Bryusov, Hippius, Ivanov, Merezhkovsky, Sologub, found themselves no longer looked upon as literary pariahs.

The struggle for the recognition of symbolism had in reality been a struggle for the recognition of individualism. When the victory was won, each writer reverted to type and plunged into the pursuit of his own ends. Too many writers who had claimed that they were numbered among the symbolists saw in symbolism nothing more than an artistic method, a means for literary expression; too few within the symbolist movement saw in symbolism an outlook on life, a means for revealing the truth of the noumenal, the "real," world. Too many grasped at symbolism in order to further their own prestige. Too few regarded it as a *cause*. And, unfortunately for symbolism, those who possessed the greatest organizing ability proved mere "fellow travelers." The germ that led to the disintegration of symbolism as an organized movement lay within the movement itself. Symbolism as an artistic method had won its victory. Symbolism as a closely knit school was dead.

New literary groups emerged now to oppose the "mystics," that is, Biely and those who continued to regard symbolism as a metaphysical philosophy. One such group was the "clarists," who operated with the periodical *Apollo* as their base, and who inspired "acmeism," which is commonly regarded as the successor to symbolism. In the polemics that ensued between the mystics and the clarists, Bryusov, despite his essay "Keys to Mystery," vigorously attacked the former group and rallied to the defense of "pure poetry," unfettered by metaphysical chains.

Even after symbolism as a unified literary school had disintegrated, the quarrel between Bryusov and Biely continued. In the fall of 1911, several months after Biely and Asya Turgenev had returned from their extensive journey through Italy, Egypt, and Palestine, Biely began to negotiate with the *Russian Thought* about publishing some of his travel sketches. He addressed his correspondence to Bryusov, then literary editor of the periodical. Bryusov, apparently, was little inclined to aid his former colleague and friend. Indignantly and despairingly Biely described his experiences to Blok: "Bryusov has short-changed me." In response to his plea for an "opportunity somehow to earn some money," Bryusov advised him to prepare a few connected sketches about Egypt and about Rades, the Tunisian town where Biely had stayed.[65] In order to "avail [himself] of some free time" to continue his proposed trilogy, Biely complied with the suggestion. Accordingly, he prepared an essay on Egypt (110 pages) and a shorter one on Rades (60 pages). On reading the manuscripts, Bryusov praised them to Biely, but "would not move a finger" to have the periodical accept them.

Finally Biely received an official offer from the *Russian Thought* to submit by January, 1912, some 200 pages of his next novel.[66] Biely believed that, since his first novel, *The Silver Dove*, which during 1909 filled the pages of the *Balance*, had favorably impressed Berdyaev, Bulgakov, and Gershenzon, they had prevailed upon their friend and editor of the periodical, P. B. Struve, to solicit another of his works.[67] To him, now desperately in need of money, this offer appeared providential. But his hopes underwent one cruel disappointment after another.

As literary editor of the magazine, Bryusov undertook the negotiations with Biely and continuously bargained over the

---

[65] *Perepiska*, p. 278.
[66] *Literaturnoe Nasledstvo*, pp. 453–456; *Nachalo veka*, pp. 326–332, 447; *Epopeia*, IV (1923), 212–227; *Perepiska*, pp. 274–275.
[67] *Literaturnoe Nasledstvo*, p. 453.

proposed remuneration. "At first he promised [me] 150 rubles" for each sixteen pages, Biely told Blok, "then 125, and finally announced that 'Struve would give 100'."[68] The compensation as compared to what was customarily paid to other well-known writers was very small. Leonid Andreyev, for example, who had utilized many of the symbolist concepts, received ten times what Biely was offered. When Biely objected to such discrimination, Bryusov laughingly remarked that the periodical was heavily in debt; and that he knew that Biely was "the least mercenary person in the world" and would be the last to be offended by a comparatively small compensation.

As usual, Biely had no money, and the trifling salary, 75 rubles per month,[69] that the publishing house Musaget paid him for editorial work was inadequate to support two adults. So he saw no alternative but to yield. Although his environment, physical and mental, was quite unfavorable to creative writing, he immediately plunged into his work, especially so since he had but three months to complete his manuscript. The attitude of his mother and his aunt toward Asya made the atmosphere at home unbearable. Consequently, through the aid of friends he rented a small house in the country. But as soon as he and Asya moved in, heavy frosts made their quarters, designed as summer residence, unlivable. The couple was obliged to return to Moscow. Here they stayed at the small apartment that Asya's stepfather and her brother-in-law, V. K. Campioni and A. Pozzo, occupied. But in these cramped quarters, with people walking in and out all day, Biely could not concentrate on his work and grew quite despondent. Then a solution presented itself: his friend, G. A. Rachinsky invited him and Asya to the Rachinsky estate in Bobrovka. Gratefully, Biely accepted.

Here, writing day and night, and "rewriting each page at least three times," Biely completed, shortly before Christmas, approximately 250 pages of a novel that began as a sequel to

[68] *Perepiska*, p. 278.
[69] *Omut*, pp. 342-348.

his *Silver Dove* but branched out and became an entirely independent work. Elated he rushed with his brain child to Bryusov, hoping to collect the money promised in advance. Again, however, he was cruelly disappointed. Upon learning the nature of the new work, Bryusov hedged; and when Biely openly demanded the money that was due him, Bryusov stood on his legal rights and maintained that the manuscript would first have to be approved by Struve. Biely argued that no such stipulation had been made originally, but in vain. The real shock came when Biely learned that Struve had rejected the novel.

Angrily Biely pursued Bryusov. "Bryusov squirmed like a thief who had been caught red-handed." He gave Biely a half-dozen excuses. With a shrug of his shoulders he explained that the "greatest merit of the novel lay in its wrath," precisely the quality to which his superior objected.

Officially Struve objected to the novel for its "malice and skepticism,"[70] although Biely, seeking to explain his own failure, attributed it to the fact that he portrayed his hero as "an absent-minded liberal" who suddenly "switched his political allegiance from the extreme left to the right." His caricature of this type of intellectual understandably seemed repugnant to the editorial offices of the liberal periodical, which had housed besides its publisher, Struve, several other former Marxists who had become converted to idealism.

Biely, on the other hand, felt that he "had been cheated out of three months' pay," and painfully realized that with each succeeding day his financial plight was growing increasingly desperate. Just at that time he received a letter from Alexander Blok, who offered to lend his friend 500 rubles, part of the estate that he had received after the death of his father. To Biely this aid came like manna from heaven, and because Blok's offer had been "very delicately phrased," Biely felt that he "could not refuse it."[71]

---

[70] *Literaturnoe Nasledstvo*, p. 455.
[71] *Perepiska*, pp. 301–309.

In Blok's noble gesture Biely found the support that he badly needed, and thereupon returned to Bobrovka and completed the novel. Soon word of the incident spread throughout the Russian literary world. Vyacheslav Ivanov, another onetime friend-enemy-friend, immediately organized a group of St. Petersburg littérateurs and invited Biely to his apartment, the Tower, for a series of readings of his new novel. The book, *Petersburg*, was immediately adjudged a huge success, and a number of publishers offered to buy the manuscript for immediate publication. Biely finally gave it to K. F. Nekrasov. When, however, the publication was delayed, Biely, yielding to the advice of Blok, agreed to have the novel transferred to M. I. Tereshchenko, who published it in three serial installments in his miscellany *Sirin* during 1913 and 1914.[72]

Bryusov's role in the *Petersburg* affair appears unattractive. Whether or not he had maliciously planned the entire episode is hard to say, although he seems to have been perfectly capable of doing so. Thereafter Biely understandably maintained "only a nodding acquaintance" with his former colleague. Their cool relations continued until after the November revolution of 1917, when both men found themselves on the same side—with the Bolsheviks. To most of their former friends they now appeared as traitors of the Russian intelligentsia, and for these people both "had died."[73] As soon as the two men again felt the common bond of public ostracism, a reconciliation took place between them. But not until a few months before Bryusov's death were they able to reëstablish a genuine friendship. It happened at Koktebel, where they had gone for health reasons, and where, in August, 1924, both participated in a vaudeville sketch produced at the resort.[74] On October 8, 1924, Bryusov died of pneumonia.

[72] *Literaturnoe Nasledstvo*, p. 602.
[73] See chapter vii.
[74] *Epopeia*, IV (1923), 217.

Bryusov has been accused of opportunism and insincerity[75] in his literary career. The businesslike manner with which he pursued his policies, both literary and personal, and his sudden changes of poetic allegiance, from modernist eccentricity to revolutionary pathos in 1905, to urban realism, to chauvinism, and finally to the exaltation of the proletarian revolution, support this view. After symbolism had disintegrated, Bryusov disclaimed that he had ever had more than a passive interest in or sympathy with the movement. Yet after his essay "Keys to Mystery," and especially after the quotation "and the leader [of symbolism] shall be I! Yes, I!" his claim that "the role of *maître de l'école* of Russian symbolists was forced" on him[76] sounds somewhat grotesque. Without necessarily sharing the personal sentiments of Zinaida Hippius, one may well agree with her claim that Bryusov's literary credo lies in the following poem.

> I long have ceased believing
> One view above all views,
> And all the seas and havens
> With equal love I'd choose.
> I wish my skiff may freely
> Sail over any sea.
> Both to the Lord and Devil
> I'd give praise equally.[77]

Bryusov's inconstancy is probably explained not so much by any sinister motives as by a lack of a firm principle other than fear of falling behind times. In such a light his rapid changes of allegiance appear both comprehensible and logical.

Whatever his sins, Bryusov was a vital figure in the development of the symbolist movement in Russia. So long as he chose to remain a part of it, he was an all-important cog in the total mechanism, and when he abandoned symbolism, the movement collapsed.

[75] *Zhivyia litsa*, I, 20.
[76] *Vengerov*, I, 109.
[77] *Zhivyia litsa*, p. 90.

Biely and Bryusov 127

In 1911, Emili Medtner attempted to reëstablish symbolism as a vital and growing movement in literature, but his effort proved anticlimactic. The former pathos predicated on a "struggle for recognition" was gone, and the artificially revived symbolism again collapsed. Although symbolism as a *Weltanschauung* retained its three brilliant representatives in Biely, Ivanov, and Blok, it inspired no spontaneous, unified, organized movement. Without the organizing ability of Bryusov, symbolism lacked vitality. Symbolism as a literary movement was revived temporarily in 1919, when Biely established the journal *Notes of Daydreamers* (*Zapiski Mechtateley*), but with the success of the revolution, and the official recognition of materialistic philosophy and realistic literature, symbolism became an anachronism, and the *Notes of Daydreamers* after six issues were discontinued in 1922.

7

ANDREY BIELY AND THE MEREZHKOVSKYS

WHILE IN HIS RELATIONS with Bryusov Bugayev appeared as Andrey Biely the littérateur, to the Merezhkovskys he usually presented the Borya Bugayev face of the coin.

At the turn of the century, Dmitri Sergeyevich Merezhkovsky (1865–1941) was probably the most influential figure among the St. Petersburg symbolists. Strangely enough he owed his prestige not to his poems, which prophesied "new dawns," nor to the fact that in naming his second book of verse *Symbols* (*Simvoly*) he had been the "first in Russia" to use the word.[1] He owed it rather to his trilogy *Christ and Antichrist* (*Hristos i Antihrist*, 1894–1902) and to his books of criticism, *Causes for the Present Decline and the New Trends in Russian Literature* (1893),[2] and *Tolstoy and Dostoyevsky* (1900–1902). In these works Merezhkovsky attempts to solve such timely problems as "what does religion mean to modern man," and "how can one surmount the feeling of loneliness" to which the modern intellectual is subjected.[3] The simplicity with which Merezhkovsky seemed to solve these burning questions appealed to the public. His use of the dialectical resolution of thesis and antithesis into a resultant synthesis disarmed readers by its oversimplified logic. Merezhkovsky prophesied that the "two religions," paganism and Christianity, which he identified

[1] D. S. Merezhkovskii, "Autobiography," *Vengerov*, I, 292.
[2] See chapter ii.
[3] Introduction to his *Sobranie sochinenii* (Moscow, 1914), I, v ff.

with flesh and the spirit, respectively, would eventually emerge as Neo-Christianity, a religion that happily fused "flesh and spirit." His prediction apparently held a possible answer to some of the "accursed questions."

By the beginning of the twentieth century, Dmitri Merezhkovsky together with Vasili Vasilievich Rozanov (1856–1919), Dmitri Vladimirovich Filosofov, and several other thinkers had succeeded in establishing the Religious-Philosophical Society.⁴ Since it was the fertile brain of Merezhkovsky's wife that conceived the idea of this society, the Merezhkovsky apartment became the center of the religious-mystical, so-called "God-seeking," movement. Eventually Sundays were set aside for intellectual *jours-fixes*, and the Merezhkovskys began to cultivate a following.

Dmitri Merezhkovsky was only the nominal master of the house; the real magnet of the growing salon was his beguiling red-headed wife, Zinaida Nikolayevna Merezhkovsky (1868–1944), another prominent figure in the rising modernist literary tide. She was perhaps the most brilliant Russian woman writer of all time, certainly the greatest of the symbolist movement. To the literary world she was better known by her maiden name, Zinaida Hippius, and by the pseudonym Anton Krayni (Anthony the Extreme). Zinaida Hippius was a poet of the first rank, and Anton Krayni was a literary critic whose subtlety and rapier-like wit inevitably resolved to her advantage all arguments with the old-guard publicist critics. In a scintillating essay of his own, Andrey Biely compared Krayni's trenchant essays aimed against Mikhaylovsky and other populist critics to a skilled swordman's devastating assault against an unarmed pugilist.⁵

In her poetry, she gave Russian literature strong, fine, well-chiseled lines that combine a deep religious feeling with almost Sologubian demonolatry, which make her verse appear as un-

⁴ Z. N. Hippius, "Autobiography," *Vengerov*, I, 176 ff.
⁵ *Arabeski*, pp. 439–443.

feminine as her pseudonym. In her essays, mostly personal causeries on modern intellectual trends and scenes, Mme. Merezhkovsky is a truer representative of her sex. She discusses her subject matter from the point of view of aesthetics and religion, rather than social significance, and at every opportunity lashes out at the popular sociologist-critics. Despite the frequent brilliance of her essays, however, she was more clever than profound. On occasion she can and does write with venom, but even then she remembers to remain a poet. In this respect Anton Krayni represents the new generation of essayists, who, unlike their predecessors, strive under all circumstances to express their views artistically.

The Merezhkovskys illustrate how opposite temperaments may attract each other. According to Mme. Merezhkovsky, from the very beginning of their friendship the pair constantly "argued and even quarreled over matters of poetic taste." Merezhkovsky frankly did not care for her poetry and, also, his poetry did not appeal to her.[6] In physical appearance, too, the couple seemed oddly matched. Drab little Dmitri was not a prepossessing sight. Zinaida, on the other hand, was the feminine counterpart of the glamorous Andrey Biely. Everyone agreed that the attractive, brilliant, and ingratiating "Zinochka" (the affectionate diminutive for Zinaida) Hippius, was charming with her flaming hair, green eyes, girlish slenderness, and impish agility, and everyone connected with Russian modernism was a "little bit in love" with her. Thanks to his philosophical and critical treatises, Dmitri came to be regarded as the Delphian oracle of the Merezhkovsky ménage, and his wife as its Circe.

The most caustic comments that emanated from the religious-philosophical group issued originally either from the pen or tongue of its ultramodern, eternally virginal siren, and only afterwards would the oracle promulgate the idea in his own

---
[6] *Vengerov*, I, 175.

words. Small wonder, therefore, that such an irreconcilable foe of symbolism as Leon Trotsky should have been willing to take an oath that Zinochka Hippius was "a witch"; and he was uncertain only as to "the number of prongs on her tail."[7] Strangely enough, the husband of this "witch," the "Delphian oracle," if not the Zeus of Russian modernism, had a doleful, vaguely pathetic air about him, which seemed incongruous with his reputation. Despite such divergence of character the Merezhkovskys, married in 1888, remained a loyal and devoted couple. Moreover, their interest in "problems of contemporary individualism," formed the basis for their life-long respect for each other's personality.

With the aid of his wife and friends, Merezhkovsky became the outstanding St. Petersburg literary exponent of the religious mysticism that was popular at the turn of the century. As such he constantly toured Russia and lectured to full houses on religion, philosophy, and art.

Since Merezhkovsky and his wife were inseparable, they always traveled to these engagements together. During their first lecture trip to Moscow, in 1901, they became acquainted with Mikhail and Olga Solovyov. Although Mme. Merezhkovsky and Mme. Solovyov had been corresponding with each other for years, they had not met before this visit. Bryusov, as head of the Moscow modernists and, therefore, acting host, officially introduced the two ladies to each other. The Solovyovs in turn hastened to display their protégé to the famous literary figure. Consequently, when on December 6, 1901, Boris Bugayev returned home, probably from the university, he found a cryptic message from Olga Mikhailovna waiting for him: "Come—the Merezhkovskys will be over. O. M."[8]

Trembling with excitement born of the thought that he was about to meet the "Russian Luther," as Dmitri Merezhkovsky

---
[7] L. Trotsky, *Literature and Revolution* (New York, 1924), 8.
[8] *Nachalo veka*, pp. 172–173.

was regarded by his admirers, the young man dashed downstairs. Mme. Solovyov met him at the door, and the expression on her face told him that her "myth" of Zinaida Hippius had been shattered. She led him into the room where the Merezhkovskys and Bryusov awaited his arrival.

The picture in the drawing room that met young Bugayev's eyes left him a little dazed. From the rockingchair shone the figure of a human wasp. A lorgnette and a pair of greenish eyes, set off by a flaming mouth, gleamed through a shock of red hair which all but "hid a crooked little face." "The Beardsleian enchantress" looked every inch "The Communicant slyly Tempting the Devil," from an illustration by Félicien Rops. The "devil"—Valeri Bryusov—stood nearby and his very pose betrayed how pleased he was to be tempted. As for Dmitri Merezhkovsky, the intellectual titan, the Delphian oracle of St. Petersburg, Boris had failed to notice him at first. The "Russian Luther" sat completely swallowed up by a huge armchair.

The atmosphere in the Solovyov apartment was one of tense politeness. Nor did the fact that Vladimir Solovyov had on a number of occasions criticized members of the St. Petersburg religious-mystic group help the situation. Bugayev, naturally, regarded himself a Solovyovist and for that reason looked upon the Merezhkovskys with distrust.

Although both Vladimir Solovyov and Merezhkovsky prophesied a new era that should witness carnal paganism and ascetic Christianity fused into a new religion, they differed in their views concerning the church. Solovyov advocated theocracy as the ideal world rule, and even favored a union of the Orthodox and Roman Catholic churches. Merezhkovsky, on the other hand, opposed any greater external control over human affairs, especially by the church.

Hippius sensed that her "ultra decadent" appearance had created a poor impression on her hosts and their young friend, and because she had been particularly anxious to impress the young genius (as Mme. Solovyov described Biely), she resolved to mend matters in the immediate future.

When in the course of a day or two the Merezhkovskys once more called on the Solovyovs, an entirely new Zinaida Hippius appeared before Biely's eyes. Instead of the "Beardsleian Sataness" an unaffected young woman approached him, who, despite her thirty-four years, behaved like a high-school girl, and immediately won the friendship of the twenty-one-year-old poet.[9]

Needless to say, on the night of Dmitri Merezhkovsky's lecture, Bugayev was a member of the audience and listened eagerly to the speaker's words. After the Merezhkovskys had departed for St. Petersburg, he wrote a long, "nebulously worded" essay, in which he refuted Merezhkovsky's ideas and defended those of Vladimir Solovyov.[10] He showed his letter to the Solovyovs, signed it "a student," and dispatched it to St. Petersburg.

Within a few days, Olga Solovyov received a letter. It was from Hippius, begging to be told the identity of the "student." Hippius wrote that the entire Merezhkovsky circle—she, her husband, D. V. Filosofov, A. Kartashev, V. V. Rozanov—had been profoundly stirred by the rebuttal. She begged that Mme. Solovyov ask the anonymous writer to call on Merezhkovsky immediately after his forthcoming lecture on a new trip to Moscow. Hippius used such epithets as "brilliant" and "genius" to convey the St. Petersburg opinion of the "student." As one may expect, this sudden acclaim greatly flattered Boris Bugayev.[11]

The Merezhkovskys came once more to Moscow, and Merezhkovsky's second lecture took place. Bugayev again sat in the audience, this time a little excited. No sooner had the lecture ended, than Bugayev, flushed and a little frightened at the

---

[9] *Ibid.*
[10] See Merezhkovskii, "Nemoi prorok," *Sobranie sochinenii*, XVI, 122–135.
[11] *Nachalo veka*, p. 183.

134 The Frenzied Poets

prospect of bearding the lion in his den, rushed backstage, where he expected to have a barrage of arguments meet him. But no violent debate followed. Instead, Merezhkovsky quietly invited the young man to call on them within the next few days to have a more leisurely discussion of his views; and on the morrow the young man complied.

Bugayev called at the suite of rooms that the Merezhkovskys occupied. The atmosphere was filled with a brownish, "cinnamonlike" mist which perfectly suited Merezhkovsky's own personality. As Bugayev entered the room, "out of the cloud of blue cigar smoke, like a flower opening its petals, the figure of Dmitri Sergeyevich revealed itself."[12]

At home Merezhkovsky no longer seemed drab or suspicious. On the contrary, he was quite charming, the young man thought. In conversing with his critic Merezhkovsky displayed no tendency to question or refute. The lion showed no inclination to rip the lamb apart; the distinguished author only listened attentively to what the young upstart was saying, and after Bugayev in the role of Andrey Biely had finished talking, Merezhkovsky invited him to join his group "in its search for truth." Convinced that Merezhkovsky was seeking no arguments, but only aid and advice in his search, Biely, swelling with the feeling of self-importance and greatly pleased, agreed.

Olga Solovyov, horrified when she learned that her protégé had come to an understanding with Merezhkovsky, regarded his action equivalent to a pact with the devil.[13] She could not understand how her Borya could possibly forsake his ideals; and she could not justify his interest in the Merezhkovskys as a cultural phenomenon that paralleled his own search for an acceptable faith. Biely's newly formed alliance strained his relations with Olga Solovyov, and induced him at ever shorter intervals to seek refuge with the Argonauts at the Vladimirovs'.

[12] *Ibid.*, p. 190.
[13] *Ibid.*, p. 183.

Biely and the Merezhkovskys 135

Thus, the Solovyovs gradually faded into the background of a "completed seven-year span." Their deaths, which came a scant year after they had introduced Biely to the Merezhkovskys (and to Bryusov), ended the discord that the Merezhkovskys had caused between Olga Solovyov and Biely.

Biely's acquaintance with Bryusov and the Merezhkovskys opened new horizons to him. The life of the intellectual Bohemia presented a fascinating panorama to his eyes. By 1902 Bryusov had already begun to draw him into the orbit of the Scorpio and into the life of the Moscow modernists, and the letters that he received from Zinaida Hippius brought the life of St. Petersburg ever closer to the young man. Bryusov with his talks about the Scorpio and the Merezhkovskys with their invitation to join their proposed periodical *New Path* tempted him and promised him a brilliant future in literature. Bryusov and the Merezhkovskys were like two magnetic forces acting on a steel rod—Biely. But where Bryusov attracted only the literary instinct in Andrey Biely the poet, the Merezhkovskys appealed also as human individuals to Boris Bugayev the man. When Bryusov enlisted Biely's support for the miscellany *Northern Flowers*, he paved the way for Biely's literary activity in Moscow. The Merezhkovskys not only arranged for his contributing to such St. Petersburg periodicals as the *World of Art* and the *New Path* and thus added to his literary success, but also had a direct effect on his private life.

Young Biely had had little feeling of fellowship for Bryusov, and since their alliance was based on mere literary expediency, the friendship between the two men dissolved when the expediency disappeared.

Biely's relations with the Merezhkovskys were of an entirely different nature. Almost immediately after their first meeting, he began to correspond with Zinaida Hippius, and for a number of years regarded himself almost as a member of the family. Although their literary utility for him had ended in 1904, when both the *World of Art* and the *New Path* were discontinued, his genuine friendship for them persisted.¹⁴ For nearly two years (1905–1906) the Merezhkovsky apartment became almost a second home for the young man, who accepted literally the invitation from Hippius that "in St. Petersburg he should live with them."¹⁵ Zinaida Hippius and her two sisters "Tata" and "Nata"—Tatyana and Natalia Nikolayevna Hippius—came to replace Olga Mikhailovna Solovyov as "substitute mothers" for the young poet. Here, in the Merezhkovsky apartment, he found the comfort, appreciation, and encouragement that he craved.

Life at the Merezhkovskys' appealed to Biely. It was an existence which in its Bohemian tradition defied logic. The temple of the "little hot-house daisy" seemed always to exude a strange combination of odors, in which the fragrance of tuberoses and the aroma of cinnamon blended with the smell of Havana cigars.¹⁶ None of its inhabitants retired at night, arose in the morning, or ate meals at the same time as any other member. Each member of its household lived his own individual life.

In the brick-red living room, Biely would sit by the fireplace, stir the coals and talk with his hostess about "trinities," "the church," "the flesh." The conversations would last until 4 a.m., at which time Dmitri Merezhkovsky would begin to pound on the wall and complain that they would not let him sleep. Occasionally even the patter of slippers would resound in the hallway, and the little man's face would poke in through the door, once more to register his protest. But the conversation would go on until a fresh outburst of pounding would finally stop it.¹⁷

The house had visitors constantly. They comprised "members of the family"—Biely, Kartashev, Filosofov, Rozanov—

---

¹⁴ *Epopeia*, II (1922), 175.
¹⁵ *Zhivyia litsa*, I, 28; also *Epopeia*, II, 174.
¹⁶ *Nachalo veka*, p. 423.
¹⁷ *Epopeia*, II, 174–175.

and "strangers." Biely was ever amused to see the master, in tufted slippers, shuffling out of his study to "sniff over his callers," and growl good-naturedly for the nth time: "You are ours; we are yours. Your experience is ours; ours is yours."[18]

Most members of the Merezhkovsky circle with whom Biely came in contact interested him only in the beginning. Dmitri Vladimirovich Filosofov, "Dima" (in contradistinction to "Dmitri" Merezhkovsky), arrived every evening for tea. This dapper, tall man had a sobering effect on the atmosphere of the house. Filosofov was the "housekeeper of the intellectual inventory of the Merezhkovsky household and acted as censor of Dmitri Sergeyevich's public utterances."[19] Anton Kartashev, who with Zinaida Hippius usually formulated Merezhkovsky's theses, quarreled eternally with his hostess. Their altercations invariably resulted in "tragedy"; Kartashev fuming helplessly would bang the front door and stride out of the house. But "Tata" Hippius, Merezhkovsky's sister-in-law, always managed to bring him back for a reconciliation. Then, there was Vasili Vasilievich Rozanov, "Vasya," whose "lisp and self-satisfied smirk" together with the shower of saliva that accompanied his words, nauseated Biely.[20] All these, like Biely, were "members of the family." Among others who frequented the Merezhkovsky home were S. N. Bulgakov, N. A. Berdyaev, P. P. Pertsov, and G. I. Chulkov. These men, all prominent in Russian letters, were, however, less intimate friends. They are of little importance in connection with Biely.

Everyone argued about religious themes; everyone energetically defended his own point of view; everyone strove to prove that his own solution of the dilemmas confronting the "modern man in search of his soul" was the only correct one. For some time, Biely identified himself with their characteristic "modern

---

[18] *Nachalo veka*, p. 424.
[19] *Epopeia*, II, 176–179; *Nachalo veka*, pp. 425–426.
[20] *Nachalo veka*, pp. 436–443.

man"; for he recognized as his own the "accursed questions" which they all discussed. He, therefore, immediately plunged headfirst into this maelstrom of words and ideas, frantically hoping that its current would wash him onto the promised shore. Soon, however, he began to doubt; next, the doubts became disillusionment; and Boris Bugayev, truthseeker, became bored with this brand of searching. The visitors at the Merezhkovskys palled upon him. He felt that the "God seekers," who promised much, had deceived him and delivered nothing. Biely turned away from the philosophical atmosphere of the Merezhkovsky apartment.

What continued to attract him there, however, was the company of Zinaida or "Zina" Hippius, and her two unmarried sisters, Tata and Nata, both painters. It was Tata who became a special friend of Biely. Her attitude towards him may well have transported him mentally back to his childhood and early boyhood, and recreated the memories of happy hours with Raisa Ivanova or Mlle. Radin. She would take him to her room, seat him on the gray couch and show him her sketch-album diary. During his "drama with Blok" (1906),[21] Zina and Tata became his confidantes, to whom he could come for support and sympathy. It was they, who "strengthened in [him] the belief that he was destined for 'Shch.' [Lyubov Blok], and she—for him."[22] Thus, even though he had tired of the intellectual fare he had found at the Merezhkovskys', he was grateful for the spiritual sustenance he received from the sisters Hippius, whom he "had initiated into the entire maze of his relations" with Lyubov and Alexander Blok."[23]

Shortly after the unsuccessful revolution of 1905–1906, in a period when reaction had once more gripped Russia, the Merezhkovskys went abroad. Since in a number of his earlier works Dmitri had criticized the Orthodox church, he now

---

[21] See chapter viii.
[22] *Omut*, p. 58.
[23] *Ibid.*, p. 62.

KONSTANTIN BALMONT

ZINAIDA HIPPIUS

DMITRI MEREZHKOVSKY

VALERI BRYUSOV

feared a possible reprisal. With their departure, Biely lost his shelter.

Although Biely had professed great friendship for Zinaida Merezhkovsky, he now wrote no letters to her; he was apparently too busy with his own affairs. The Merezhkovskys heard nothing from him until the winter of 1906–1907, which they were spending in Paris. One day their doorbell rang, and in walked Biely—"the picture of despair."[24] He had been tramping through Germany, and was now planning to spend an indefinite time in Paris. Inasmuch as the Merezhkovskys had no place to accommodate him at the time in their apartment, Biely rented a room in a near-by *pension*. Suddenly he fell ill; his ailment, an inflammation of the inner ear, became progressively more painful, until he finally decided to submit to surgical treatment.[25] Throughout the illness, operation, and the tedious period of convalescence, Zinaida Hippius looked after him with all the loving tenderness of a sister.

To Biely this illness appeared as the crowning blow of his misfortunes. His "ego, disillusioned in its religious and ethical strivings, oppressed by the ... political and moral reaction, disillusioned in ... love as well as in philosophical paths," now became a "corpse that was buried alive."[26] Such a mood produced the cycle *Corpse* with frequent motifs of self-pity.

> I came out of my wretched grave.
> No one was there to greet me—
> No one: only a sickly bush above
> Nodded its bare twigs at me.[27]

Although the *Corpse* hardly merits inclusion in future anthologies of Russian poetry, the following poem of another cycle of this same period,[28] certainly deserves that distinction. Despite

---

[24] *Zhivyia litsa*, I, 31.
[25] *Omut*, p. 182 ff.
[26] Belyi, *Stikhotvoreniia* (1922), p. 329.
[27] *Ibid.*
[28] *Zolotoe Runo* (January, 1907), 96–99.

ill-chosen epithets, despite repetitions, despite its subjectivity, it ranks for its pathos and the dramatic quality of its lame rhythm on a level with the truly great poems of the Russian language.

An Epitaph

Once I trusted the arrows of gold,
Yet from shafts of the sun I fell.
I had solved the riddle of ages;
Could not solve my life's as well.

Do not scorn the departed poet,
Take a wreath to his grave.
On my cross during summer and winter
Let the porcelain flowers wave.

Their petals are shattered.
The holy image grown dim.
Oh, the weight of my gravestone!
Will it ne'er be removed from my tomb?

I had loved the bells in their tolling
And the setting sun, aflame.
Why must I be thus tormented?
I am really not to blame.

Come to me. Take pity.
As a wreath toward you I shall sweep.
Hold me dear—oh, learn to love me.
I perhaps have not died,
I perhaps shall return:

From my sleep.

Zinaida Hippius may be proud that Biely originally dedicated this poem to her, even though in his later edition, he rededicated it to Nina Petrovsky.

Many Russians, particularly among the émigrés have come to regard this poem as a prophecy and a part of the Biely legend. According to some rumors,[29] Biely died not of arterio-

---
[29] Osorgin, "Vstrechi," *Posledniia Novosti,* January 18, 1934.

sclerosis, as officially reported by the press, but of sunstroke. If this be true, Biely—like Pushkin, Lermontov, Solovyov, Gumilyov—had a prevision of his own death. Another intuition of the truth lies within the words of the opening stanza, "I had solved the riddle of ages, Could not solve my life's as well." Ironic as they are, the words describe Biely perfectly. Despite his tremendous talent, even genius, he "did not know, and did not want to know how to live."[30]

Biely spent three months in Paris. Although he "had fallen in love with the vernal picture of Paris," and was sorry to leave it, he decided to return to Russia. Writing in Soviet Russia, a short time before he died, Biely recalled that in taking leave of the Merezhkovskys and Filosofov, he "thanked them for the brotherly aid that they had given an ailing man."[31]

On his return to Moscow, Biely plunged into a bitter polemical campaign that the *Balance* was waging against the *Golden Fleece*, the *Torches*, Ivanov, Blok, Chulkov, and "other former friends." Throughout the first year of the controversy, Zinaida Hippius was Biely's ally. She not only contributed articles under her own name and her pseudonym, Anton Krayni, but used also several other pseudonyms,[32] the most important of which was Comrade Hermann. She continued as Biely's colleague for a year. In 1908 she forsook the *Balance* in favor of the more popular *Russian Thought*.

When the Merezhkovskys returned to St. Petersburg in 1909, they found themselves out of touch with the world and the interests that they had formerly shared with Biely. By 1909, Biely had adjusted his differences with Ivanov; he had lost his bitterness against Blok; and the polemic between the *Balance* and the *Golden Fleece* had lost much of its former personal character.

Moreover, Biely had not only made peace with his former

---
[30] *Nekropol'*, p. 99.
[31] *Omut*, p. 188.
[32] *Zhivyia litsa*, I, 93.

Biely and the Merezhkovskys 143

"enemies," but found new friends and new interests. During his adolescence and early manhood he had regarded Olga Mikhailovna Solovyov as an older sister and substitute mother. In 1905–1907, Zinaida Hippius had played that role. The same "search for friendship and human kindness," that had determined his "relations... and the spirit of the games and jokes at Hippius' fireside," now brought him temporarily under the protective wing of Margarita Kirillovna Morozov.[33] She was the wife of a wealthy Russian merchant, M. A. Morozov, and although she was neither poet nor writer herself, she was interested in the intellectual life of Moscow. She founded the Moscow Religious-Philosophical Society and the publishing house *The Path*. (It had no connection with the former periodical *New Path*.) During some of the distressing moments of Biely's life, she tried to cheer him. Margarita Morozov, whose "eyes shone with [the fire] of sapphires and emeralds," replaced Hippius as his confidante. About 1909, Biely was drawn intimately also to the family of P. I. d'Alheim, host of The House of Song. In 1910 d'Alheim's ward, Asya Turgenev, became the poet's wife. Thus, although he still remained on amicable terms with the Merezhkovskys, Biely had drifted away from their sphere of influence. Once Zinaida Hippius realized this she—like Olga Solovyov and Bryusov—became resentful of "Borya's inconstancy," and soon broke off relations with him.

The break came a few months after the Merezhkovskys had returned to St. Petersburg. Biely came to St. Petersburg to give a lecture; and as had been his custom in the past, he lodged with the Merezhkovskys. While there, he fell ill, and Zinaida Hippius, as in Paris, assumed the role of a nurse.[34] Thanks to her ministrations, by the evening of his lecture Biely was able to fulfill his engagement and went with Zinaida Hippius to

[33] *Nachalo veka*, p. 465.
[34] *Ibid.*, p. 319.

144   The Frenzied Poets

the lecture hall. There they met Vyacheslav Ivanov, with whom Biely had quarreled during his polemical campaign and with whom he had but recently become reconciled. Ivanov had just read Biely's book of verse, *Ashes,* and, feeling that he had to talk with Biely about it, insisted that his friend come with him to the Ivanov apartment, the Tower, after the lecture.

Sensing in Ivanov another rival for Biely's regard, Hippius hissed into her escort's ear that if he dared accept Ivanov's invitation "she would never forgive" him and that he need "not return to them." Trying to comply with her demand, Biely excused himself by saying that he was ill. But after the lecture Ivanov "forcibly tore [him] away from Hippius" and "dragged [him] to the Tower."[35]

The incident with Ivanov ended Biely's friendship with Zinaida Hippius, who never forgave him. Soon afterwards Biely married, and began the series of journeys which eventually led him to the anthroposophical colony of Dr. Rudolf Steiner in Switzerland. On his return to Russia in 1916 Biely once more met the Merezhkovskys, at their villa in Finland.[36] Zinaida Hippius now saw him through different eyes. Borya Bugayev now seemed completely transformed into Andrey Biely. His moustache and the golden fuzz that had once adorned his head had vanished. The bald-headed, close-shaved man was a stranger. Although as formerly, he still "danced about, humorously and cutely crossed his eyes, and chattered incessantly," he talked no longer about religion, truth, or beauty, but about Dr. Steiner and anthroposophy. The man now bored her.

Biely's political views completed Zinaida's disillusion. Biely, who seemed destined to arrive at the Merezhkovskys' on historically fateful days, appeared at their apartment on the day the Bolshevik revolution broke out. In the past, he had appeared on Bloody Sunday, on the first day of the general

---
[35] *Ibid.*
[36] *Zhivyia litsa,* I, 45.

Biely and the Merezhkovskys 145

strike, on days marked by some political assassination or other. To the Merezhkovskys Biely's present arrival augured ill. Biely again talked, heatedly, with inspiration; but now it was about the revolution. When he informed Zinaida Hippius that he welcomed the new revolution, she was not surprised; she felt only "pity and contempt" for him.[37]

Soon the Merezhkovskys left for the Caucasus, where they received two or three letters from Biely. As usual, they were "insanely brilliant, but their eulogies for ... the Social Democrats ... left an unsavory taste in [her] mouth." So far as the Merezhkovskys were concerned Biely might have been dead.[38]

[37] *Ibid.*, I, 63.
[38] *Ibid.*, I, 20.

8

ANDREY BIELY AND ALEXANDER BLOK

With no other person were Andrey Biely's connections so turbulent, so complicated, and so confused as with Alexander Blok. Few people, indeed, were so dear to Biely at one time and so odious at another. The curve of their relations ran an eccentric course, climbing peaks of ecstasy and then catapulting into abysses of despair. Their correspondence testifies quite eloquently to their association, and for the better part of a decade reads like a fever chart of a man desperately ill. Not until 1910 do the fervor and intensity of their emotional reactions towards one another abate and their relations subside into a calm, straight line of simple friendship. During the intervening years, 1903–1909, Blok appeared to Biely now as a heaven-sent "brother," now as an implacable demoniacal enemy.[1]

Blok and Biely or Biely and Blok are usually regarded as the youngest pair of the several Siamese twins of the symbolist movement. The mention of either name has come to suggest also the other. Yet Biely was partly justified in insisting that the idyll of Blok and Biely was only imaginary.[2] Although the two poets undeniably shared many characteristics, their dissimilarities are nearly equally basic and deep-rooted. Perhaps one may more correctly say that the two poets mutually complement each other, rather than that they resemble each other.

---
[1] *Nachalo veka*, p. 8.
[2] *Ibid.*

The similarities between the two were great. Alexander Alexandrovich Blok was born on November 28, 1880, and was thus but one month younger than Andrey Biely. Both were the only sons of university professors—Blok's father was professor of political jurisprudence at the University of Warsaw,[3] while Biely's father was the outstanding mathematician of Moscow university. During their adolescence and youth both became saturated with the mystical currents that floated in the air, and were strongly affected by Vladimir Solovyov's eschatological poetry. Both men were distinct individualists in character, and both were endowed with a remarkable natural sense for rhythm. Both men, moreover, felt uprooted and vainly strove to recover harmonious relations with their surroundings. And, finally, the Russian symbolist movement reached its apex in the writings of the two poets. Their rise in Russian literature was nearly synchronous, and recognition crowned the efforts of both young men as soon as the modernist public discovered their work.

But here the similarity between them ends. Geographically, Blok belonged to urbane, European St. Petersburg, and Biely to patriarchal, colorfully Russian Moscow. Spiritually, the two men were also far apart; the grave, dignified, reticent Blok was surely no mirrored image of the mercurial, garrulous, gyrating Bugayev-Biely. In the life of the Russian literary Bohemia, Blok was a static piece of marble, and Biely a veritable human dynamo of words, actions, and mannerisms.[4] Blok's life was directed almost entirely by intuition; Biely, though by nature perhaps as prone as Blok to let emotions guide his actions, usually tried to subordinate his feelings to reason, or at least to compromise between intuition and intellect. In a letter to Biely, Blok very pointedly characterized this difference.

[3] A. Blok, "Autobiography," *Vengerov*, II, 315–316.
[4] See *Zhivyia litsa*.

148 The Frenzied Poets

Do not be angry because I write you always less than you write me. This is because I do not understand my own words when they are many. It is better when they are fewer in number.[5]

Bugayev was ever intent on finding out the cause of every phenomenon. He thirsted most of all for "infallible" knowledge.[6] Blok, on the other hand, confessed that "finding out" was not within his nature.[7]

Like many other children of the "lost generation" ("children of Russia's terrifying years," as Blok later referred to them), both Biely and Blok possessed two natures: the one essentially religious and moral; the other, lying beyond good and evil and characterized by an amoral, capricious, irresponsibile, gypsy-like, lyrical strain.

In his writings, Blok was first and foremost a lyricist, who followed blindly the dictates of his poetic will and intuition. "I want it thus," he once formulated his credo. "And should a lyrical poet lose this motto . . . he ceases to be a lyricist."[8] Since during the earlier period of his creative activity, the first of his two natures prevailed, Blok's outlook resembled that of Biely. Later, however, Blok yielded to the dictates of his second nature and proclaimed that none had the right to demand of a poet that "green pastures appeal to him more than houses of prostitution."

Biely, on the other hand, insisted (with Sergey Solovyov) that a necessary condition for art was "the realization of another, a higher will," to which a poet must subject his inspiration, and that a true lyricist created therefore "not in his own name."[9] Fearing that Blok might discard this theurgical principle of art, Biely as early as 1903 begged Blok not to "cast off the church, nor the 'crutches' of Vladimir Solovyov." How far Blok allowed himself to be guided by his creative intuition

---
[5] *Perepiska*, p. 53.
[6] *Ibid.*, p. 32.
[7] *Ibid.*, p. 204.
[8] Blok, "O lirike," *Sobranie sochinenii* (Leningrad, 1935), X, 61–90.
[9] Sergei Solov'ev, "O gospodine Bloke," *Crurifragium* (Moscow, 1908), pp. 153–169.

may be seen from his admission[10] that in his famous poem *The Twelve*, the figure of Christ in the van of the twelve revolutionaries came as a surprise to him; and yet, because it had come, Blok refused to delete it.

Although in his poetry Biely was chiefly guided by inspiration, his works rarely reflect pure intuition. Usually a deep-rooted rational factor is also present. Blok's works to a large extent are mirrors of his inner, spiritual life. Biely's works portray an external reality, as seen through the prism of his imagination. In a word, generally speaking, Blok is intimate, Biely is personal; Blok tells of his visions, Biely of his experiences; Blok is lyrical, Biely is dramatic (or, at his worst, melodramatic); Blok is wholly intuitive, Biely is half-rational.

The childhood of the two poets also differed greatly. To be sure, the home environment of neither was quite normal. We have already seen what Boris Bugayev had to endure as a child. Alexander Blok spent his childhood in a fatherless home, because shortly after he was born his parents separated and were officially divorced when the child was nine; soon afterwards, his mother remarried. Thus Blok, like Biely and, as a matter of fact, like most of the other Russian symbolist poets, lacked a "normal" childhood. Yet Alexander Blok received some compensation. Unlike Biely, whose precocity was discouraged at home, Blok found his early environment favorable to his artistic inclinations. He grew up under the devoted care of his mother, Alexandra Andreyevna Kublitsky-Piottukh (by her second marriage), who encouraged every effort of her son.[11]

In 1898, Blok graduated from the Vvedensky gymnasium of St. Petersburg and enrolled in the College of Jurisprudence at St. Petersburg university. He found, however, the curriculum not to his liking and in 1901 transferred to the historico-philological faculty.[12]

[10] M. Nemerovskaia, ed., *Sud'ba Bloka* (Leningrad, 1930), p. 226.
[11] M. A. Beketova, *Aleksandr Blok i ego mat'* (Leningrad, 1925), pp. 95–106.
[12] *Vengerov*, II, 316.

The Frenzied Poets

Although he had been scribbling "poetry" since early childhood, Blok claims that he remained singularly ignorant of the new poetic trends until after he had entered the university. Here, at the age of eighteen, he became acquainted with the poetry of Vladimir Solovyov, which, he was amazed to discover, expressed precisely his own intimate feelings.[13] At the university he learned of the "new art" and eventually came in contact with its representatives. One of his first friends among them was Andrey Biely, whom he got to know through the Mikhail Solovyovs. In 1898, when Boris was just beginning to think seriously of himself as a writer, he learned from the Solovyovs that "Seryozha had a relative . . . 'Sasha' [diminutive for 'Alexander'] Blok, who, like themselves, wrote verses."[14] Just that summer, at Dedovo (the Solovyovs' summer estate) Sergey Solovyov had renewed his acquaintance with his second cousin Blok and had become fast friends with him. Before long Sergey Solovyov found himself corresponding with Alexander Blok, and their mothers soon followed their example.

In the fall of 1901, Mme. Kublitsky-Piottukh sent a few of her son's poems to Mme. Solovyov. Olga Solovyov was so impressed with them that she showed them to the members of her family circle, including Boris Bugayev. Blok's poetry created such an impression on Bugayev that he immediately composed a poem of his own in answer to it. Mme. Solovyov's letter to Mme. Kublitsky-Piottukh may be worth quoting in full.

Dear Alya,   3/IX/1901

> I wanted to tell you as quickly as possible one pleasant bit of news. Sasha's poetry created an unusual, almost indescribable, amazing, tremendous impression on Borya Bugayev, whose opinions we value very highly, and whom we regard as the most understanding person we know. Boris showed the poems to his friend Petrovsky, [no connection with Nina] a very strange, mystically inclined young man, whom we

---
[13] *Ibid.*, p. 317.
[14] *Epopeia*, I, 137.

VLADIMIR SOLOVYOV

ALEXANDER BLOK

VYACHESLAV IVANOV

ANDREY BIELY IN 1923

The Frenzied Poets

do not know personally. He, too, reacted in the same way. What Borya said concerning the poems may perhaps better remain unsaid, because it sounds too exaggerated, but I am pleased, and I think that you should be, also. More than ever before, I advise Sasha to send his poems without fail to the *World of Art*, or to Bryusov.... Borya immediately wrote some verses that were prompted by Sasha's poetry, and dedicated them to Sergey. Here they are:

> Let it be foggy at dawn.
> I know, what I've longed for is near!
> Look: all at once disappears
> the basilisk's shadow afar!
> Let all be strange and austere ...
> Let it be foggy at dawn.
> I know, what I've longed for is near.
>
> Tender and pale, the east glows aflame.
> Do you realize—night is a-wane?
> Do you recognize freedom's refrain—
> like the sigh of a breeze—come and gone—
> spreading the news of the sun?
> Slumbers the cypress grown numb ...
> Do you realize—night is a-wane?
>
> Yielding, I press once again
> tender white flowers to my heart ...
> Those tender visions of gold,
> those sacred greetings of old,
> painfully pierce through my heart.
> Yielding, I press once again
> "tender white flowers to my heart."[15]

Blok appreciated this show of esteem and, thanks to Solovyov and Bugayev, came to believe that Moscow was closer to him than his native St. Petersburg. In one of his letters to Sergey Solovyov he stated that Moscow, unlike St. Petersburg, was "pure, white, primordial."[16] He also referred to Bugayev.

---

[15] Cf. Vladimir Solov'ev, "Belye kolokol'chiki," and "Vnov' belye kolokol'chiki." *Stikhotvoreniia* (6th ed.; Moscow, 1915), pp. 208, 213.
[16] Blok, *Pis'ma* (Leningrad, 1925), p. 48.

"It is strange that I have never met this man, who is so near and dear to me, and have not yet exchanged a single word with him."[17]

The Solovyov apartment became a clearing house for communications with Blok. Blok's many letters to Sergey Solovyov were not only read by the Solovyov family, but also formed the basis for their discussions.[18] Mme. Solovyov acted as Biely's special agent and delivered his messages to Blok, through Mme. Kublitsky-Piottukh. A peculiar sensitivity existed between the two men, which at first prevented them from writing directly to each other. Finally on December 22, 1902 (less than a month before her death) Olga Solovyov informed Blok's mother that Bugayev wanted to write to Sasha, but that he lacked the "courage to do so," and that for that reason he asked her to find out whether Alexandra Andreyevna might think it either "strange or out of place."[19]

Blok, too, had been interested in communicating directly with Bugayev, and Mme. Solovyov's letter served as an impulse for the two young men simultaneously to write each other letters that crossed in the mails. Both interpreted this coincidental meeting of minds as an act of fate.

On January 4, 1903, Bugayev wrote Blok a flowery letter "in the nature of a philosophical dissertation."[20] To his amazement, on the very next day he received a blue envelope that was characteristic of Blok—mailed from St. Petersburg on January 3. Blok's letter was a critical essay discussing Biely's article "Forms of Art," which had appeared in the *World of Art*.[21] Blok in his letter sought to clarify what Biely had meant by the term "music," and stressed his belief that Biely had used the term too loosely. Blok insisted that "music" in its

[17] *Ibid.*
[18] *Epopeia*, I, 157–158.
[19] *Perepiska*, p. 208.
[20] *Epopeia*, I, 159 ff; *Perepiska*, pp. 7–12.
[21] See *Mir Iskusstva* (December, 1902), 343–361; also *Nachalo veka*, p. 259.

154 The Frenzied Poets

ordinary connotation did not convey the Pythagorean meaning "music of the spheres,"[22] to which Biely had apparently confined it. Blok's further discussion of the term "music of the spheres" revealed that he too was inclined toward the mysticism of Vladimir Solovyov. "Music of the spheres" was the symbol of symbols toward which culture was striving; it symbolized "her," who is one in all muses. She was the muse of music, and at the same time, she was the Sophia of Vladimir Solovyov's poetry. Biely had already written about her in his *Dramatic Symphony*.

The fact that both young men had written simultaneously to each other created a profound impression on them. It gave rise to an unusual friendship between the two poets, a friendship not devoid of elements of humor and tragedy, and one that brought with it bitterness, misunderstanding, and yet a sense of mystic gratification. Blok wrote to Biely in later years that he "could not help feeling that their relations were based on something more significant" than they themselves.[23]

Strangely enough, although Blok was the less voluble of the two men, in this correspondence it was he who brought their relationship to a plane of ecstatic spiritual intimacy. Upon his initiative each of the two poets was soon addressing the other as "dear brother" and regarding him as a heaven-sent companion. In one of his first letters, Blok confessed that he had felt a natural necessity to become more closely acquainted with his correspondent,[24] and that he longed to "hear Biely's heart blossom."[25] And whereas Biely ended his letters merely "Sincerely yours,"[26] Blok was the first to write a letter that bordered on the ecstatic.

---
[22] *Perepiska*, pp. 3–4.
[23] *Ibid.*, p. 232.
[24] *Ibid.*, p. 7.
[25] *Ibid.*, p. 5.
[26] *Ibid.*, p. 14.

17/1/1903

Dear and sweet [*Mily i dorogoy*] Boris Nikolayevich,
    Received your letter today. At the same time I learned all about the deaths of O. M. and M. S. Solovyov. I embrace you; kiss you. Apparently this is just as it had to be. If it is not too difficult, write a few words. How is Seryozha? Dearest, beloved one [*mily, vozlyublenny*], I am with you. I love you.

Deeply faithfully yours,
Alexander Blok.[27]

Only after the ice had been broken, did Biely respond in kind and end his next letter, "joyfully I kiss you." The non-Russian reader must be cautioned not to misinterpret the relations that arose between the two poets. Nothing indicates that they regarded each other as anything other than "spiritual brothers," and the terms of endearment in their correspondence must not be looked upon as anything transcending the bounds of propriety.

After the death of the Solovyovs, Bugayev continued to broadcast his praise of Blok's muse in Moscow. Thanks to Biely's efforts, the Argonauts[28] came to regard Blok as the foremost Russian poet of the time several years before he was known to the average reader. Not content, however, with such missionary work, Biely took it upon himself to act as Blok's literary agent and began to acquaint the Moscow modernist publishers with his verse. In a letter dated September 13, 1903, he asked Blok to send him a few poems that he might submit to the Gryphon miscellany.[29] Blok repaid Biely in kind and went a step further. Not only did he show Biely's poetry to such modernists as P. P. Pertsov (editor of the *New Path*),[30] but occasionally submitted his friend's letters for publication, even without first notifying Biely.

Early in 1903 Blok's review of Biely's *Dramatic Symphony*

---
[27] *Ibid.*, p. 15.
[28] See chapter v.
[29] *Perepiska*, p. 51.
[30] *Ibid.*, pp. 19–21, 51.

156 The Frenzied Poets

appeared in the *New Path*. Blok's essay is not so much a review in the conventional sense as a lyrical "echo" to Biely's poem in prose. Blok's composition shows how a symbolist interprets a symbolist work. In it Blok made no effort to reason out the contents of Biely's *Symphony;* he made no effort to "interpret" it in the usual sense of the word. Blok's "review" was, rather, a poetic response to the mood that Biely's novelette had created in him. It was purely a lyrical expression of his own mystic mood, a perfect example of the irrationality of symbolism:

I dreamed of all this once. Or rather, it all had appeared before my imagination in the uncertain flickering strip that separates the brief sleep of rest from the eternal sleep of life. Upon waking suddenly, after labors and cares, I would walk to the window and see in the clear distance seemingly strange contours of buildings. And above moved a curtain that concealed from me the twilight of all-perceiving God. And the curtain was about to drop! Is this what I have dreamed, I who has emerged from weariness and who now departs into weariness, a timid passer-by? And like a candle, the light of which the wind causes to flicker in the window, I would gaze forward—into the calmness of the night—and then look back into the daily abode of my toil.

"The morning cometh and also the night" (Isaiah).[31] The music of the night is dim. The twinkling stars keep ringing. The light of dawn appears. The pearls pour down. *Incarnation* approaches. Someone has risen and whispers from above, "Dear one, is it you?"

"Something seeks to be put into words. Something is still unsaid. Something is happening. But it is neither here nor there" (Vl.[adimir] Solovyov).[32] I turn around. No one.

But "he that hath the bride is the bridegroom" (St. John).[33] He shall recognize the voice of his Companion before the others. He who yearns to rush headlong into the mountains hears the voice beyond the divide. You shall not fall asleep in the "gold-crimson" night. In the morning you shall say softly at her window: "Greetings, O rose-colored Companion, O fairy tale that is the dawn!" Who was it that had told this to you? "What has happened to you this night? Has the Angel of Hopes talked with you?" (Vl.[adimir] Solovyov).[34]

[31] Isaiah, xxi:12.
[32] Vladimir Solov'ev, *Stikhotvoreniia*, p. 210.
[33] St. John, iii:29.
[34] Vladimir Solov'ev, *op. cit.*, p. 137.

Biely and Blok 157

I insist, this is not a book. Let the seer tell his prophecy; let the belated traveler hasten; and let the monk pray. As for me, "I have already dreamed this dream."[35]

When Blok became engaged to be married, few people outside his immediate family knew of the event. Two of those whom Blok took into his confidence were Sergey Solovyov and Andrey Biely. On March 20, 1903, Blok wrote Solovyov of his impending marriage, the date of which was still uncertain. Blok gave Solovyov this news in confidence, and begged his younger friend to "tell no one of this—not even Boris Nikolayevich Bugayev, to say nothing of relatives [!]."[36] A few weeks later, however, Blok notified Biely also of his engagement, and at the same time asked both young men to act as ushers at his wedding. The two readily accepted the invitation, but the death of Professor Bugayev forced his son soon to alter his plans,[37] and Solovyov alone attended the wedding.

Blok's fiancée was Lyubov Dmitrievna Mendeleyev, daughter of the famous Russian chemist, Dmitri Ivanovich Mendeleyev (1834–1907). To Blok she appeared as the Lady Beautiful, in whom he was startled to recognize the incarnate divine Sophia. Consequently, the love that she aroused in him was akin to a lofty, devout adoration. He wooed her passionately. Several times, when she was cool, he was on the verge of suicide, and when he finally won her consent he was beside himself with rapture. On August 17, 1903, they were married.

As his Lady Beautiful, Lyubov inspired Blok to write hundreds of poems. They were hymns that he sang to his deity in expectation of the great mysteries that would soon come to pass. With a feeling of ecstasy and alarm, Blok (like Biely) awaited the end of the world, and in his mind he therefore connected the image of his Lady Beautiful—his vision of the Woman Clothed with the Sun—with his own eschatological expec-

[35] *Novyi Put'* (April, 1903), 164–165.
[36] Blok, *Pis'ma*, p. 50.
[37] *Perepiska*, p. 33.

158   The Frenzied Poets

tations. He, therefore, hailed the apocalyptic writings of Vladimir Solovyov as inspired revelations and came to regard himself as a disciple of the philosopher. The imprint of Solovyov is unmistakable in the entire cycle, *Poems of the Lady Beautiful.*

> My prophecy has been fulfilled:
> Before the end of days,
> I see your shrine glow bright once more
> Mysteriously ablaze.
> Enraptured by a mystery great,
> Triumphantly I stand
> And know full well that not by chance
> Are prophecies at hand.
>
> (March, 1901)

Such was the *leitmotif* of Blok's *Poems of the Lady Beautiful,* and the spirit in which he conducted his courtship suited his verse. Only after his marriage did Blok gradually realize that the woman whom he had regarded as a metaphysical entity, as a fourth hypostasis of God, was only a very real flesh-and-blood human and "devoid of all metaphysics."[38] He saw now that Lyubov Blok had no desire to remain an incarnated deity and asked to be just a woman. This discovery undoubtedly shocked the sensitive poet. The mood of his poetry as well as the image of his muse were soon completely transformed.

Strangely enough, Blok seems to have prophesied the change three years before the event:

> I have a prescience of You. The years go by:
> And yet You in Your single image still I see
> Aflame and clear beyond endurance is the sky
> While I with sorrow and with love wait silently.
>
> Aflame is the horizon; close Your appearance seen.
> And yet a bold suspicion in me you'll excite
> And finally will change Your customary mien.
> I dread to see Your face in its new light.

---
[38] *Omut,* p. 11.

How I shall sink—so low, so piteous—I fear
Unable my mortal reveries to overcome!
How clear is the horizon! Your radiance—how near!
And yet I dread the change that You'll have undergone.
                                            (June, 1901)

Disillusioned in his dreams, Blok discovered that the vision of the Lady Beautiful, which had long haunted his reveries, was gone. Even though subconsciously he had apparently desired a tragic outcome for his love affair and was prepared for it, the loss struck him as a stunning, mortal blow. Poetic inspiration—which, he discovered, depended on her image—meant his very life to him. His notebooks reflect the torment that he felt arising from a growing spiritual deafness—an inability to hear his "music of the spheres." Thus in April, 1904, Blok complained that he could no longer sense her. On May 1, he recorded that although she was gone, he was "still in love with her." In vain he tried to resurrect her image and finally, left without inspiration, cried out in despair: "Lord! How long have I been without poetry! How will this end? How black my soul feels! How tortured!" By June, 1904, he felt spiritually utterly destitute. Still seeking her, he turned for inspiration to the philosophical writings of Vladimir Solovyov, but found no solace there, "only unbelievable boredom."[89] Rebellious now, Blok renounced his belief in Christ as well as in Solovyov. Frantically he continued his search and, as his desperation grew, began to yield to his gypsylike Dostoyevskian other nature.

Inspiration returned slowly and in an unexpected guise. Gone was his former mood of religious mysticism, as seen in the following example. Here Blok appears as one of the pioneers of the Russian "tonic verse" with its disregard of the classical meter.

---

[89] Blok, *Pis'ma k E.P. Ivanovu* (Moscow-Leningrad, 1936), p. 21.

We Two Old Men

We two old men wander on solitarily,
About us a misty night.
Before us windows glow in the distance,
And the far-off sky is light.

But whence into our mysterious twilight
Has come this azure gleam?
We tremble with but a single vision
Before you, the unseen.

Oh, whence have come the hazy clouds
That burst into crimson sparks,
The threads of gold that onward stream
The dawn that lights the dark?

We two old men press ahead towards the twilight;
The windows glow again.
We tremble now with a single vision—
For we've learned the price of pain.

(December, 1901)

Now, however, self-mockery and irony replaced adoration and ecstasy. Blok's next cycle of poetry *Earth Bubbles* with its Shakespearean epigraph, "The earth hath bubbles as the water has, and these are of them," suggested that the Lady Beautiful had yielded to one of Macbeth's witches. By January, 1905, demons seem to have possessed Blok. The following poem typifies his new mood.

Swamp Imps

I had chased you with a whip
Through the brush at noon,
So that we two might await
Quiet oblivion.

Here we two sit on the moss
Midst a swamp: the while
A third—the crescent moon above—
Has wanly crooked its smile.

> I'm like you—a child of woods;
> My features are effaced.
> Still as water, low as grass,
> A devil self-abased.
>
> And upon my dunce cap hangs
> The bell of parting friends;
> Beyond our shoulders, far off lies
> A chain of river bends ...
>
> Water's wretched dream are we;
> A billow turned to rust,
> A forgotten trace are we
> Of souls that have been lost.

By April, 1905, Blok was convinced that she was irretrievably gone. With tortured reverence he penned his last prayer to her:

> Thou art gone to the fields—forever—
> Hallowed be Thy name ....

Blok's world then gradually changed into a puppet show, peopled by characters with berry juice flowing through their veins. In a poem, "Puppet Show," written in July, 1905, Blok has his hero, Buffoon, bleed to death with cranberry juice. What ought to be soldiers of Buffoon's Queen coming to his rescue ironically prove to be minions of the Evil One, and the hero perishes. The show closes, and the two children in the audience go home weeping over the fate of poor Buffoon. Within six months Blok had begun his first lyrical drama (also named *Puppet Show*). Here, its three main characters—Pierrot, Harlequin, and Columbine—are identified with Blok himself, Andrey Biely, and Lyubov Blok. The hero pursues his betrothed Columbine in vain and, as the curtain falls, is left on the stage alone, singing of his bitter, loveless lot. His friend Harlequin—whose image and autobiographical significance may be seen in Biely's poem "The Eternal Call" (1903)[40]—

---

[40] *Perepiska*, p. 40.

pursues Columbine with greater success, but, just as he is about to ride off with his prize in a sleigh, he sees her topple over into the snow, and discovers that she is made of cardboard. The Maiden of the Rainbow Gates (*Dieva Raduzhnykh Vorot*) had thus become the Cardboard Bride!

The next step in the transformation of Blok's muse was logical and almost inevitable. As the result of his despondent roaming through the streets and alleyways of St. Petersburg, she, the Woman Clothed with the Sun, now changed into the Woman Arrayed in Purple and Scarlet. Lilac and scarlet displaced azure and white as the dominant colors of his poetry. The poem "Nocturnal Violet" (*"Nochnaya Fialka"*), according to Blok was "almost the exact reproduction of a dream" (November 16, 1905); the color of that flower—violet—became the dominant hue of his new palette. The air of ethereal mystery that had enshrouded the Lady Beautiful, became one of physical, sensuous allure, and Sophia finally became the Unknown Demi-mondaine!

The Unknown Woman

At eventide above the restaurants
The sultry air is thick and mute
And o'er the city's din of drunken taunts
A noxious spirit waits its loot . . .

Far off above the dust of alleyways,
Above the bored suburban scene
The glitter of a golden pretzel plays
And one can hear an infant's scream.

And every evening past the city gates,
Their derbies rakishly askew,
Amidst the gutters, tried sophisticates
Parade their ladies fro to to.

Above the lake a rusty oarlock grates:
And now a girl will shrilly scream,
While in the skies, accustomed to its fate,
Insipidly a disk of silver gleams.

And every night reflected in my glass
I see my one and only friend.
The tart, mysterious fluid now he grasps
And o'er the table numbly bends.

And by the tables just adjoining mine
The sleepy waiters loll about;
I hear the drunken men with rabbit eyes
"In vino veritas!" cry out.

And every night at the appointed time
(Or have I only dreamed all this?)
A girlish form in rustling silks entwined
Floats past the window through the mist.

And slowly walking past the drunken guests,
With ne'er an escort, all alone,
Exuding fragrance of a perfumed mist
She seeks a table, all her own.

And memories of ancient lore, resumed,
Float from resilient silks quite bland
And from her hat with long, black ostrich plumes,
And from her slender jeweled hand.

And there, transfixed by strange propinquity
Beyond her heavy veil I gaze.
I see beyond it the enchanted sea
And an enchanted azure space.

To me mute mysteries have been assigned,
In my hands someone's sun is placed;
Each recess of my soul (I am resigned),
Shall be suffused by bitter taste.

And ostrich feathers, dipping gracefully
Still sway within my drink-dimmed brain,
And I see eyes of azure tracelessly
Abloom upon a far terrain.

164   The Frenzied Poets

> Within my heart a priceless treasure lies;
> Alone, I have its only key.
> I know, truth is in wine, your words are wise
> Inebriate monstrosity!
>
> (April, 1906)

One explanation for the change in Blok's mood is that, in striving to recover the image of his muse, Blok had yielded to his second, the lyrical, nature and deliberately cast aside his religious leanings. His mystical half had led him to perceive and to fall in love with Lyubov as incarnated Sophia. Since dissillusion cost him his inspiration, it prompted him not only to cast off his "Solovyovan crutches" but to disavow Christ. Blok's Titanic mood coincided chronologically with the Russo-Japanese War of 1904–1905, which ended in Russian disaster, and with the Russian revolution of 1905, which to the more extreme intelligentsia also seemed an abortive failure. Besides Blok, various other Russian intellectuals also yielded to their "lyrical" natures. Restless, and disillusioned with his own life, Blok in the fall of 1906 found himself among people who constantly talked of revolution, rebellion, anarchy, madness. There he found "beautiful women . . . their heads raised, their lips half-parted. Wine flowed in rivers, and everyone acted insane and as though he sought to destroy family and home—his own as well as anyone else's."[41]

A dozen years later, among the recollections that he entered in his diary, Blok summarized with remarkable candor what had happened to him:

> Scarcely had my fiancée become my wife than the lilac [!] worlds of the first revolution seized us and carried us into their whirlpool. First I, who had so long secretly wished to perish [!] was drawn into the grey-scarlet, silvery stars, the pearls and amethysts [!] of the blizzard. My wife followed me, and for her this transition (from the difficult to the easy, from the unpermissible to the permissible) was tortuous, and much more difficult than for myself.[42]

[41] M.A. Beketova, *Aleksandr Blok* (Petersburg, 1922), p. 102.
[42] Blok, *Dnevniki* (Leningrad, 1928), II, 72.

The color scheme, as Blok gives it here, illustrates what he believed had happened. There seems little doubt in his mind that the Mother of Harlots from St. John (Revelations xii, 1–6) had displaced the Woman Clothed with the Sun as the inspiration of his verse! Be that as it may, after years had passed and after both Blok and his wife had betrayed their marriage vows many times over, he stated that, gossip to the contrary, he did not have one hundred, two hundred, or three hundred different paramours. "I have only two. One of them is Lyuba; the other—all the rest."[43] (Lyuba is a diminutive of Lyubov.) The pages of his diaries support his claim, for they abound in professions of his love for Lyubov Blok.

Although Blok seems to assume all the blame for the family "drama," as he termed it (because he had "not yet matured sufficiently to experience a tragedy"), perhaps not even the main burden of guilt lies on his shoulders. Andrey Biely, Lyubov Blok, and others were also responsible.

Biely unquestionably played the leading role in the "drama." However, until unpublished materials pertaining to it become available, it will be impossible to reconstruct with certainty the entire story. Biely's notebooks and dairies should shed considerable light on the affair, as may his correspondence with *all* the principals involved, along with their own letters. At present the most important single source is the large volume of correspondence between Biely and Blok; since, however, one of the principals, Lyubov Blok, was still alive at the time of publication, the editors of the correspondence chose to omit five letters crucial for clarifying the affair. Also available are two sets of Biely's memoirs. They give a fairly consistent version of Biely's side of the matter. In addition, V. F. Hodasevich published another version of Biely's story, which he claims to have received from Biely in Berlin in 1922. But, as pointed out earlier, Hodasevich had quarreled with Biely, and on one occa-

---

[43] Blok, *Zapisnye knizhki* (Leningrad, 1930), p. 180 (May 30, 1915).

sion Biely had publicly insulted him and referred to him by some very unsavory epithets. Since the two men never became reconciled, it is quite possible that the Hodasevich revelations are not entirely trustworthy. The following account has been pieced together from the mentioned sources and from Blok's notebooks, diaries, and letters to his family and friends.

Before Biely had ever met the Bloks he already envisaged the couple in a romantic aura. From the beginning of their epistolary friendship, Biely (and with him Sergey Solovyov) accepted Blok's view of his fiancée. Even before Biely saw the young woman, he had indulged in a romantic sort of adoration for her. He did so because, believing in the eschatological prophecies of Vladimir Solovyov, he expected the Woman Clothed with the Sun to appear, and therefore was half-way willing to think that Lyubov was Sophia.

Biely and Sergey Solovyov often pretended that Lyubov's true identity revealed itself to them in her very name—Lyubov (love), which, when "spelled with a capital letter represented an attempt by Blok to resurrect allegorically the cult of Demeter in his lyrics."[44] Biely and Solovyov half in jest, half in earnest argued further that Lyubov's patronymic, Dmitrievna, supported their belief, because it was "actually 'Demetrovna.' " Unhappily for himself, as well as for Blok and his wife, Biely was destined to fall in love with this incarnation of the divine Sophia.

Biely first saw the Bloks on January 10, 1904,[45] when the young couple came to Moscow. Thus, the "spiritual brothers" met almost exactly one year after they had first exchanged letters. Biely had anxiously anticipated this personal acquaintance. Despite Sergey Solovyov's descriptions of Lyubov Blok, Biely was stunned by her physical appearance. According to Hodasevich, he fell "head over heels in love with her" at this meeting. Biely seemed struck by the *woman* he beheld, and

---

[44] *Nachalo veka*, p. 344.
[45] See Blok, *Pis'ma k rodnym* (Leningrad, 1932), I, 101.

not by a metaphysical ideal. Flattered by his attentions, she in turn permitted this Prince Charming of the Moscow modernists to captivate her. Blok, already disillusioned in his bride, and ever seeking, and even desiring a tragic outcome, probably quickly sensed the common bond that soon sprang up between his wife and his "brother." Inasmuch as such a situation would have underscored the earthly quality in his wife it may well have hastened the change in Blok's muse.

Nevertheless, the Bloks' fortnight stay in Moscow seemed to proceed according to plan, except that Biely was "quite different from what [Blok] had expected,"[46] as Blok observed. The couple made friends everywhere. Tall, handsome, dignified Alexander Blok was the perfect match for the "retiring, unpretentious, and graceful" young lady whose blend of "old Russian beauty with a touch of the Titianesque" instantly captivated everyone.[47] The famous romantic poet Balmont composed a sonnet for her, while Sergey Solovyov and Andrey Biely showered her with bouquets. The entire visit passed in a major key. The young people enjoyed themselves hugely, read poetry, and exchanged compliments. Biely and Solovyov acted as self-appointed guides to the Bloks, whom they introduced to the Argonauts and to the local literary set. Nothing suggested the drama that was soon to begin.

The first indication of the coming storm was Blok's inability to compose more than two poems during the subsequent two months. When the young people met again at the Bloks' summer home in Shakhmatovo, Blok had already fully realized the loss of his Lady Beautiful. He longed to take some violent action and confessed to his friend Y. P. Ivanov that he felt like "going on a drunken spree."

The following summer, when Biely and Solovyov again came to Shakhmatovo, they could feel the tautness in the atmosphere. In the evenings, after they had gathered in the living

[46] *Ibid.*, pp. 101–102.
[47] *Epopeia*, I, 187; Blok, *Pis'ma* (1925), pp. 23–25.

room, Blok would suddenly rise and without warning stride out into the night and roam among the marshes. On occasion he would read his latest poems about imps and other denizens of the swamps. His attitude toward his wife had changed. Andrey Biely was nonplussed, and Sergey Solovyov was indignant. Both blamed Blok for the change. Young Solovyov felt that Blok, who three short years previously had solemnly assured him that he accepted even the most extreme aspects of Vladimir Solovyov's mysticism, now defiled the memory of the philosopher. "If Blok's Lady is the breed of lust," Sergey Solovyov would explode, "I wish him a child by her. But in that case stop capitalizing her name and stop this winking at the divine Sophia!" When the Unknown Demi-mondaine appeared in the place of Sophia, Sergey Solovyov decided that Blok had met his doom and that he and Biely were morally obliged to rescue Lyubov Blok.

Blok's new mood marked the turning point also in his relations with Biely, and their ecstatic friendship soon changed to one that may be called "hysterical." The new phase in their association arose from their personal relationship, which soon, however, took on an ideological flavor. The open clash that developed between the two poets was waged in the name of high moral principles.

At first, Biely remained aloof from the family drama of the Bloks. His moral scruples (fortified just then by an earnest study of Neo-Kantian philosophy) would not permit his taking any but a passive part in the affair. He insisted that he regarded Lyubov Blok as a "sister" and restricted himself to corresponding with her. Before long, however, other persons persuaded him to change his attitude.

The first of these was Sergey Solovyov, Blok's second cousin and one of his earliest admirers. Sergey, like many other disciples of Vladimir Solovyov, saw in Blok's new motifs blasphemy and the defilement of everything that Blok himself had once proclaimed as sacred. Sergey failed to see in Blok's new verses the technical perfection of a great artist; nor did he make any effort to account for the sudden change in Blok's muse; he did not even try to sympathize with Blok's position, nor to justify him; he saw only that Blok had betrayed a cherished ideal.[48]

Since Andrey Biely was Sergey Solovyov's closest friend, Sergey quite naturally exercised his powers to convert Biely to his point of view. Ignoring the personal factors in the situation, Sergey was the first to argue with his comrade that Blok was heading for spiritual bankruptcy.

The second person that changed Biely's passive attitude was Blok's mother, Alexandra Kublitsky-Piottukh. Her one concern in life was her son, and she unquestionably had a deep spiritual understanding of him.[49] She was one of the first people to become aware that all was not well between her son and his wife, and she probably also knew or guessed that Biely was in some way involved in the affair. She naturally sympathized with her son and regarded with hostility anyone who acted against the welfare of her only child. Consequently she was antagonistic not only toward Biely, but also to Sergey Solovyov, who was the professed friend of Andrey Biely. Furthermore, since Mme. Kublitsky insisted on sharing her son's apartment, Lyubov Blok undoubtedly resented the presence of an overprotective mother-in-law. Several of Blok's letters to his mother testify to the tension that existed in his home. He protested too strongly that his filial affection for his mother had undergone no change. Eventually, the relations between Blok's mother and wife became so strained that during his last illness, in 1921, Lyubov Blok forbade his mother to see him. Even during 1905 Lyubov Blok apparently found her mother-in-law's constant interference so unbearable that she must have complained to her "brother." Biely thereupon addressed one of his letters in-

[48] Blok, *Pis'ma* (1925), pp. 32 ff.
[49] M. A. Beketova, *Aleksandr Blok i ego mat'*, *passim*.

The Frenzied Poets

tended for Lyubov Blok directly to Mme. Kublitsky—ostensibly for "inspection." Undoubtedly, the split of allegiance that Blok felt, further contributed to his dissatisfaction with life.

The third person was Zinaida Hippius. Some of her interest in the Biely-Blok triangle was probably prompted by rancor that she felt against Alexander Blok. Hippius became acquainted with Blok through Mme. Solovyov. Soon she had him as a regular visitor at the Merezhkovsky gatherings, and for some time regarded him as one of her prize protégés. As late as 1904 Blok admitted that he was completely under their influence.[50] But by 1905 he had quite changed his opinion. He could find "nothing at all in Dmitri Sergeyevich," and he often saw Hippius, as a "complete blank."[51] Biely, on the other hand, was still on excellent terms with them. Zinaida Hippius zealously guarded the prestige of Merezhkovsky's following and, therefore, not only resented that Biely remained an intimate friend of Blok, but also was jealous of the influence that Blok, as well as his wife, exercised on Biely. Time and again she attempted in some petty manner to undermine their friendship.[52] When Biely finally confided to her that he was in love with Blok's wife, Hippius not only lent a sympathetic ear to his troubles but encouraged him to plan more definitely how to further his interests with Lyubov Blok.

The first open break between the two poets occurred in the summer of 1905, after Biely and Solovyov had joined the Bloks in Shakhmatovo. From the beginning this visit produced a certain tenseness.[53] Sergey Solovyov, apparently brooding over Blok's "betrayal" of his muse, was looking for an excuse to provoke a quarrel. Since Blok was by nature too inoffensive to give a valid reason for a clash, Solovyov chose Mme. Kublit-

---

[50] Blok, *Pis'ma* (1925), p. 101.
[51] *Ibid.*, p. 178.
[52] *Nachalo veka*, pp. 433–435.
[53] *Epopeia*, II, 240 ff.; Beketova, *Aleksandr Blok*, pp. 97–99; Blok, *Pis'ma* (1925), 28 ff.; *Omut*, p. 27 ff.

sky as the target of his attack. One evening he aroused her temper, and she replied sharply, whereupon Biely entered the scene.

Biely not only had sensed the hidden antipathy that Blok's mother felt against him, but was secretly vexed that he had become involved in such strange relations with the Bloks. He felt that by allowing himself to fall in love with Blok's wife, he had betrayed his "spiritual brother." Realizing his guilt, he nevertheless sought in his own mind to shift the blame to Blok. Then, since he could not wholly accept such exoneration, he became dissatisfied with himself and with the world in general. This irritation had just began to reach the seething point within him and prompted him to vent his emotions. The opportunity presented itself when Blok's mother poured out her wrath upon the head of Sergey Solovyov. Biely immediately came to the defense of his friend. Unfortunately, in answering Mme. Kublitsky-Piottukh he lost his temper and made a scene, which he concluded with a dramatic exit.

Blok's attitude in the quarrel seemed to have been one of quiet, sad understanding. He had probably sensed what had happened. He could attach no blame to anyone. And although he felt somewhat apologetic for the entire affair, he also felt innocent of any active wrongdoing. He was grateful to his mother because she had defended him, but at the same time he sympathized with Biely's position, and accepted the blame for his wife's unhappiness and dissatisfaction. Thereupon, Blok, ever a fatalist, passively let matters take their course, even though he realized that his former relationship with Biely would be "irretrievably lost."[54] The following morning, when Biely mounted his horse to ride off, Blok kept his eyes fixed on the ground; Lyubov, the real cause of the trouble, quietly dabbed her tears with a handkerchief. Sergey Solovyov, the apparent cause of the quarrel, stayed on for a few days "probably out of sheer spite,"[55] as Biely expressed it.

[54] *Epopeia*, II, 260.
[55] *Ibid.*, p. 262.

The Frenzied Poets

Thereafter a series of climaxes and anticlimaxes occurred in the relations between the two men. Rapidly touching reconciliations yielded to flares of anger. In August, 1906, Biely challenged Blok to a duel, and Blok in turn challenged Biely a year later. Fortunately for the young poets, neither duel took place.

The initial break with Blok profoundly affected Biely's literary outlook. When later in that summer of 1905 he joined Solovyov in Dedovo, they "no longer read Zhukovsky."[56] Instead, they now "drank in Gogol," particularly his weird tales, such as *The Earth Goblin (Viy)* and *The Terrible Vengeance (Strashnaya Mest)*. Biely now sacrificed the lyric romanticism of Vladimir Solovyov's poetry to the "heartrending anguish of Gogol, Nekrasov, and Dostoyevsky." Their former preoccupation with problems of individualism gave way to themes of revolution, the people, and, especially, pain. That summer Solovyov succeeded in converting Biely to his belief that Blok's path led straight to ruin. As time went on, Biely's relations with Blok became increasingly muddled. After Biely had left Shakhmatovo, Blok wrote him a conciliatory letter,[57] and in his reply Biely eagerly accepted the hand which his "brother" proffered him, and thanked Blok for his "tender words."[58] This exchange of placating letters, however, marked merely an armistice, not peace, and within a few months Biely was demanding that Blok explain how he planned to reconcile with his new themes his "call to serve the Lady Beautiful."[59] In conclusion Biely admonished his fellow poet:

> Dear Sasha, forgive me my words, addressed to you out of love. I have written them because I am bound by the responsibility of preserving the purity of a mystery—which you are betraying, or are about to betray. Take heed! Whither are you going? Come to your senses! ... Either stop, or forget *mystery*. It is impossible to be simultaneously with God and the devil.

---
[56] *Ibid.*, p. 263.
[57] *Perepiska*, pp. 136–137.
[58] *Ibid.*, p. 138.
[59] *Ibid.*, p. 155.

Biely and Blok 173

May the powers that be help you. Forgive me my frankness. But right now nothing can prevent my speaking, for I am—

Mighty[60]

Blok's reply again was surprisingly conciliatory. In it he seemed to admit his sins, and, terming himself unworthy to be called Biely's "brother,"[61] Blok conceded that Biely's wrath was justifiable and confessed that he "still loved" him. But in his own behalf Blok argued that he was unable to become anything other than what he was. He even begged his friend "to cross him off, if he so wished," and added half apologetically that perhaps he should have been crossed off long ago. Thus Blok appeared to admit Sergey Solovyov's accusation that he was headed for ruin, yet he claimed that he saw no other course that he could take, for "the huge void that unfolded within" him made him "feel gay." Blok's gypsy *alter ego* was taking possession, and leaving his former self devoid of will power and the ability to struggle. Blok granted that Biely was morally superior to him, even though an outsider may have well believed that Andrey Biely was trying to make off with his best friend's wife. Blok concluded his letter with a lyrical confession:

If I am a traitor—damn me and forget me. And do this as quickly as possible, so that I may not stand in your way. If you see any possibility of showing me the path, do so. I know that you are—mighty [*vlastnyi*] ... All that I have written to you is in many respects not to the point. It is more important for me to tell you ... that no one but I weeps over you, just as no one weeps over Time. If you were crucified, I would stand by the cross and look at the red moon in the black heavens above your head .... I would stand near your cross, even though my soul then might turn completely to ashes.[62]

Biely was eager to clarify his own position in the odd triangle. He keenly felt his moral obligation toward Blok; yet

---

[60] *Ibid.* In his works of this period Belyi visualizes himself not only as a prophet, but even as a "New Adam." His signature to the letter cited here, "Vlastnyi," sounds as startling in Russian as does "Mighty" in English.
[61] *Ibid.*, p. 158.
[62] *Ibid.*, p. 159.

he tried to find some means of justifying to himself his own hidden desires, striving to rationalize his position on moral grounds. He got support not only from Sergey Solovyov, but also from Zinaida Hippius. Both of them tried to persuade him that Blok was immoral, because Blok in his lyric mood recognized no restriction for his own actions. Biely permitted Zinaida Hippius to convince him that his "duty" lay in taking Lyubov Blok away from St. Petersburg.[63] The arguments of Solovyov and Hippius gave Biely precisely the excuse that he needed to justify his position in the affair.

Now, armed with a moral purpose, Biely became a crusader whose aim ostensibly was to save Lyubov Blok from her husband. He had found a cause that placed justice on his side. He saw now that their "communal vessel" was sinking, that its captain, Blok, was unable to realize his mistake, and that it was therefore his own duty to "rescue the passenger, Lyubov Blok, while he still had time."[64] But despite the lofty reason that he found for rescuing the doomed woman, Biely could not wholly dismiss his rival's rights in the case. Each time that he received Blok's conciliatory letters he seemed to suffer pangs of contrition. He could never find any fitting reply to Blok's letters.[65] He realized that Blok was not to blame, yet stoutly averred that neither could any blame be attached to himself. On receiving Blok's above-mentioned "tender letter," Biely begged him to arrange a meeting for them "together with Lyubov Dmitrievna, if she should be willing."[66] Blok consented, and Biely started for St. Petersburg.

At that time (October, 1905) everything in Moscow was in a state of revolutionary turmoil. Meetings were held everywhere. Complete disorganization reigned at the university. Anarchy ruled the country as a result of the general strike.

---
[63] *Omut*, p. 58.
[64] *Epopeia*, II, 154–155.
[65] *Perepiska*, p. 160.
[66] *Ibid.*, p. 161.

Biely and Blok 175

Though public utilities discontinued service, and the regular train service between Moscow and St. Petersburg was disrupted, Biely managed to reach the Russian capital.[67] Here he asked the Bloks to meet him in a restaurant, to avoid the tense atmosphere of the Blok apartment.[68] The mood of the meeting seemed to Biely conciliatory. Blok's attitude was one of understanding, and in their rivalry for the affections of his wife he seemed willing to "step aside" in favor of his rival.[69] Biely felt quite reassured of his success and left the meeting with his mind at ease both as to his course of action and the outcome.

Yet here Biely's calculations met with unexpected reverses, primarily because he had made his plans without taking into account the possibility that Blok might still love his wife. She, on the other hand, realizing this, refused to decide whom of the two men she preferred.

Since Lyubov Blok burned Biely's letters to her, and since Biely's diaries and her letters to the poet are still unpublished, our most reliable source for the affair are Biely's memoirs.

Judging by this account, Lyubov Blok was a paragon of vacillation. One day she would tell Biely that she loved both him and Blok; the next day she would be in love with neither him nor Blok; the following day her love for Blok would be purely platonic, and her feelings for Biely would be more concrete; and the day after it would just be the reverse.[70]

As the intellectual that he was, Blok could take no positive action; he let his fatalism take possession of his will. He seemed to admit passively that he had betrayed his wife and therefore had no right to influence her verdict. Therefore he remained silent throughout the affair, stoically noble, and left the final decision entirely up to her. With the solution thus depending on her own sense of honor, Lyubov Blok could not bring her-

---
[67] *Epopeia*, II, 262.
[68] *Perepiska*, p. 179.
[69] *Omut*, p. 58.
[70] *Ibid.*, p. 78.

176   The Frenzied Poets

self to take the decisive step. And Biely, thinking that Blok had renounced all claims to his own wife, could not understand why she should hesitate to leave her husband.

From February, 1906, to September, Biely sat astride a fuming volcano of emotion, knowing that sooner or later it would erupt, yet uncertain what he should do in the meantime. He spent those months dashing back and forth frantically between Moscow and St. Petersburg, each time conferring with Mme. Merezhkovsky, who each time would reassure him not only that he was morally right, but also that success would inevitably be his. His morale thus fortified, he would rush to the Bloks' apartment, forever hoping that his rival's wife would consent to flee abroad with him immediately. At the Bloks', however, he would receive only equivocal assurances, which he, nevertheless, wishfully would interpret as acquiescence. Then he would dash madly back to Moscow, to make financial arrangements necessary for their trip abroad.[71]

Meanwhile a veritable torrent of letters broke loose between Biely, the two Bloks, and Mme. Kublitsky-Piottukh. Within three days, for example, Lyubov Blok received as many as eight letters from Biely.[72] During the same period, Biely wrote also three letters to Blok, and one more to his mother. Meanwhile, an avalanche of letters from Lyubov Blok fanned the flame of her suitor's aroused passions. Each succeeding letter from her would be a direct contradiction of the one before. In the morning she would beg Biely to speed to St. Petersburg, and that same afternoon she would forbid him to come. Meanwhile Biely continued rushing to St. Petersburg for meetings with Blok alone or with Blok and his wife. Then in Moscow a stormy meeting with Blok took place. Finally war was formally declared.

On five occasions Biely was thoroughly convinced that Lyubov Blok was in love with him, each time only to have to

---
[71] *Ibid.*, p. 79.   [72] *Perepiska*, p. 165.

change his opinion.[73] On three different occasions they were on the point of leaving for Italy, but each time at the last moment, Lyubov Blok experienced a change of heart.[74] The situation, according to Biely, resembled the plot of an Ibsen drama.

Life became a nightmare. The affair was so unbearable as to demand an immediate solution, one way or another. The uncertainty had driven Biely frantic; he was quite beside himself and nearly insane. He felt that he was honor-bound to challenge Blok to a duel, and at the same time he recoiled from the thought that a duel would mean "murder" for one of them. The realization that the solution lay in murder, and that he for his part was incapable of killing, only heightened the horror of his nightmare.[75] The phantom of death overshadowed everything else in his mind. His poetry of this period is one of drunken abandon through which a Karamazovan bestiality resounds. Futility and despair can be sensed through the vapors of alcoholic gaiety. In rhythmical perfection Biely's "drunken ditties" know no equal in Russian poetry. He has caught in them the spirit of the orgiastic abandon of the drunken, vulgar, muzhik *plyas* (jig). Biely spares no sensibilities. Nothing matters; let there be joy in Russia!

> *Joy in Russia*
> How we hauled flask after flask,
> drank the fire from the cask,
> An' I
> drank my fill,
> An' I
> danced my fill.
>
> The deacon, scribe, the priest, and sexton,
> On the meadow come a'mincing.
>
> Ekh!
> What a shame for men!
> Ekh!
> What laughs for a hen!

---
[73] *Omut*, p. 93.   [74] *Ibid.*   [75] *Ibid.*, p. 90.

The Frenzied Poets

There they go in wild abandon in their dance.
Dance, my heart—go on, go to it, prance!

What a dance out on the meadows
In the woods and 'midst the furrows—

Go to work on it!

O'er the highway every which way let your footsteps fly
O'er the footpaths cut them loose—oh my!

Then, stomp your feet!

No need to think; no need to wait:
Just huff and spit, and to hell with it!
Spit it out, then rub it out.
Just make merry, stuff your snout!

Homiletics and canonics!
Roar, accordion, and screech, harmonicas!

The deacon's jigging,
    "Deacon, deacon!"
His robes a-flinging
    "Deacon, deacon,

"Tell me, deacon, what is death?"

"Death? It's this and that, it's, why ...
"Your nose hits a puddle, your heels—the sky."
. . . .

In the wind a leaping perch,
its arms akimbó, flies.

Its sloshing shaking branch
waves in the skies.

With turquoise waves
The skies it covers

And o'er my native land
Death hovers.

                                      (August, 1906)

Both men felt that a personal combat had become inevitable. The excuse for a duel presented itself when, after a brief meeting with Biely (in one more effort to reach an understanding), Blok sent him the following note:

Shakhmatovo,
August 9, 1906.
Borya!

I had planned to dedicate my book Unexpected Joy to you, as a memory of the past. But now such a dedication would be false; because I have ceased to understand you. For this reason alone do I refrain from dedicating the volume to you.

Al. Blok[76]

Having resolved that a duel was the only means by which he could settle their complicated relations, on August 9 or 10[77] Biely sent Blok two "hysterical" letters, both of which the editors of the Biely-Blok correspondence, unfortunately, decided to suppress. And on August 10, Biely composed his challenge to the man whom he had once called his "dear brother." Biely asked his friend Ellis (pseudonym for Lev Lvovich Kobylinsky) to deliver it and at the same time requested Ellis and Sergey Solovyov to act as his seconds.

When Blok received Biely's challenge, he replied in his typical calm manner that he saw "no cause for a duel," and charitably explained Biely's action by supposing that "Borya was simply very tired."[78] Ellis returned to Moscow bearing the news that *Blok* was very tired and that no duel was really necessary.[79] Biely, happy to forego the combat, accepted Ellis' explanations with great relief.

On August 12, Blok wrote Biely a warm, intimate letter, in which he said that he felt again that he "loved" Biely. He said quite plainly that he regarded their friendship as something created by fate and therefore above personalities. For that

---
[76] *Perepiska*, p. 177.
[77] See note to letter No. 134 in *Perepiska*, p. 178.
[78] *Omut*, p. 92.
[79] *Ibid.*

reason he found that Biely's "relations with Lyuba were often unimportant" [!], although he admitted that he had often thought of his rival "with spleen and hatred."[80]

As usual, Blok's letter completely disarmed Biely. Within the next few days Biely wrote Blok a number of very touching letters, in which he begged forgiveness of his "dearest, most beloved friend."[81] Nevertheless, despite such mutual assurances, the affair between Biely and the Bloks had not yet ended.

In September Biely once more journeyed to St. Petersburg, expressly to have one final conversation with Lyubov Blok. She let her suitor cool his heels for nearly a week, and then sent him a message ordering him to "come—and immediately!"[82] The meeting proved somewhat calmer than might have been expected, and the two decided to part for a year, at the end of which period they would meet again.[83] Lyubov persuaded Biely to take a trip to Italy and promised to write him to maintain his "will to Good."

Biely was soon en route to Munich where his friend V. V. Vladmirov[84] had begun his art studies. From Munich Biely went to Paris where he met the Merezhkovskys and where he fell ill.[85] The misery that his Paris illness caused him he regarded as a catharsis that cleansed his soul and body of the accumulation of evil.[86] The personal drama over Lyubov Blok had passed its crisis.

But the drama with Alexander Blok was not ended, and under the surface Biely still harbored a deep resentment against him. In March, 1907, Biely returned to Moscow and joined Bryusov in an active campaign against Georgy Chulkov, Vyacheslav Ivanov, the group of mystical anarchists, and the *Golden Fleece.*[87] Because Blok had permitted his name to be

---

[80] *Perepiska*, pp. 177–178.
[81] *Ibid.*, pp. 179 ff.
[82] *Omut*, p. 99.
[83] *Ibid.*
[84] See chapter v.
[85] See chapter vii.
[86] *Omut*, pp. 182 ff.
[87] See chapter ix.

linked with the mystical anarchists,[88] he naturally became an ideological foe of the Bryusovites.

Bryusov had persuaded Biely that the mystical anarchists, in denying that a poet should recognize any authority save his own caprice, would inevitably vulgarize art; therefore, argued Bryusov, the successes of mystical anarchism had to be checked. Since Blok's lyrical mood, which apparently bore the stamp of mystical anarchism, had won him popular acclaim, Biely regarded his latest success as another victory for mystical anarchism. Probably hoping to assuage his own injured ego, Biely now flung himself into a campaign against Blok, his victorious rival in love and in art.

Persuading himself that his duty as a critic compelled him to expose the ideological bankruptcy of Blok's "blasphemous" verse, Biely launched a series of attacks against his "brother." He appeared frantically trying to justify himself for his role in the "affaire Blok," as though by proving Blok guilty of moral defection he might absolve himself of guilt. In one of his essays he accused Blok of having no ideological principles. For this lack he blamed the demoralizing influence of mystical anarchism, which, according to Biely, had transformed Blok into "a painter of vacuity ... whose Lady Beautiful had disintegrated into a prostitute, into an imaginary quantity, something like $\sqrt{-1}$."[89] Although under the pressure of Biely's attacks Blok wrote an open letter to the *Balance*[90] and publicly denied being a mystical anarchist, he refused to sever his relations with the *Golden Fleece*. In fact, he accepted the post of literary editor, a position that on Bryusov's advice Biely had already refused. To Biely, Blok's accepting the position that he had rejected constituted literary "strike breaking,"[91] and only further increased his irritation with Blok.

---

[88] See E. Semenov, "Le mysticisme anarchique," *Mercure de France*, 242 (July 16, 1907), 216 ff.
[89] Cf. *Arabeski*, p. 465.
[90] *Vesy* (August, 1907), 81.
[91] *Omut*, pp. 246–247.

182   The Frenzied Poets

Meanwhile, on August 6, 1907, feeling the urge to reëstablish his former friendly relations, Blok wrote Biely that he was willing to listen to Biely's criticism of his works, but that he believed that personal feuds were out of place in literary polemics.[92] At the same time he avowed that he "never had had and never would have anything in common with 'mystical realism,' or 'mystical anarchism,' or 'collective individualism.'" At the close of his letter he begged Biely to "indicate, even though briefly, their basic point of difference" and stated that he agreed with Biely's views concerning "those new half-baked theories."

In the meantime, and with no knowledge of Blok's letter, Biely sent Blok a sharp note in which he accused him of trying to ingratiate himself with the realists, followers of Maxim Gorky, who were grouped around the miscellany *Knowledge (Znanie)*. Biely quoted an article in which Blok had favorably reviewed a book by Skitalets ("Vagabond"), a mediocre realist writer.[93] Biely wrote:

> When I saw your petition [to the public], pardon me, your "article" in the "Golden Fleece" about realists, in which you wrote something that you did not really believe, everything became perfectly clear.... Our relations may be considered severed for all time.[94]

When Blok received Biely's challenging letter, after the conciliatory message that he himself had just dispatched, he felt justifiably outraged. He immediately wrote a heated answer (August 8), in which he accused Biely of being a "spy and a lackey" and ended with an ultimatum:

> Whatever the reasons that may have prompted your attacks on me, I give you ten days either to retract your words (which you yourself do not believe to be true) or to send me your second. If prior to August 18 you shall have complied with neither, I shall be forced to take appropriate measures of my own.
>
> Alexander Blok[95]

---
[92] *Literaturnoe Nasledstvo*, p. 383.
[93] Blok, *Sobranie sochinenii* (Leningrad, 1935), X, 42–43.
[94] *Literaturnoe Nasledstvo*, pp. 384–385; 406.
[95] *Ibid.*, p. 385.

Blok simultaneously notified his friend E. P. Ivanov of Biely's letter and of his own reply. He felt that the time had arrived for "positive action." For, unless Biely was insane (in which case Blok felt "infinitely sorry" for the man), it was "necessary to stop this kind of conduct."[96] Blok thought that a duel was the only means to achieve this end and requested Ivanov to act as his second.

On hearing of Blok's challenge, Ivanov was terror-stricken and begged him to abandon his plans:

> I beg you ... not to do this .... You know that you are older [a mistake on Ivanov's part], and healthier, and wiser than Andrey Biely. Besides, you are an aristocrat .... You yourself will no doubt guess that I shall decline to serve as your second .... I somehow feel at fault in my relations with Biely .... He is close to insanity. I understand what has given rise to his slanderous accusations .... It is obvious that the man has been driven insane by love.[97]

Before Blok's challenge had been delivered, Biely received Blok's conciliatory letter of August 6, quieted down immediately, and began to answer it in detail. On August 11, when he had one-half of his reply written, he received Blok's letter of August 8. He put aside his original answer and proceeded immediately to reply to Blok's furious note.

Just as a year previously Blok had refused to accept Biely's challenge, now Biely refused his, saying that Blok had now become a stranger, "one of many," and that it was impossible to fight duels with "anyone and everyone."[98] Nevertheless, Biely ended his letter in a conciliatory tone and asked for an intimate private talk that would enable them to "grasp not only with the intellect, but also with the heart, whatever might be taking place between us."[99] The challenge thus disposed of, Biely returned to answering Blok's earlier letter.

---

[96] Blok, *Pis'ma k ... Ivanovu*, p. 60.
[97] *Ibid.*, pp. 118–119.
[98] *Literaturnoe Nasledstvo*, pp. 394–395.
[99] *Ibid.*

184 The Frenzied Poets

Unwilling to face the real issues involved in their quarrel, Biely claimed that his chief difference with Blok had arisen because Blok adhered to mystical anarchism and yet called himself a symbolist. He asked Blok to reveal to him his *"Weltanschauung* and philosophy,"[100] the "exact formula" and nature of which he did not know.

> I do not know your literary, social, religious, ethical, philosophical credo.... I know that I am profoundly appreciative of your poetry... (as art). Much in your recent works that is mystical in spirit seems absolutely foreign to me. In your dramas I see constant blasphemy.... I repeat that "inwardly" I have lost sight of you.... Too many of my attacks against St. Petersburg in general you have probably taken to be directed at you.... When I write of pretzels[101]... I do not address myself to you, but to the whole circle of littérateurs in which you revolve. In this particular case, I merely express the sentiment of a great many people in Moscow who, because they will not shout about "collectivity," "daring," "333 embraces,"[102] by no means think that they are behind the times, or that they are decadents or individualists. Individualism among many of us is just a mask of shyness and fear lest we profane what is still very vague and dear to the heart.[103]

After receiving Biely's two letters, Blok, as mentioned above, wrote an open letter to the *Balance* and renounced mystical anarchism. On August 15, he started another conciliatory letter to Biely, in which he acknowledged that the duel was out of question and that he retracted his words about Biely's being a "spy and lackey," words which, he admitted, "had been evoked by anger." Some of Blok's admissions in this letter are important for a fuller understanding of the poet.

> Our very first letters... disclosed a difference in our temperaments and the strange—even fateful—incongruity between us.... Your thoughts were unusually important to me, and, what is most important, I felt that a *mysterious bond* existed between us, a bond the name of which I never knew, nor sought. At that time I was under the stress of

---
[100] *Ibid.*, p. 391.
[101] Cf. "The Unknown," p. 162.
[102] Cf. chapter ix; "Veneris figurae."
[103] *Literaturnoe Nasledstvo*, p. 391.

two forces: either a terrific tension arising out of mystical experiences ... or a terrible mental lassitude, fatigue, inertia, toward everything.... From the very first I had difficulty in understanding you ... and at our first meeting I found it difficult to speak with you.... Nor was my lack of ambition the only reason for this. The first evening we went walking together in the moonlight—at Shakhmatovo—I remember you talked a great deal, while I, as usual, was silent. After we took leave of each other and went to our rooms, I suddenly felt a mystical dread of you.... That night I realized that ... spiritually, we were enemies.... I believe that you, too, sensed a great deal of this....[104]

In answering Biely's request to explain his *credo*, Blok stated that, unlike Biely, who was always determined to "find out the reasons" for everything, he, Blok, intuitively either accepted or rejected, believed or disbelieved, but that he did not find things out through reason, because reasoning was alien to him.[105]

Blok further explained that he had praised Skitalets because he himself had felt an urge to simplify himself; because he felt that Skitalets represented not a mere handful of "repentant nobles with complications," but 40,000,000 common people. Blok felt that Skitalets was closer to Russia than he himself to the coachman with whom Blok "talked during one entire journey" to St. Petersburg.

The coachman cannot help being ignorant, nor I—being more ignorant. I cannot do anything about Mystical Anarchism, to say nothing of the important things. But I am healthy and unpretentious and am becoming as unpretentious as I can.

You will say that ... action is needed, not repentance, that I do not understand epistemology. This is all true. But even Leonid Andreyev ... whom you respect, is tortured by damnable, clumsy, uncultured questions, and is tormented by Russia, which he knows probably a little better than I. This is the reason that I clutch at Skitalets ... the healthy, warm pain of the Volga. I do not claim that it is art....

The drama (I have not yet matured sufficiently to experience tragedy) of my Weltanschauung—lies in the fact that I am a *lyricist* by nature. Lyricism is both eerie and joyous. But beyond the eeriness and the joy lies hidden a chasm into which we may fly headlong—so that

---
[104] *Ibid.*, pp. 395–396.
[105] *Ibid.*

nothing shall remain of us. Were it not for this cloak, were I not guided by the fearful Unknown, from which my soul alone shields me, I should not have written a single one of the poems that you find to some degree significant."[106]

Blok ended his letter with assurances that he was ready to talk over with Biely their mutual problem, and that he was certain that they could clarify their relations. Blok was convinced that they could then determine how much each had wronged the other in the "more intimate things, concerning which one cannot write."[107] Biely's answer to this letter once more ended the personal feud between the two poets. But its closing phrase, "Firmly clasping your hand, I remain deeply respecting you," also definitely marked the end of the ecstatic period of their friendship.[108]

On August 24, 1907, Blok came to Moscow. The two men met, still under a certain tension. Although they greeted each other cordially enough, their relations obviously lacked intimacy. During the twelve hours that they spent talking in Biely's study, Blok tried to persuade Biely that Sergey Solovyov had been at the bottom of their misunderstanding, while Biely insisted that the source of their trouble had been Lyubov Blok.[109] Biely's view of the matter was probably nearer the truth. As the result of their talk they agreed that although in many points of literary policy they belonged to rival camps, personally they should thereafter respect each other. Gradually their conversation changed from the formal *vy* (you) to the informal *ty*.[110]

Nevertheless, even this meeting failed to provide lasting peace. For about six months their relations continued cordial, though quite devoid of intimacy. In April, 1908, Biely published his fourth (and last) symphony, *The Goblet of Blizzards*, a lyrical record of his emotional experiences of the few years

[106] *Ibid.*, p. 397.
[107] *Ibid.*, p. 400.
[108] *Ibid.*, pp. 402–403.
[109] *Omut*, p. 329.
[110] *Ibid.*

just passed. Here he recorded a poeticized version of his relations with the Bloks, and in thinly veiled scenes described some passionate moments of his affair with Sophia incarnate! He sent a copy of his book, with a "tender inscription" to Blok. The reasons that the *Symphony* failed to appeal to Blok are readily understandable. In a letter to his mother Blok wrote of Biely's work: "I go around spitting, as though a roach had crawled into my mouth. To hell with Bugayev!"[111] At the same time he candidly notified Biely that he was obliged to regard the *Symphony* as hostile to himself.[112] In that same letter he confessed that, although he could not help believing that their relations were based on something more significant than they were themselves, in his entire life he had never experienced anything more complicated than these relations.[113]

Biely apparently failed to understand why Blok should have been annoyed by his "masterpiece." Now he, in turn, became insulted and heatedly replied to Blok that, in view of the "complexity" of their relations, he was breaking them off in order to "liquidate the trouble."[114] In conclusion, he begged Blok not to bother answering.

Both men believed that their connection had been severed for all time. Outwardly Blok (and probably Biely) seemed relieved now that they had clarified their positions. At least Blok jotted down in his notebooks: "Glory be to the Creator! I have broken off spiritually with my best friends and 'protectors' (headed by A. Biely)—forever. At last!"[115] Even a year later, Blok maintained that he could do without Biely and Solovyov.[116] Not until the end of the summer of 1909 did Blok begin to mention Biely's name once more without rancor and irony,[117] and within a year after that the two poets made their lasting peace.

[111] Blok, *Pis'ma k rodnym*, I, 208.
[112] *Perepiska*, p. 232.
[113] *Ibid.*
[114] *Ibid.*
[115] Blok, *Zapisnye knizhki*, p. 81.
[116] *Ibid.*, p. 117.
[117] *Ibid.*, pp. 128, 138.

188   *The Frenzied Poets*

Of prime importance to their final reconciliation was the fact that Biely had at last found his "soul companion." She was the charming Asya Turgenev, with whom Biely went abroad in the fall of 1910.[118] Her image eclipsed that of Lyubov Blok, which had persisted until then in his mind. The summer of 1910 brought a promise of peace to Biely's restless spirit, and with peace came a feeling of relief. At last he could be happy.[119] The sense of his own inferiority to Blok, a sentiment that had grown out of jealousy and envy, was now dissipated.

While spending the summer with the Campionis—V. K. Campioni was Asya Turgenev's stepfather—Biely made the happy discovery that Blok's muse had changed once more. In a periodical Biely chanced to see Blok's latest cycle of poetry, *On the Battlefield of Kulikovo* (*Na pole Kulikovom*). Blok's "decadent" themes that Biely had found objectionable had been replaced by patriotic motifs, treated with a pervading, mystic fear of the Oriental Menace that once more showed the influence of Vladimir Solovyov.[120] Biely rejoiced to note that Blok's muse had undergone one more transformation; Russia had displaced the Unknown Demi-mondaine.

To what extent the personal events of Blok's life, and particularly his break with Biely, had affected his return to Solovyovan themes, will remain a subject of controversy. Nevertheless, since Blok himself has written that all his poetry "may be regarded as a diary,"[121] the fact that almost immediately following his break with Biely he turned to mysticism, seems to indicate that he felt the loss of this spiritual "brother" more deeply than he cared to admit even to himself.[122] The split between the two poets had occurred in May, 1908, and already by June of that year Blok had written three poems of the cycle *On the*

---
[118] See chapter v.
[119] *Omut*, pp. 362 ff.
[120] Cf. Vladimir Solov'ev, "Panmongolizm."
[121] Blok, *Zapisnye knizhki*, p. 226.
[122] See for example the ironical remarks that he makes about Belyi, *Zapisnye knizhki*, pp. 81, 89, 90, 97, 117.

Battlefield of Kulikovo, which clearly reflect again the influence of Vladimir Solovyov. Within a year Blok's poetry turned again to mysticism and now to the theme of Russia. Family tragedy—the death of the poet's infant son in February, 1909, and the death of his father in December—undoubtedly had a tendency to deepen his new mystical mood. Blok's return to mysticism gave Biely the excuse to resume their "fateful" friendship.

Meanwhile, Biely had succeeded in overcoming his despair through philosophical study. In his *Metaphysical Melancholy* cycle (*Metafizicheskaya grust'*) light irony displaced the mood of his "drunken ditties." The poem "Despair" was one of the last shrieks of pain from his agonized soul.

Despair

Enough! Hope no longer; be scattered,
My battered long-suffering folk!
Each torturous eon fall shattered
    And vanish beyond all revoke.

Those ages of want and oppression ...
My Russia, belovéd of lands,
Give way to my blinding obsession
    To sob in your hollow expanse.

Out there on the yellow-humped prairie,
Where clusters of oaks catch the eye,
Their paws sweeping—clumsy and hairy—
    The shaggy dull lead of the sky;

Where horror lurks under each shadow,
And each weary tree top becomes
A toy of the wind, while the meadow
    Sinks under its brown leafy crumbs;

Where over the hillocks, like caverns,
Unblinking arise from the night,
Cruel yellowish eyes of your taverns
    To scatter their mad, gloomy light;

190 The Frenzied Poets

> Where pestilence, warfare, and illness
> Have etched their infernal design ...
> Dissolve in that chasm of stillness, ·
> O, Russia, belovéd of mine!
>
> (Summer, 1908)

By the fall of 1908 Biely was already hard at work on his first novel, the *Silver Dove*, which mystically, with apparent calm, dealt with the peril of the Orient to Russia.

When Biely accidentally came upon Blok's new verses he was impressed by their strength.[123] But he was even more impressed by the fact that they coincided "line for line" with his own most intimate thoughts of those past few years: of the impending threat from the Orient.[124] These verses marked "the final 'yes' along [their] road."[125]

Shortly afterward the periodical *Apollo* carried Blok's article "The Present Condition of Symbolism,"[126] in which he once more called Vladimir Solovyov his "teacher." As his chief thesis Blok stated that the poet is "free in this mysterious world which is full of correspondences. . . . he is the solitary possessor of a secret treasure, although about him are others who know of the treasure."[127] "Hence," concluded Blok, "we, *the few knowing ones*, are the Symbolists." Blok himself must have been seeking inwardly to reconcile himself with Biely, for in this same article he referred to Biely's novel, the *Silver Dove*, as "the work of a genius."[128]

Taking the next step to restore his friendship with Blok, Biely wrote him a long, friendly letter, to which he received a "bright, fragrant reply."[129] This exchange of letters permanently ended their differences. Although they had lost their

---

[123] *Zapiski Mechtatelei*, VI (Petersburg, 1922), 120.
[124] *Epopeia*, IV, 173; Belyi's novels of this period, *Serebrianyi golub'* and *Peterburg* also reflect the same theme.
[125] *Zapiski Mechtatelei*, VI, 120.
[126] Blok, *Sobranie sochineii*, IX, 76–87.
[127] *Ibid.*, p. 77.
[128] *Ibid.*, p. 85.
[129] *Perepiska*, p. 234 ff.; *Epopeia*, IV, 173.

Biely and Blok 191

former ecstatic "soul brotherhood," they now found a calm "spiritual brotherhood."[130]

The period from November, 1910, to April of the following year, was the time when Andrey Biely toured the Near East with Asya Turgenev. From there he wrote Blok long letters in which he described their experiences and his new-found joy.[131] Blok also rejoiced in his friend's happiness. On January 13, 1911, he wrote his mother:

> I have received a letter from Borya in Africa. He is living in a village near Tunis. He is terribly happy with his new life and his newly discovered joy after six years of suffering! I am happy for him.[132]

Nevertheless, Biely discovered that his bliss was short-lived. On his return from abroad he found himself in desperate financial straits.[133] Because of the bitter polemical campaign that he had waged in the *Balance*, he learned that his former literary antagonists had practically ruined his literary career. Having a young, equally penniless bride to support, Biely once more seemed on the verge of nervous collapse. Then, as described in chapter vi, he suddenly received Bryusov's request for a long novel, an offer that appeared nothing short of providential. Nevertheless, Biely's joy died almost stillborn when he learned that Bryusov would pay nothing in advance, and that until he had completed a large part of the novel the tantalizing offer could mean to him no more than does a desert mirage to a thirsty traveler. The fact that Biely could not bear the thought of "subjecting Asya to hunger, rheumatism, and the other concomitants of the literary profession,"[134] only added to his anguish.

Biely's nervous letters[135] kept Blok informed of the situation. In an effort to raise some funds that might enable him to finish

---
[130] *Epopeia*, IV, 174.
[131] *Perepiska*, pp. 253–254.
[132] Blok, *Pis'ma k rodnym*, II, 111.
[133] See chapter v.
[134] *Perepiska*, p. 277.
[135] Blok, *Dnevniki*, II, 321.

192   The Frenzied Poets

the novel, Biely wrote Blok a "despairing letter,"[136] in which he begged Blok to try to find a market for some of his unpublished literary works.

> I need 500 rubles immediately. Isn't it possible to receive that sum for literary labor that has been accumulating in vain? ... Unless I get the money within two weeks, I shall howl at the top of my lungs to the bourgeois rabble, "For the sake of Christ, give alms to Andrey Biely!" But I will howl with pride, for I am, by the grace of God, an artist, a man whom society must provide at least with *bread* and *clothing*, unless art, literature, thoughts, ideas, images, have become superfluous for everybody![137]

Blok who had received from his father an inheritance of more than 40,000 rubles, immediately offered his friend a loan of 500 rubles.[138] Biely retained some measure of self-respect by accepting the money only on the condition that it really came from Blok's inheritance and "not from hard earned literary fees."[139] How Bryusov and *Russian Thought* refused to accept the ordered novel, and how Biely was left dangling once more above a financial abyss, has been recounted.[140] Here Blok once more came to his financial assistance and loaned him an additional 350 rubles to give him and Asya a chance to go abroad and thus escape the suffocating Russian literary scene. In time, Biely repaid his entire debt to Blok.[141]

Once he had joined the anthroposophical colony in Dornach, Switzerland, Biely apparently broke all ties with his former friends excepting Blok. During the next four years even his relation with Blok was rather impersonal; it can be judged only from Biely's letters and from an occasional rough draft of Blok's answers preserved in his notebooks and diaries, for the letters themselves repose with Anna Alexeyevna Turgenev

---
[136] *Ibid.*, p. 41.
[137] *Perepiska*, p. 277.
[138] *Epopeia*, IV, 264; *Perepiska*, p. 227.
[139] *Perepiska*, pp. 277–278.
[140] See chapters v and vi.
[141] *Perepiska*, pp. 333–334.

and are still inaccessible.[142] Biely's letters to Blok deal for the most part either purely with business matters—arrangements for the publication of his various works, in which Blok took an active interest—or with information concerning anthroposophy, a subject that intensely irritated Blok, because it claimed to reconcile mysticism with science.[143]

Sick of life among the anthroposophists, Biely returned to Russia without Asya in July, 1916, ostensibly in order to join the army reserve.[144] Since Blok also was liable for military service, Biely felt a new bond rising between them. "After I return from the 'front' (you know, both of us will be going soon)," wrote Biely, "I shall resume my literary work."[145] Biely, however, saw no army service. Before he was conscripted the Bolshevik revolution of 1917 broke out; he may have been exempted from military service on medical grounds.

The two poets, although they were not Communists, found themselves aligned against the old world and supporting the Bolsheviks. Accepting the November revolution as a mystical manifestation of the Second Coming,[146] both men were irreconcilably opposed to the ideology of most of their former literary comrades. Consequently, for such writers as the Merezhkovskys, the two poets became "traitors."[147]

Though the fervor of their earlier friendship had died out, Biely and Blok maintained their cordial relations, which the common bond of ostracism now further cemented. During the first few years of the revolution the two men saw each other occasionally. Both suffered from cold and hunger and both took an active part in the various cultural projects that the new government had launched. Nevertheless, the revolution affected

---

[142] Cf. A. A. Turgeneva's unpublished letter to the author; also the introduction to the Blok-Belyi correspondence, *Perepiska*, v–lxiv.
[143] Blok, *Dnevniki*, II, 99, 101, 148, 163, 170.
[144] Cf. Osorgin's unpublished letter to the author.
[145] *Perepiska*, p. 331.
[146] Cf. Blok's *Dvenadtsat'* and Belyi's *Khristos voskres*.
[147] See chapter vii.

194 The Frenzied Poets

the creative work of the two men quite differently. While it soon stifled Blok's poetic genius, it seemed to stimulate Biely's imagination. Blok wrote practically no poetry after his famous poems "Scythians" and "The Twelve." Biely, however, found the five or six years immediately following the revolution among the most productive of his career. Although at first both poets sincerely welcomed the Bolshevik successes and tried to adapt themselves to the new life, they soon discovered how far they were inherently removed from the proletariat.

In his diary Blok discussed the tragedy that a poet must expect on meeting the "rabble":

> The poet in his struggle with the rabble will necessarily end by yielding to the demands of the mob . . . and, therefore, by perishing.[148]

Blok later developed this Pushkinian theme into an essay "On the Destiny of a Poet" (*"O naznachenii poêta"*). Although in speaking of the rabble Blok had in mind the "bourgeois rabble" of the "old world," the words were fateful. Blok found himself a misfit in the "new world" as well. The realization that even the revolution failed to produce a world into which he, a poet, would fit drove Blok to quiet despair and to the verge of insanity. On August 7, 1921, he died a dispirited, prematurely old man of forty.

Andrey Biely was one of the pallbearers at Blok's funeral, and the *Volfila* (Free Philosophical Association) soon arranged a special memorial meeting in honor of the poet. Biely presided at the meeting and delivered the main address.[149] "He spoke with such inspiration and feeling; so beautifully and concretely did he portray the image of the poet of his youthful period that the entire auditorium was profoundly moved...."[150]

With the coming of the revolution Biely, like Blok, realized that he had no roots in the new Russia. Yet, unlike Blok, he

---
[148] Blok, *Dnevniki*, II, 216–218.
[149] Cf. Vol'fila, *Pamiati Bloka* (Petersburg, 1922), with its record of the meeting and the speeches by Belyi and Ivanov-Razumnik.
[150] Beketova, *Aleksandr Blok*, p. 305.

surrendered to the driving urge to create. He sensed that he still had a vast treasure which he could give to Russian literature. Like Blok, he felt that revolutionary conditions had greatly restricted his creative freedom. During the severe winter of 1921, apartment houses were without fuel, and the people were often starving. For this reason he, like many another Russian writer, sought to go abroad and thus escape conditions that physically limited a writer's ability to express himself.

That year, after Blok died almost insane, and Gumilyov, another poet of real talent, was executed, Biely redoubled his efforts to leave the country, because he feared that, if he were to remain in Russia, a fate similar to that of Blok might overtake him. Blok's death prompted the authorities to relax their rules for granting exit visas, and many prominent writers and artists were able to leave Russia. Thanks chiefly to this fact and to the efforts of such men as M. O. Gershenzon and P. S. Kogan,[151] Biely, as already recounted, received permission to leave Russia for Berlin in the fall of 1921.

Biely's friendship with Blok was one of the most significant factors in his existence. Not only did it determine to a large extent the course of his life, but it was one of the vital influences in shaping—or, perhaps, misshaping—his literary career. His drama with Blok determined the furious bitterness of Biely's polemics, in which he found the needful outlet for the spleen that his feud with Blok produced. Biely's lack of restraint in his polemics, in turn, converted his adversaries into lasting enemies, who as a matter of principle later opposed his contributing to most periodicals, and who by ignoring his writings deliberately belittled whatever literary glory was due him. In fact, not until after the revolution of 1917 were books by Andrey Biely readily reviewed.

In literary significance, the most important result of the Biely-Blok friendship was Biely's brilliant memoirs, prompted

---

[151] See chapter v.

196   The Frenzied Poets

directly by Blok's death. Following his address at Blok's funeral, Biely published the series of his *Reminiscences of Blok*, mentioned in chapter v.[152] He expanded them in his *Epopée* in which he described their relations during the age of symbolism. The success of the *Reminiscences* prompted him to write his (unfinished) memoirs,[153] in which he pungently narrates the intellectual background of the symbolist movement in twentieth-century Russia. Yet, scintillating as these memoirs are, Biely is incomplete without Blok. For here, more than ever before, Biely portrays primarily the external experiences of a symbolist poet. His memoirs, therefore, lack the intimate visions and spiritual experiences, which, except for some of Biely's earlier poetry and for his *Symphonies,* have so far been revealed only in Blok's diaries and notebooks. In fairness to Biely, however, final judgment should be postponed until his own diaries and notebooks are published. To the end, Biely remained personal, Blok intimate. And for that reason they complement each other and make the one almost indispensable for the understanding and evaluation of the other.

---

[152] *Zapiski Mechtatelei,* IV (1921), VI (1922) ; *Literaturnye Zapiski,* February, 1922; *Severnye Dni,* II (1922) ; *Golos Rossii* (Berlin), February 26, 1922, April 2, 1922; *Posledniia Novosti,* April 7, 1922.

[153] *Na rubezhe dvukh stoletii; Nachalo veka; Mezhdu dvukh revoliutsii.*

9

BIELY AND VYACHESLAV IVANOV

> "Should aught transpire quite unexpected—
> You stand before me—resurrected
> In your dress coat of ancient black:
> Amidst old armchairs, old divans,
> A printed volume in your hands:
> *Translucence:* Vyacheslav Ivanov."
>
> —A. BIELY, "TO VYACHESLAV IVANOV"

THROUGHOUT THE 1890's and the opening years of the twentieth century, Dmitri Sergeyevich Merezhkovsky was the undisputed leader of the St. Petersburg symbolists. Then in 1903, Vyacheslav Ivanov, "Vyacheslav the Magnificent,"[1] spectacularly appeared from nowhere, bedazzled the Russian literary public, and quickly won eminence among the younger symbolists.[2] Like the mercurial Biely, the satanic Bryusov, the sibyllic Hippius, and the romantic Blok, the new luminary was distinctly a personality and as such appealed to the intelligentsia.

Born in Moscow in 1866, Ivanov made his appearance in literature rather late in life, at thirty-seven. He was unknown in literary circles until 1903, when his first collection of verse, *Guiding Stars (Kormchie Zvyozdy)*,[3] appeared in print and immediately won him recognition as one of the ranking poets of his day. No sooner was his book released than Ivanov himself streaked cometlike upon the scene. He remained in Russia

---
[1] L. Shestov, "Viacheslav Velikolepnyi," *Russkaia Mysl'* (October, 1916), 80–110.
[2] E. Anichkov, *Novaia russkaia poeziia* (Berlin, 1922), pp. 42–51.
[3] Viacheslav I. Ivanov, *Kormchiia zvezdy* (Moscow, 1903).

just long enough to intrigue and charm those with whom he came in contact; then suddenly he vanished, cometlike again, into the West, whence he had come.

During his brief sojourn, Ivanov's affability, maturity, and erudition won him many friends.[4] Although he was older than most of his modernist friends, Ivanov treated them not with the condescension of a superior, but with the deference of a novice. Nevertheless, intellectually he was in no way behind the times, for his somewhat ambiguous pronouncements concerning a "new organic era," of a "universal" yet "national" art, of "Eros" as the guiding spirit of life coincided with the moods then current among the Russian intelligentsia. As for his erudition, Ivanov was recognized as a rare scholar even among the symbolists, who, taken as a whole, were probably the best-educated group of writers Russia has ever known.

Ivanov's new friends soon discovered that he had spent the better part of the preceding two decades in travel and study abroad. His journeys had taken him to practically every corner of Europe and the Near East. His special field of scholarly investigation proved to be classical antiquity, which he had pursued under the expert guidance of Professor Theodor Mommsen in Germany; in 1910 Ivanov published his dissertation, written in impeccable Latin, *De societatibus vectigalium populi Romani*. His combined gifts as poet, critic, philosopher, scholar, and last but not least, host *par excellence*, quickly made him a legendary figure of the symbolist pantheon. "Vyacheslav the Magnificent," because of his appearance and encyclopedic knowledge became the "wizard" of symbolism.[5]

When Ivanov made his first appearance as a poet in Moscow, Biely was away in Nizhni-Novgorod, where he had fled to escape the attentions of Nina Petrovsky.[6] On returning home,

---
[4] F. Steppun, "Viacheslav Ivanov," *Sovremennyia Zapiski*, LXIII (1938), 231.
[5] L. Shestov, "Viacheslav Velikolepnyi"; see also Ol'ga Forsh, *Voron* (Leningrad, 1934).
[6] See chapter vii.

he found his circle of friends in a state of commotion. One name was on everyone's lips—Ivanov.

"Ivanov said this!" "Ivanov was here!" "You know, Boris—he's got red hair and a wart on his nose." "Can't decide whether he is a genuine eccentric, or just posing simply to impress the crowd." "Don't tell me, you haven't met Ivanov!" "Oh, Ivanov and I . . ."[7] Ivanov had come to, seen, and, apparently, conquered the Argonauts. Biely's curiosity was piqued.

Someone had told Biely that Ivanov "was dying to meet" him,[8] and within a few days Ivanov did actually call at Biely's apartment. When Biely went to the door to meet the caller, "a dark figure stumbled near-sightedly over the threshold." The mysterious man was clad in a badly wrinkled frock coat, and his outstretched left hand "clutched a pair of black gloves and a top hat of antique vintage and reddish hue. . . . A mop of orange hair overshadowed a pointed nose, set in a roundish, ruddy face."[9] The figure entered on squeaking shoes, bumped into a chair, and sang out: "Ivanov."

Despite his irreverence in describing Ivanov, Biely was genuinely impressed. No sooner had Biely acknowledged the introduction, than Ivanov astonished him by addressing him with the familiar *ty* and by insisting that his young host follow his example.[10] A friendship immediately sprang up between the two poets, but before it had a chance to develop further Ivanov returned to Italy and Switzerland.

During his visit to Russia in 1903, Ivanov merely surveyed the ground and prepared the foundation upon which he later built his following.

From the first, Ivanov's poetry struck a responsive chord among those intellectuals who appreciated the air of romantic incongruity, religious mystery, and ultrarefinement that char-

---
[7] *Nachalo veka*, pp. 308–309.
[8] *Ibid.*, p. 311.
[9] *Ibid.*, p. 315.
[10] *Ibid.*

acterized his verse and seemed to reflect the man's bizarre nature. His lyrics combined ponderously dignified, archaic Russian phraseology with ultramodernistic concepts and figures of speech. This poetry with its mood of erotic longing for esoteric mystery and its ancient Greek verse forms startled its Russian readers by its novelty. It was unquestionably "different" and for this reason appeared fresh. In a long critical analysis of Ivanov's style,[11] Biely calls him a "twentieth-century Alexandrian."[12] The definition is very apt, for in Ivanov's poetry one feels a striving to harmonize the supersaturated culture of ancient decadent Alexandria with the mysticism of early twentieth-century decadent Russia. Despite their resultant modern ultra-aestheticism, Ivanov's verses contain barbaric strength, thanks chiefly to his propensity for dissonances. A poem typical of Ivanov is his "Sweet Mystery."

Sweet Mystery

Hark to my word; unadorned it is beautiful,
   if only my word be
True. Be it false, O my friends, vain is the
   life I have lived,
Long, if my word be untrue, is the road I have
   erringly wandered;
Death shall have charmed me, alas! and love proved
   to be false.

Into my heart, by the ring of departure has Love's
   benediction been written,
Death, by the circle of return has sealed, forever,
   the vow.
Lips and desires speak falsehood; only the all-knowing
   heart speaks the truth.
If during my life I have loved, know this then: that
   Mystery is sweet.

---

[11] A. Belyi, *Poeziia slova* (Petersburg, 1922), pp. 20–105.
[12] *Ibid.*, p. 22.

> Mystery is sweet, such my word—and life is a
>   lullaby.
> Death—a midwife; in her earth a new cradle
>   awaits us.
> Mystery is sweet; peace eternal—a wedlock;
>   the creation—a bride.
> The Bride chamber of the Universe is the all-starry
>   night of the Lord.
>
> Mystery is sweet! Love kisses all, and Forgiveness
>   caresses.
> All that I see hath the Bridegroom embraced with
>   his luminous crown.
> Every last drop of many a bliss that has passed
>   undiscovered
> Falls into the chalice Life's crater so sweet
>   has preserved.
>
> All that has tasted its joys shall bloom like
>   the seed
> With the flower of bliss—and shall give to
>   the lone Rose its blossom.
> Mystery, O brothers, is sweet: be it designate then,
>   by the sign of the Rose,
> By the calm, quiet smile of the grave, by the
>   tender seal that is Love.[13]

On embarking upon his literary career, Ivanov associated himself with the younger generation of poets. They differed from their predecessors in that they demanded of a poet a striving toward a new life, rather than a Buddhistic detachment from the present. Their philosophy reflected also the concept of Vladimir Solovyov that the world, as it was known to them, was soon to meet its end.[14] Some of them awaited the end of their era in the year 1900, which according to an interpretation of the prophecy of Agrippa of Nettesheim, was destined to usher in a new age of mankind.[15] Ivanov adapted Nietzsche's

---
[13] V. I. Ivanov, "Nezhnaia taina."
[14] See V. Solov'ev, "Tri razgovora," *Sobranie sochinenii*, X, 193–218.
[15] V. I. Ivanov, *Po zvezdam* (Moscow, 1909), p. 311.

terminology to the eschatological presentiments of Vladimir Solovyov, and expounded his philosophy in terms of the "new organic era,"[16] on the brink of which he visualized the world to be tottering.

Important to the symbolist movement was Ivanov's definition of symbolism, as opposed to decadence. Decadence, he stated, was an escape from life, but symbolism was the anticipation of and the striving toward the "new" life.[17] Similarly, romanticism was a reflection of the past, a "longing for the unattainable," but symbolism was a "striving to the future—a longing for what had not yet been attained."[18]

In his definition of symbolism, Ivanov, like Biely and Blok, typified the younger generation of symbolists. Unlike Bryusov, who saw in symbolism only a poetry of nuances and subtle shadings,[19] designed to convey the emotions of a modern poet, Ivanov regarded it as a means by which ultimate reality might be revealed to a poet during creative frenzy. To Bryusov, symbolism was merely a literary method; to Ivanov, symbolism represented a philosophy. Bryusov used symbols to convey his moods and emotions, Ivanov regarded symbols as instruments by means of which a poet could convey images of the "ultimate reality." According to Ivanov, through symbolism a poet depicted the *realiora* of the more real world in terms of its shadows, the *realia* of the visible world—the only aspect in which the greater reality is perceptible to the average man.[20] Therefore, the motto that Ivanov adopted for symbolism was *a realibus ad realiora*,[21] from the real to the more real.

Interesting, too, was Ivanov's interpretation of a symbolist poet's relation to the masses. Like the rest of the symbolists,

---

[16] Friedrich Nietzsche, "Die Geburt der Tragödie," *Gesammelte Werke* (München, 1922), II, 119 ff.
[17] Ivanov, *Po zvezdam, passim.*
[18] *Ibid.*
[19] N. Ashukin, ed., *Valerii Briusov*, p. 65.
[20] Ivanov's concept is basically Platonic, as developed in the allegory of the cave, in book vii of the *Republic*.
[21] V. I. Ivanov, *Po zvezdam*, pp. 277, 305, and *passim*.

Ivanov accepted the view of Pushkin[22] (and of the German romantic philosophers) that a poet is a superman, endowed with powers beyond the reach of an average mortal. But unlike Pushkin, Ivanov did not believe that between a poet and his public lay an unbridgeable chasm. On the contrary, Ivanov urged that the poet should embrace the "rabble."[23] Ivanov saw symbolism as the art of the future, intelligible at the time only to the poets and a few individuals who had already attained a certain level of spiritual and cultural development. Realizing that without a symbolist audience symbolist art could not exist,[24] Ivanov declared that symbolism must raise the masses to the required cultural level.[25] He believed that eventually every individual would become an artist in his own right. Art would then become a broadly communal enterprise, rather than a narrowly individualistic effort. In such communal art, the symbol would, therefore, expand itself into a myth, and art become "mythurgy," myth-creation.[26]

Ivanov thus proposed to democratize symbolism. He succeeded in this purpose only too well. Primarily because of his efforts, symbolism as a literary genre eventually gained popular recognition as a legitimate vehicle of artistic expression. Unfortunately, however, for symbolist art, the recognition came too rapidly. It came before the reading public had become elevated to what the symbolists considered the proper cultural level. The mass of readers came to accept symbolism as a technique in art, without understanding its principles as a philosophy. The philosophical tenets of symbolism were usually couched in such obscure and ambiguous terminology as to make comprehension difficult. The public, therefore, selected those ideas that appealed to its mood, and in so doing frequently misinterpreted them to suit its own fancy. The ethical

---

[22] A. Pushkin, "Chern'" (1828).
[23] Ivanov, *Po zvezdam*, pp. 33–42.
[24] V. I. Ivanov, *Borozdy i mezhi* (Moscow, 1916), p. 156.
[25] Ivanov, *Po zvezdam*, pp. 326–327.
[26] *Ibid.*, pp. 285–290, and *passim*.

204   The Frenzied Poets

tenets of symbolism, as a philosophy, were altogether ignored. Therefore, instead of elevating the masses to a higher plane, as Ivanov had hoped, symbolism itself became vulgarized and descended to their level.

The misinterpretation of Vladimir Solovyov's concept of "love" illustrates how Ivanov's followers transformed a strictly ethical notion into something primarily sensual. According to Solovyov, love is the primary moving power of life; death is one of the greatest positive evils,[27] and only the power of all-embracing true love can overcome it. Solovyov believed that Christ in arising from the dead had demonstrated to mankind the power of love.[28] Ivanov took Solovyov's concept of love and, because of his predilection for classical antiquity, renamed it "Eros." Although Ivanov employed the term basically in its Platonic sense, he was prone to interpret it also in its physical meaning, as a Dionysian force.

To the uninitiated, Eros was synonymous with erotic, and Ivanov's idea soon became distorted. The distortion proved all the easier, since it occurred at a time when part of the intelligentsia, disillusioned after the attempted revolution of 1905, was wallowing in the mire of spiritual decay and sought to justify its sensual cravings. Therefore, the so-called "third wave" of symbolism produced a veritable shower of pornography, which horrified some older poets, who looked upon "true" poets (like themselves) as priests and prophets, consecrated to a sacred task.[29] Such followers of Ivanov as Margarita Sergeyev, I. Gurvich, A. Bronin, L. M. Vasilevsky, Lensky, creatures whom Biely castigated as "baggage-train refuse," were too prone to seize upon a term like "Eros" in order to sanctify their own erotic mood. They had really nothing in common with the ideals of the symbolists, who sought in love

---
[27] V. Solov'ev, "Smysl liubvi," *Sobranie sochinenii*, VI, 3–56; "Tri razgovora," *Sobranie sochinenii*, X, 83–221.
[28] V. Solov'ev, "Tri razgovora."
[29] *Omut*, p. 196.

a source of inspiration that would lead to the ecstatic rapture that enabled the poet to grasp intuitively the real essence of the universe. Bronin and his colleagues held no such lofty aspirations of art. They were mere rhymesters, who had gleefully seized upon a symbolist tenet that they found a useful tool. Small wonder then that Biely, who at that time (1907) envisaged himself as a crusader to keep the muse of poetry unsullied, should have descended upon the heads of the renegade defilers.[30]

Since at the literary *jours fixes* in his apartment, the Tower, Ivanov preferred to listen to the ideas of others, rather than express his own, he made little effort to correct misconceptions of his philosophical notions. In fact, by harboring in his Tower such devotees of erotica as Kuzmin,[31] and through some of his own poems (for example "Veneris figurae," in which he rhapsodized "the three hundred and thirty-three embraces"),[32] Ivanov seemed to lend the erotic trend at least his tacit approval; in time, moreover, his Wednesdays became symposia for mystical anarchism, mystical individualism, collective individualism, and other similar trends of the period 1905–1910.

The Wednesday gatherings in the Tower began in 1905, when Ivanov and his wife (also a writer, Lidia Zinovyeva-Annibal) returned from a recent visit to Italy and Switzerland. During his absence of a year or more from Russia, Ivanov's external appearance had undergone a change. He had raised a small, flaxen goatee, which, together with a perpetually slipping *pince-nez*, added to his air of absent-minded detachment. The Ivanovs came directly to St. Petersburg and rented an apartment that overlooked the Potyomkin Palace (at 25, Tavricheskaya Street, the building that eventually housed the Russian State Duma).[33] This was the seventh-floor penthouse that soon

---
[30] *Vesy* (June, 1907), 68; (July, 1907), 72.
[31] Cf. M. Kuzmin, *Aleksandriiskiia pesni* (St. Petersburg, 1909).
[32] *Vesy* (January, 1907).
[33] *Nachalo veka*, p. 313.

206   The Frenzied Poets

acquired the nickname of the "Ivanov Tower"; and here, overlooking the treetops of the Taurid Gardens, came into being the lavish "Ivanov Wednesdays," which became famous in the history of Russian cultural life.

It was not so much the St. Petersburg literary world that bade welcome to the Vyacheslav Ivanovs, as it was the Ivanovs who opened their arms to all those of the intellectual and artistic world whom they regarded interesting.[34]

The Wednesday night gatherings started unpretentiously enough, and at first consisted only of a small group of intimate friends.[35] Thanks to Mme. Ivanov's charm as hostess and her husband's geniality as host, their *salon* soon grew to amazing proportions. The Ivanovs had a gift of creating an atmosphere of pleasant intimacy and had the ability of attracting people of widely diversified interests.[36] Perhaps a still greater gift that the Ivanovs possessed was their ability to unite the people who joined them in their *soirées* into a homogeneous group.

Ivanov quickly proved that the rumors of his erudition were no idle gossip, and that he was not only a most amiable host and poet, but also a brilliantly educated scholar, a philosopher of mystical inclinations, and, above all, a man of broad and varied interests. He had an uncanny facility of unfailingly hitting upon the very core of any matter discussed.[37] Like Biely, he had the ability of conversing intelligently with any person on whatever topic was closest to that person's heart. But, unlike Biely, Ivanov refrained from burying people with whom he talked under an avalanche of his own words and ideas. He preferred to listen.[38] Each person, whether scientist, philologist, actor, philosopher, musician, or archaeologist, thus felt comfortably at home in the unusual surroundings of the Tower. The thought-provoking questions that Ivanov would pose to his

---
[34] E. Anichkov, *op. cit.*, pp. 45–46.
[35] V. Piast, *Vstrechi*, pp. 166–180.
[36] M. Nemerovskaia, ed., *Sud'ba Bloka*, pp. 96–101.
[37] Piast, *op. cit.*, p. 47.
[38] F. Steppun, "Viacheslav Ivanov," p. 231.

guests frequently transformed his evenings into veritable symposia. These qualities in Ivanov favored the creation of a spiritual laboratory in which ideas would be exchanged and literary currents formulated.[39] Amidst the din of arguments and repartee of paradoxes, would float the reddish-blond figure of the master of the Tower, perpetually tossing upward the ever-slipping *pince-nez*, rubbing his hands, now pacifying two antagonists, now raising himself on tiptoes and tossing a remark of his own into an argument, now listening with interest to a newly formulated theory.[40]

Actually the Wednesdays soon became Thursdays. The initiated remained long after supper had been served at 2 A.M.[41] The gatherings continued to grow, so that the guests were soon obliged to sit on the floor, leaving a small circle in the center of the room for anyone who wished to read from his own works or to speak on some social or philosophical theme.[42] Anyone with the slightest spark of talent was welcome here.

Many of Ivanov's out-of-town friends stayed at the Tower during their visits in St. Petersburg. Some of them lived there for weeks and months, and one of them, M. A. Kuzmin, who had "dropped in for a visit," stayed on for years![43] Occasionally the walls had to be torn down and another room added to the ever-growing penthouse. Even the death of Mme. Ivanov in 1907, failed to disrupt the life of the Tower, which continued its eccentric course until 1912, when Ivanov went abroad and everything ended.[44]

To an intellect that sought to clarify its own *Weltanschauung* Ivanov's attraction was obvious. In search of a philosophy that might disperse his doubts, Biely was drawn quite naturally into the orbit of Ivanov's influence. Biely was impressed by the

[39] M. Nemerovskaia, ed., *Sud'ba Bloka*, pp. 96–101.
[40] E. Anichkov, *op. cit.*, p. 43; cf. also Piast, *loc. cit.*
[41] V. N. Kniazhnin, *O Bloke* (Petersburg, 1922), p. 97.
[42] *Nachalo veka*, p. 321.
[43] *Ibid.*, p. 322.
[44] *Ibid.*, p. 318.

older man's mind and felt a genuine kinship with the strange, illusive host of the Tower, whose contradictory and complex nature seemed to echo Biely's own duality. Ivanov, in turn, sensed in Biely a disciple who should prove worthy of his master. Since Zinaida Hippius and Valeri Bryusov feared in Ivanov a serious rival for leadership among the symbolists, they made an effort to keep Biely within their own fold, and out of Ivanov's clutches. Nonetheless, an alliance between Andrey Biely and Vyacheslav Ivanov was inevitable.

Biely's initial friendship with Ivanov, however, evaporated rather quickly. As soon as Ivanov returned from Switzerland in 1905 and renewed his acquaintance with Biely, the new symbolist current, mystical anarchism, alienated the two poets. Ivanov became one of the leaders of the new trend, Biely became its bitterest critic.

Mystical anarchism was originated by Georgy Chulkov, a poet of little merit, who once had been a collaborator of the *New Path* and an editor of *Questions of Life* (*Voprosy Zhizni*, 1905). It answered the popular demand for self-assertion and mysticism that followed in the wake of the revolution of 1905. Mystical anarchism was based on an urge to surmount the "antinomy of freedom and necessity" by means of an irrational "assertion of one's individuality."[45] Since "Eros is always a miracle worker—an intermediary between gods and men," Eros was seen as the means for attaining the goal.[46] Since "individuality, which asserts itself through the will, is the Absolute," it expresses itself not in "secluded individualism, but in ... that perfect individualism which seeks expression in society."[47] According to Chulkov, however, one's individual personality can be free only in a society "based on a free *anarchical* union in love."

---
[45] Georgii Chulkov, "Ob utverzhdenii lichnosti," *Fakely*, II (St. Petersburg, 1907), 24.
[46] *Ibid.*
[47] *Ibid.*, p. 25.

Therefore, mystical anarchism actually expresses an irreconcilable and rebellious attitude toward any authority. It believes that individualism must destroy any regime that restricts the activity of the human spirit. It is, therefore, a force destructive to social order. Yet mystical anarchism "creates as well as destroys." Its creative activity expresses itself in art, a process that is independent of any force except Eros. Through Eros alone lay the path to renewed mystical experiences[48] and to a new humanity.

Ivanov shared Chulkov's views on love as the primary moving force in the universe. But while Chulkov saw it only as a motivating power, Ivanov accepted it as a cognitive agent that could reveal Schopenhauer's world of ideas. Reality, wrote Ivanov, could be grasped only through an action of mystical knowledge, which in turn was predicated on an action of love.[49]

Although Chulkov was the father of mystical anarchism, the movement—or rather, mood—owed its following primarily to Vyacheslav Ivanov. Chulkov as a personality, thinker, and poet lacked not only the talent but also the appeal necessary for a successful leader. Unlike Ivanov, Chulkov commanded neither the affection nor the esteem of the symbolists. Such men as Alexander Blok, Meierhold, and Maier soon had gravitated into the orbit of mystical anarchism, not because of Chulkov's efforts, but because of Ivanov's influence. Thus, Ivanov and not Chulkov, had become its central figure.[50]

Chulkov and Ivanov soon found a wealthy Moscow merchant, N. P. Ryabushinsky, who was willing to finance a periodical. While they were discussing what name to give their journal, someone happened to mention the Argonauts, and the title *Golden Fleece* immediately suggested itself. Therefore, without even consulting the Argonauts, who had no formal organization, Ryabushinsky and friends started their lavishly printed

---
[48] *Ibid.*
[49] Ivanov, *Po zvezdam*, pp. 372–376.
[50] *Nachalo veka*, p. 315.

magazine *Golden Fleece* in the winter of 1905–1906. The fact that that journal with a title obviously taken from the Argonauts and the Argonautic cycle of Biely's *Gold in Azure* came to represent the St. Petersburg group of poets, quite foreign in spirit to the Argonauts, the House of Song, and similar related modernist groups of Moscow, naturally irked Andrey Biely. Biely and his fellow Argonauts fumed indignantly at the plagiarism, but were powerless to take any action against Ryabushinsky.[51] Chulkov did not confine his publishing activities to creating the *Golden Fleece*; he succeeded in establishing also the miscellany *Torches* (1906–1907), in which the theories of mystical anarchism were discussed.

The *Golden Fleece* at first was nonpartisan in its symbolist views. It welcomed Bryusovites and Ivanovites alike. In fact, in order to consolidate the symbolist factions, Ryabushinsky first offered its literary editorship to Bryusov.[52] But Bryusov, who was at that time the *de facto* editor of the *Balance*, became alarmed lest the *Golden Fleece* might undermine his own brain child. He not only refused to support the Ryabushinsky magazine, but actively campaigned against it. He withdrew from its editorial board and soon had persuaded his own disciples to follow his example.[53] By 1907 Biely, Merezhkovsky, Hippius, Sergey Solovyov, and lesser lights, had published statements in the *Balance* declaring that they had withdrawn from the rival periodical.[54]

Although the loss of such collaborators hurt the prestige of the *Golden Fleece*, the magazine continued to exist. Consequently Bryusov continued his polemic campaign against it and its most important contributors, Ivanov, Blok, and Chulkov. The better to carry on his struggle, Bryusov appealed for support to his "faithful dogs,"[55] among whom Andrey Biely

---

[51] *Ibid.*, p. 108.
[52] *Omut*, p. 245.
[53] *Ibid.*, pp. 245–248.
[54] *Vesy* (September, 1907), 75–76.
[55] *Nachalo veka*, p. 160.

was the first to come to his aid. Bryusov convinced his followers that mystical anarchism and the group supporting it were working to the detriment of the symbolist cause, and would inevitably vulgarize it.[56] The mystical anarchists were too careless in formulating their mottoes; they appealed to the sensational elements in literature; for them art no longer remained a sacred principle. Bryusov argued, Biely agreed, and subsequent events justified their fears, that any attempt to disseminate a philosophy of art that held that art was inspired by an ecstasy born of Eros would necessarily profane the lofty aspirations of the true symbolists; the average "Philistine" versificator, who had no conception of the "sacred sacrifice" a poet was expected to make on behalf of the mob, would vulgarize the principle of the "erotic impulse," which the Solovyovan symbolists translated in the Platonic sense. The *Balance*, which heretofore had no specific program other than to win an audience for symbolism, both Russian and foreign, now adopted the principle that symbolism had to evolve its aesthetic canons before it could proceed with democratizing its doctrines.

Brooding over the unhappy outcome of his love affair, Biely explained it as the result of his own betrayal of his idealized muse of poetry. He blamed himself for allowing his search of the erotic ecstasy to carry him away. He, therefore, began to seek a means of exonerating himself of his defection and coincidentally of shifting the guilt on other shoulders. Mystical anarchists, as devotees of Eros, loomed as the natural scapegoats. Being therefore quickly persuaded that in attacking mystical anarchism he would be fighting for a principle, he clutched at this straw in hopes of vindicating himself before his own eyes. Biely went into action with the fanatic frenzy of a Savonarola. He flung one lashing tirade after another and cast vituperations at Ivanov, Chulkov, Blok, and their followers. During the years 1907–1908, Biely published some of the most stinging and

---
[56] *Ibid.*

fiery polemics that Russian literature has known. Chulkov, against whom he held no personal grievance, he castigated because he regarded him as an upstart, a pretender who claimed to be a poet. Although Biely's diatribes against Ivanov were less vehement, they strained to the breaking point the relations between the two men. In one of his attacks against the mystical anarchists and their publishing house, Ory, Biely wrote that their "banner ... was a stamped galosh."[57] He was referring to the trademark, the mystic triangle, which the Ory happened to share with a well-known Russian galosh factory. Since the word "galosh" in Russian carries a connotation of opprobrium, Ivanov became offended at Biely and the erstwhile friends severed relations. Even when Ivanov, during one of his visits to Moscow, attempted to regain Biely's friendship, Biely though somewhat mollified, only snarled back obstinately.

The reconciliation came two years later. Meanwhile both men had printed numerous recriminations against each other, each accusing the other of ignorance and of lack of good taste and ethical principles.[58] Nevertheless, by 1909, most of the spleen had drained from their polemic, and their tempers subsided. The fact that Biely's second book of verse, *Ashes*, stamped him as a pupil of Ivanov also helped to restore their friendship. The central theme of *Ashes* is Russia and therefore coincides with one of Ivanov's artistic principles that art must reflect the spirit of the *demos*, the people.[59] The two poets met at the Tenishevsky Hall in St. Petersburg, where Biely had come to deliver a lecture. Here, he noticed in the doorway to the lecturer's study, a figure in a small, soft, fur cap and "a fur coat resembling a priest's." Suddenly his hands were seized, pressed under a golden twin beard to the fur coat's bosom, and the stooped figure of Vyacheslav Ivanov was suddenly whispering into his ear: "I've just read your book, *Ashes*.

[57] *Vesy* (May, 1907), 49.
[58] *Vesy* (May, 1908), 59–63; (July, 1908), 73.
[59] Ivanov, *Po zvezdam*, pp. 243–246.

It is tremendous! I've got to talk with you tonight." During this visit to St. Petersburg, Biely was unwell and stayed with the Merezhkovskys, where Zinaida Hippius looked after the ailing poet as described earlier. Ivanov, nevertheless, snatched him from her hands. Willy-nilly, Biely allowed Ivanov to drag him to the Tower, while the words of Zinaida Hippius, "if you go, I'll never forgive you; don't bother to return," resounded malignantly in his ear. In the Tower, over a glass of steaming tea, the two poets once more became fast friends.[60]

By 1909, symbolism was showing signs of disintegration. Within it, a movement directly opposed to some of the symbolist tenets had begun to crystallize. It opposed the symbolist principles of vagueness and mysticism, and proposed clarity and concreteness in their place. In 1909 a new periodical, significantly named *Apollo*, as though to stress its opposition to the Dionysian concept, appeared, backed by such renegade symbolists as Innokenti Annensky, Mikhail Kuzmin, Nikolay Gumilyov, and Sergey Gorodetsky. The *Apollo* supplemented the *Balance* and the *Golden Fleece* and, when both these periodicals were discontinued, logically became their spiritual heir. By 1912 the new current had become a full-fledged school, the "acmeists," with slogans of their own and a fully developed system of principles.[61]

Paradoxically enough, acmeism, the successor to symbolism, had been reared under the roof of the Ivanov Tower. Kuzmin, who in 1909 was still quartered in the Tower, sheltered in his apartment the "Apolloites" Nikolay Gumilyov, Sergey Makovsky (publisher of the *Apollo*), and Znosko-Borovsky, who were convinced that symbolism was about to disintegrate.

Ivanov also was aware that a crisis faced symbolism. In order to restore some of its former vitality, he strove to reconcile Biely and Blok, the other outstanding representatives of symbolism as a *Weltanschauung*, who had been estranged since

[60] *Nachalo veka*, p. 326.
[61] *Ibid.*

214 The Frenzied Poets

1906. Ivanov now apparently realized to what extent his ambiguous pronouncements on Eros in its equivocal meaning of "passion" both as an active and a suffering urge had demoralized the symbolist movement.[62] He therefore not only renounced his former claims that passion leads a poet to conceive reality, but in a public lecture proclaimed that only "truth, as a *moral* value could lead one to . . . conceive 'reality.' "[63] Thus Ivanov capitulated to Biely's thesis that art cannot exist without an ethical as well as an aesthetic basis. Furthermore, Ivanov induced Blok to retract his assertion that a lyrical poet need seek no other guide save his intuition. Blok appeared with Ivanov at the same public lecture and paraphrased the sentiments that Ivanov had expressed. Harmony was once more restored among the three poets. With a few such minor exceptions as Biely's attack against Ivanov for approving the brutality of war in the name of Greek paganism, it proved enduring to the end of their days. Thereafter, no jarring discord interrupted the continuous course of friendship.

Ivanov sought also to revive symbolism as an active force in Russian literature and thought. He obtained Emili Medtner's support for the periodical *Works and Days* (*Trudy i Dni*, 1911–1913), which was to provide "the big three" of the younger symbolists—Blok, Biely, and Ivanov—with an outlet for their critical and theoretical writings.[64] But the fervor that had characterized the writers' earlier struggle on behalf of symbolism was now gone, and the magazine was soon discontinued.

The role that Ivanov had played in securing a publisher for Biely's novel *Petersburg* (1912) has already been briefly mentioned.[65] As soon as Ivanov learned the details of Biely's incident with Bryusov, he invited Biely to St. Petersburg. Here at his Tower he convoked all his literary associates and had

---
[62] *Fakely*, II, 234.
[63] *Apollon* (May–June, 1910), 10.
[64] See chapter vi.
[65] *Nachalo veka*, p. 326.

Biely read his novel "aloud to the Anichkovs, Sologub, Alexey Tolstoy . . . and other important figures of the Russian literary world." His eyes flashing with indignation about Bryusov's action, Ivanov shouted that the novel was "epoch-making!"[66]

Thanks to Ivanov's spirited campaign, Biely's "defeat at the hands of the *Russian Thought* was turned into a victory."[67] After all the "fuss that Ivanov had raised," publishers came begging to print the novel. Ivanov was directly responsible also for naming Biely's book. Biely had originally intended to call it "The Admiralty Spire" or "The Lacquered Coach,"[68] but Ivanov insisted, "Boris, there is only one title for your work—*Petersburg*."[69] Soon after the novel was accepted for publication, Biely and Asya Turgenev went abroad; nor did Ivanov remain in Russia long afterward.

In 1914 the two poets met in Basel, Switzerland, where Biely, still searching for an all-embracing philosophy, had become interested in the anthroposophical movement of Dr. Rudolf Steiner as related earlier. For two days the friends "discussed the crises in each other's life, and the impending doom of Symbolism" should both decide to remain abroad. Ivanov and Biely agreed that symbolism, as they had once understood it, was dead. They found that they had to relinquish their belief that art could provide man with a concept of the ultimate reality. At the end of his visit Ivanov departed for Neuchâtel and the adjacent lakes, and Biely and Asya for the Vierwaldstätter lake.[70]

Eventually Ivanov returned to Russia, where he remained until 1924. Feeling out of sympathy with the proletarian revolution, he finally emigrated to Italy. In his later years he became converted to Catholicism, and took up residence in one of the old Italian monasteries. He died in September, 1949.

---

[66] *Ibid.*
[67] *Ibid.*, p. 318.
[68] *Perepiska*, pp. 268, 279.
[69] *Nachalo veka*, pp. 318–319.
[70] *Ibid.*, p. 327.

216 The Frenzied Poets

In Ivanov's conversion to Catholicism one senses the drama of the symbolist mentality and a parallel with Biely's attempt to find an all-explaining way of life first in symbolism, then in Neo-Kantian philosophy, and finally in anthroposophy. Basically yearning to believe in the existence of another world and yet restrained by intellect from doing so, both Biely and Ivanov had sought in symbolist art a *Weltanschauung* that would satisfy their inner craving. Yet symbolism erected no dogmas to uphold its theories. Its intellectual freedom left too much room for doubt and questioning, and therefore failed to overcome the uprootedness of a romantic mentality[71]—the uprootedness which plagued the "children of the lost generation"; children who could not accept the world as their age depicted it, who had to believe in the existence of another world, and yet found themselves organically unable to do so. Disillusioned in his expectations of symbolism, Biely had turned to the dogmatic rationalized mysticism of anthroposophy,[72] which closely paralleled the symbolist ideas, and apparently accepted its main principles. Biely's nature demanded rational explanations for everything, and in anthroposophy, therefore, found a measure of temporary satisfaction. Ivanov, on the other hand, was organically more of a mystic than Biely. Failing to find a satisfactory answer to his questions, Ivanov submitted to the dogmas of the Catholic church like Verlaine, and others, before him. Neither Biely nor Ivanov gave up believing that this world was only a shadow and an echo of another world. But for support of this basic belief Biely was obliged to turn to the rational dogmas of anthroposophy and Ivanov to the authoritarian dogmas of the Roman church.

[71] *Ibid.*
[72] See chapter v.

10

CONCLUSION

THE LIFE AND WORKS of Boris Bugayev vividly illustrate the course of the Russian symbolist movement during the first decade of the present century. In Andrey Biely, Russian symbolism, at its greatest complexity and in its various connotations, found a striking representative. Symbolism as a state of mentality, symbolism as an art, symbolism as a way of life, are all reflected in his life and works.

Andrey Biely was a characteristic child of a generation that was lost in the wilderness of life. He typifies the intellectual who had discovered that, because of his background, he was beset with two irreconcilable desires: to *know* and to *believe.* Yet he realized that no absolute knowledge existed and also that he could not believe unquestioningly. Owing to nineteenth-century philosophical trends, to the progress of the machine age and the natural sciences, as well as to political, social, and economic conditions, Biely, like many other intellectuals, felt that the new ideas had robbed man of his immortality and dwarfed the importance of the individual. He felt that the validity of intuition had been scientifically disproved; that science had defined all that was knowable; and that no mysteries remained for men to probe or to hope for. He, like other intellectuals, rebelled against all these trends and attempted to reëstablish the importance of the individual, to reassert the validity of intuitive revelation and mystery, and to rehabilitate the value of imagination. In a word, he sought to disprove the entire system of scientific thought that found expression in positivism and materialism.

In attempting to reëstablish the importance of the individual, Biely first turned to himself. He began to regard himself, an artist, as a superior being. In his own mind he therefore placed himself above the throng of "Philistines." He wanted to be different from them, and consequently developed his own individuality to the point of eccentricity, which he reflected in his art.

In attempting to reassert the validity of intuitive knowledge, he turned to the irrational, to the emotions. He strove to prefer intuitive apprehension to rational comprehension. He desired to restore mystery to its former place in the world. He sought a religious expression of his emotional experiences. He wanted to interpret art as a religious sacrament, as theurgy. Yet so thoroughly was he grounded in the scientific tradition of his day that he could not fully accept any notion based on an irrational interpretation of reality, despite the inner urge to do so. Therefore he found himself dangling over the void between the cliffs of belief and skepticism.

In attempting to reject the world that science had created for man, Biely turned to his imagination to find the real world. He tried to reject completely the reality of the physical, phenomenal universe; he asserted that it comprised mere shadows and echoes of the real world. Since in reëstablishing his own ego he had come to regard himself as a superior being, he now sought to accept the view that he, an artist, could in moments of inspiration glimpse a vision of the higher reality. Nevertheless, because of his scientific training, Biely could not suppress an urge to seek rational proof, irrefutable substantiation for such belief. Failing to be completely satisfied by his findings, he turned to other systems of knowledge in search of support for his urgent will to believe.

Throughout his life Biely was unable to discard the duality

Conclusion 219

of his mental outlook. Throughout his life he longed to believe wholeheartedly that the other world did exist, and yet he could never completely accept it. Torn between the two poles, he spent his lifetime searching frantically, yet in vain, for peace of spirit. In his feverish, futile search Biely resembles another great Russian poet, Lermontov. Without ever openly acknowledging the resemblance, Biely nevertheless characterized himself in the following quatrain:

> Like a stone, flung from a fateful sling,
>   You plough through wretched mists
> In search of peace. Search not for peace:
>   No peace exists. (1908)

The similarity between these lines and the concluding lines of Lermontov's "Sail" is striking:

> But he, the rebel, thirsts for tempests,
>   As though in tempests there be peace!

Biely's *Weltanschauung* explains much of his art. It is the force that constantly drives him to deny the reality of the material, phenomenal, physical world; it is the power that activates his attempts to disprove and disavow what reason and science accept as fact; it is the basis for his entire artistic creation and for the individualism that underlies his work.

Biely's philosophical idealism drives him to stress the emotional and intuitive elements over the rational. He therefore stresses mood rather than narrative. He expresses himself vaguely, and frequently borders on the obscure. He seeks to transmit feelings rather than thoughts. Since he believes that music can best convey emotions, he stresses the musical element in his writing and goes so far as to attempt (in his *Symphonies*) to apply the principles of musical composition to literature. The religious trend in Biely's works is unmistakable. In following Vladimir Solovyov, Biely proclaims his teacher, together with himself and every true poet, as seer and prophet. Furthermore, since he senses subconsciously that the social structure of his day is doomed, his works possess an aspect of apocalyptic vision. Yet Biely, believing that the change will usher in the millenium, sees himself as a prophet of a new life. In rejecting science and its truth Biely proclaims the reality of the noumenal, transphysical world. Accepting the creative process of art as an infallible cognitive process, as a revelation of the absolute reality, he claims that art affords a creative artist glimpses of this reality. Consequently, he believes that artists should be leaders and teachers as well as creators, and that their duty lies in showing humanity their visions of eternity. Since a poet must, therefore, be different from the crowd, Biely attempts to make his art as individualistic as possible. His individualism also prompts him to make it subjective to the highest degree. For this reason he, like all symbolists, is largely autobiographical.

Biely's philosophical outlook also determines his acceptance of symbolism as a way of life. Since he believed that a poet's duty was to teach, to lead, he thought that his mission was to show mankind how to attain the new, beautiful life that he prophesied; a poet was to demonstrate how man should live. Biely believed that life should strive to reveal the higher truth, and since truth might be glimpsed in moments of creative ecstasy, he believed that one's life should yield the maximum of such moments. Nevertheless, when he himself sought such a life, his efforts ended with complete failure that spelled tragedy, not only in his own life, but in Blok's as well. Since all his works reflect the subjective factors in his life, a thorough knowledge of Biely's biography is indispensable to a full understanding of his work.

Biely's life and works of the period 1901–1909 clearly demonstrate the success and failure of symbolism as he had interpreted it. His own epitaph,

> I solved the riddle of the ages
> Could not solve my life's as well

speaks volumes. His failure in living his life, however, did not become apparent at once.

Throughout his earliest period, Biely's personality, his faith in himself, elevated him far above the average littérateur. To others who exemplified the symbolist mentality Biely appeared as a prophet. His works of the earliest period clearly reflect vitality and faith. Art was revelation, and through it lay the road to a new culture and to a new mankind. His writings reflect a predominantly intuitive approach and interpretation of reality.

No exact boundary can be placed to mark the end of his early, rapturous period. The change was deeply connected with the deaths of the Solovyovs and of his father in 1903. His love affair with Lyubov Blok intensified his despair. Certainly by 1906, with the Blok affair reaching its climax, and with the political events in Russia increasing Biely's hopelessness, the new mood, one of hysteria and despondency, came into full sway. All his earlier hopes for a new, beautiful life fell shattered. His faith in symbolism as a way of life dissipated into thin air. Seeking to maintain even a trace of hope for the future, he turned to philosophy.

Although chronologically Biely's philosophical studies coincided with the most despairing period of his life, they mitigated the despondency of his mood. Philosophy bred meditation, which in turn brought him to seek a *rational* justification for his beliefs. When he realized what change his mood had undergone, his despair yielded to disillusionment, his hysteria to irony. Symbolism as an intuitive revelation of truth, as a universally infallible cognitive principle was discarded. Symbolism for him had failed, and with this realization a definite period in his life came to an end.

When others who had believed in symbolism as a way of life, as a revelation of the truth, realized that their prophet had failed them, they necessarily rejected symbolism as an infallible philosophy. Thus, the crisis in Biely's life also played an important role in the crisis that developed in symbolism, which soon spelled the doom of that movement. Yet, in a measure, symbolism had succeeded.

The symbolist movement was, in fact, one of the peaks in the history of Russian culture. It opened a new era in Russian literature and restored lyrical poetry as an accepted, legitimate means of expression. Thanks to the work of the symbolists and of such sympathetic groups as the Argonauts, an ever-increasing number of readers came to appreciate modernism in art and music, and the new verse forms of Russian poetry. If symbolism as a philosophy and a way of life failed, symbolism as an artistic method and artistic style won a complete victory and thereby became one of the most significant phenomena in the cultural history of Russia.

Biely's own life reflects the success and failure of symbolism. He failed in his attempt to realize symbolism as a revelation of the absolute and as a way of life; nevertheless, as a symbolist artist he became a leading figure in twentieth-century Russian literature. His theoretical writings reflect his own mental outlook on reality and illustrate the philosophy typical for the "children of a lost generation," intellectuals who frantically, yet vainly, searched for an unshakable truth. Biely's *Symphonies* are a direct outgrowth of his philosophy and determined the structure and content of his later novels, of which *Petersburg* and *The Silver Dove*, for originality, brilliance, and effect reach the apogee of symbolist prose and are rivaled only by Sologub's *Petty Demon*. Biely's memoirs of the symbolist period remain unequaled even today. Although as a poet Biely is held in lesser regard than Alexander Blok, his influence on Russian literature has been great. His prose works have left an unmistakable imprint on Russian *belles-lettres* of the 1920's. His researches in prosody have placed their stamp on nearly every first-rate poet of Soviet Russia. Few symbolist writers have influenced modern Russian literature as much as has Biely, and the most permanent achievements of symbolism have been attained largely through him. Russian literature of the twentieth century eloquently testifies that Boris Bugayev, Andrey Biely, was the most original writer of the symbolist movement.

BIBLIOGRAPHY

THE FOLLOWING BIBLIOGRAPHY seeks primarily to indicate the sources actually quoted in the present manuscript and to give a selected list of the main works of Andrey Biely. Since a complete bibliography of his works would comprise more than five hundred titles, no attempt was made here to list his essays individually. Instead, the periodicals and miscellanies are listed in the first part of the bibliography, since they contain the bulk of the remaining writings of Andrey Biely, critical materials pertaining to his work, as well as many of the remaining sources dealing with the symbolist movement. Such items as *Tertium Organum* by P. D. Ouspensky (New York, 1945) and *Philosophy in a New Key* by Susanne K. Langer (New York, 1942) are not included in the bibliography; although both these books help to clarify what Biely sought to express in his own essays, they, and many like them, are not germane to the present study. The transliteration, as mentioned in the preface, coincides with that of the Library of Congress.

PERIODICALS

CONNECTED WITH SYMBOLIST AND OTHER MODERNIST GROUPS

Apollon (Apollo). St. Petersburg, 1909–1917.
Mir Iskusstva (World of Art). St. Petersburg, 1899–1904.
Novyi Put' (New Path). St. Petersburg, 1903–1904. Supplement: *Zapiski Religiozno-Filosofskikh Sobranii* (Records of Religious-Philosophical Meetings).
Pereval (Divide). Moscow, 1906–1907.
Severnyi Vestnik (Northern Herald). St. Petersburg, 1882–1898.
Trudy i Dni (Toils and Days). Moscow, 1912–1916.
Vesy (Balance). Moscow, 1904–1909.
Voprosy Zhizni (Questions of Life). St. Petersburg, 1905.
Zapiski Mechtatelei (Notes of Daydreamers). Petersburg, 1919–1922.
Zolotoe Runo (Golden Fleece). Moscow, 1906–1909.

NOT CONNECTED WITH SYMBOLIST AND MODERNIST GROUPS

PREREVOLUTIONARY

Mir Bozhii (God's World). St. Petersburg, 1892–1906.
Obrazovanie (Education). St. Petersburg, 1892–1909.

226 Bibliography

Russkaia Mysl' (Russian Thought). Moscow, 1880–1918; Sofia, 1920–1922; Praha-Berlin, 1922–1923; Paris, 1927.
Russkoe Bogatstvo (Russian Wealth). St. Petersburg, 1876–1918.
Sovremennyi Mir (Contemporary World). St. Petersburg, 1907–1918.
Vestnik Evropy (European Herald). Moscow, 1866–1917.

EMIGRÉ

Beseda (Causerie). Berlin, 1923–1924.
Epopeia (Epopée). Berlin, 1922–1923.
Novaia Russkaia Kniga (New Russian Book). Berlin, 1922–1923.
Novosel'e (Housewarming). New York, 1942–
Novyi Zhurnal (New Journal). New York, 1941–
Russkaia Kniga (Russian Book). Berlin, 1921.
Russkiia Zapiski (Russian Annals). Shanghai, 1937; Paris, 1938–1940.
Sovremennyia Zapiski (Contemporary Annals). Paris, 1920–1940.
Volia Rossii (The Will of Russia). Praha, 1922–1934.
Zveno (The Link). Paris, 1923–1928.

SOVIET

Gorn (The Forge). Moscow, 1919–1923.
Kniga i Proletarskaia Revoliutsiia (Book and Proletarian Revolution). Moscow, 1932–1940.
Kniga i Revoliutsiia (Book and Revolution). Moscow, 1920–1933.
Krasnaia Nov' (Red Virgin Soil). Moscow, 1921–1940.
Literaturnoe Obozrenie (Literary Review). Moscow, 1936–1941.
Literaturnyi Kritik (Literary Critic). Moscow, 1933–1940.
Literaturnyi Sovremennik (Literary Contemporary). Leningrad, 1933–1941.
Na Literaturnom Postu (On Literary Guard). Moscow, 1926–1932.
Na Postu (On Guard). Moscow, 1923–1925.
Novyi Mir (New World). Moscow, 1925–
Oktiabr' (October). Moscow, 1924–
Pechat' i Revoliutsiia (Press and Revolution). Moscow, 1921–1930.
Rossiia (Russia). Moscow, 1922–1925.
Vestnik Literatury (Literary Herald). Petersburg, 1919–1921.
Zhizn' Iskusstva (Life of Art). Petersburg-Leningrad, 1919–1929.
Znamia (Banner). Moscow, 1931–
Zvezda (Star). Leningrad, 1924–

MISCELLANIES

Fakely (Torches). St. Petersburg, 1906–1908.
Grif (Gryphon). Moscow, 1903–1914.
Literaturnyi Raspad (Literary Decay). St. Petersburg, 1908–1909.
Logos (Logos). Moscow, Petrograd, Praha, 1910–1928.
Problemy Idealizma (Problems of Idealism). Moscow, 1902.
Severnye Tsvety (Northern Flowers). Moscow, 1901–1911.
Shipovnik (Wild Rose). St. Petersburg, 1907–1917.
Sirin (The "Sirin"). St. Petersburg, 1913–1914.
Skify (Scythians). Petrograd, 1917–1918.
Sofiia (Sophia). Moscow, 1914.

Svobodnaia Sovest' (Free Conscience). Moscow, 1906.
Tsvetnik Or (Flowerbed of the Horae). St. Petersburg, 1907.
Znanie (Knowledge). St. Petersburg, 1903–1914.

NEWSPAPERS

Dni (Days). Berlin.
Golos Rossii (Voice of Russia). Berlin.
Izvestiia (News). Moscow.
Kievskaia Mysl' (Kievan Thought). Kiev.
Literaturnaia Gazeta (Literary Gazette). Moscow.
Novoe Vremia (New Time). St. Petersburg.
Posledniia Novosti (Latest News). Paris.
Pravda (Truth). Moscow.
Rech' (Speech). St. Petersburg.
Russkoe Slovo (Russian Word). Moscow.
Novoe Russkoe Slovo (New Russian Word). New York.
Slovo (Word). St. Petersburg.
Utro Rossii (Morning of Russia). Moscow.
Vozrozhdenie (Rebirth). Paris.
Znamia Truda (Banner of Labor). Petersburg, Moscow.

SOURCES

CORRESPONDENCE

Blok, A. A. *Pis'ma* (Letters). Edited by Sergei Solov'ev and others. Leningrad, 1925.
Blok, A. A. *Pis'ma ... k rodnym* (Letters to his family). Moscow-Leningrad, 1927–1932. 2 vols.
Blok, A. A. *Pis'ma ... k E. P. Ivanovu* (Letters to E. P. Ivanov). Leningrad, 1928.
Blok, A. A. "Pis'ma" (Letters), *Zvezda* (May, 1930; October, 1931; February, 1932; May, 1932).
Blok, A. A. and Belyi, Andrei [pseudonym of B. N. Bugaev]. *Perepiska* (Correspondence). Published as vol. VII of the *Letopisi Gosudarstvennogo literaturnogo muzeia* (Chronicles of the State Literary Museum). Moscow, 1940.
Briusov, V. Ia. *Pis'ma k P. P. Pertsovu, 1894–1895* (Letters to P. P. Pertsov, 1894–1895). Moscow, 1927.
Briusov, V. Ia. "Pis'ma" (Letters), *Novyi Mir* (June, 1926; February, 1932).
Briusov, V. Ia. "Pis'ma" (Letters), *Literaturnyi Kritik* (October–November, 1939).
Belyi, Andrei. "Tri pis'ma" (Three letters), *Sovremennye Zapiski*, LIV (1934).
Solov'ev, V. S. *Pis'ma* (Letters). Moscow, 1908. 3 vols.; St. Petersburg, 1922.

DIARIES, NOTEBOOKS, ETC.

Blok, A. A. "Dnevnik 1902 goda" (Diary for 1902). In *Literaturnoe Nasledstvo*, vols. 27–28 (Moscow, 1937).
Blok, A. A. *Dnevniki* (Diaries). I, 1911–1913; II, 1917–1921. Leningrad, 1928. 2 vols.
Blok, A. A. *Zapisnye knizhki* (Notebooks). Leningrad, 1932.
Briusov, V. Ia. *Dnevniki, 1891–1910* (Diaries, 1891–1910). Moscow, 1927.
Gippius, Z. N. [pseudonym of Z. N. Merezhkovskaia]. "Chernaia kniga" (The Black Book) in *Russkaia Mysl'* (January–April, 1921).

Gippius, Z. N. *Siniaia kniga* (The Blue Book). Beograd, 1926.
Merezhkovskii, D. S. *Bylo i budet, 1910–1914* (What Has Been and Shall Be, 1910–1914). Petrograd, 1915.
Shaginian, Marietta. *Literaturnyi dnevnik, 1917–1931* (Literary Diary, 1917–1931). Leningrad, 1932.

MEMOIRS AND REMINISCENCES

Ashukin, V., comp. *V. Ia. Briusov*. Moscow, 1929.
Beketova, M. A. *Aleksandr Blok*. Petersburg, 1922.
Beketova, M. A. *Aleksandr Blok i ego mat'* (Alexander Blok and his Mother). Leningrad, 1925.
Belousov, I. A. *Literaturnaia sreda, 1880–1928* (The Literary Wednesday, 1880–1928). Moscow, 1928.
Briusov, V. Ia. *Iz moei zhizni. Moia iunost'* (From my Life. My youth). Moscow, 1927.
Briusov, V. Ia. *Za moim oknom* (Outside my Window). Moscow, 1913.
Belyi, Andrei. See works of Belyi, memoirs.
Chukovskii, Kornei [pseud. of K. I. Korneichuk]. *Repin, Gor'kii, Maiakovskii, Briusov: Vospominaniia* (Repin, Gor'kii, Maiakovskii, Briusov: Reminiscences). Moscow, 1940.
Chulkov, Georgii. *Gody Stranstvii* (Years of Wandering). Moscow, 1930.
Gippius, Z. N. *Zhivyia litsa* (Living Faces). Praha, 1925. 2 vols.
Ivanov, Georgii. *Peterburgskiia zimy* (Petersburg Winters). Paris, 1928.
Pertsov, P. P. *Literaturnye vospominaniia* (Literary Reminiscences). Leningrad, 1933.
Gor'kii, M. [pseud. of A. M. Peshkov] *Zametki iz dnevnika, vospominaniia* (Notes from the Diary, Reminiscences). Berlin, 1924.
Piast, Vladimir. *Vstrechi* (Meetings). Leningrad, 1929.
Teleshov, N. *Zapiski pisatelia* (A Writer's Notes). Moscow, 1943.
Tsvetaeva, Marina. "Plennyi dukh" (Captive Spirit) in *Sovremennyia Zapiski*, LV (1934).
Zaitsev, Boris. *Moskva* (Moscow). Paris, 1939.

COLLECTED AUTOBIOGRAPHICAL DATA

Fidler, F. F., comp. *Pervye literaturnye shagi* (First Literary Steps). Moscow, 1911.
Vengerov, S. A., ed. *Russkaia literatura XX veka* (Russian Literature of the Twentieth Century). Moscow, 1914–1916. 8 fasc. Unfinished.

WORKS OF ANDREI BELYI

COLLECTED WORKS

Sobranie sochinenii (Collected Works). Moscow, Pashukanis, 1917; only vols. IV and VII.
Stikhotvoreniia (Verses). Berlin, Grzhebin, 1923.
Stikhotvoreniia (Verses). Malaia seriia poetov. Leningrad, Sovetskii pisatel', 1940.

LONGER POEMS

Khristos voskres (Christ is Arisen). Petrograd, Alkonost, 1918.
Pervoe svidanie (The First Meeting). Petrograd, Alkonost, 1921. 2d ed.: Berlin, Slovo, 1922.

BOOKS OF VERSE

Zoloto v lazuri (Gold in Azure). Moscow, Skorpion, 1904.
Pepel (Ashes). St. Petersburg, Shipovnik, 1909. 2d ed.: Moscow, Nikitinskie subbotniki, 1929. 3d ed.: Moscow-Leningrad, GIZ, 1935.
Urna (The Urn). Moscow, Grif, 1909.
Korolevna i rytsari (The Queen and her Knights). Petrograd, Alkonost, 1919.
Stikhi o Rossii (Poems of Russia). Berlin, Epokha, 1922.
Zvezda (The Star). Moscow-Leningrad, GIZ, 1922.
Posle razluki (After the Parting). Berlin, Epokha, 1922.

NOVELS

Serebrianyi golub' (The Silver Dove). In *Vesy* (April–December, 1909. 2d ed.: Moscow, Skorpion, 1910. 3d ed.: as vol. VII of the *Sobranie sochinenii* (Moscow, 1917). 4th ed.: Berlin, Epokha, 1922; 2 vols.
Peterburg (Petersburg). Iaroslavl', Nekrasov, 1912. 2d ed.: in *Sirin*, I–III (1913–1914); separately: Petrograd, Sirin, 1916. 3d ed.: Berlin, Epokha, 1922. 2 vols. 4th ed.: Moscow, Nikitnskie subbotniki, 1928. 5th ed.: Moscow, GIZ, 1935.
Kotik Letaev (Kitten Letaev). In *Skify*, I–II (1917–1918). 2d ed.: Berlin, Epokha, 1922.
Zapiski chudaka (Notes of an Eccentric). Berlin, Gelikon, 1922; 2 vols. Also as "Ia" (I) in *Zapiski Mechtatelei*, I, II–III (1919, 1921).
Kreshchenyi kitaets (The Baptized Chinese). Moscow, Nikitinskie subbotniki, 1927. Reprinted in 1928. Also appeared as the unfinished "Prestuplenie Nikolaia Letaeva" (The Crime of Nikolai Letaev) in *Sovremennyia Zapiski*, XI, XII, XIII (1922); and in *Zapiski Mechtatelei*, IV (1921).
Moskva (Moscow). I. *Moskovskii chudak* (The Moscow Eccentric). II. *Moskva pod udarom* (Moscow Under the Blow). Moscow, Krug, 1926; 2 vols. 2d ed.: Moscow, Nikitinskie subbotniki, 1927. 3d ed.: Moscow, GIZ, 1929.
Maski (Masks). Moscow, GIKhL, 1932.

SHORT STORIES AND MYSTERIA

"Svetovaia skazka" (Luminous Fairy Tale) in *Grif*, II (1904).
"Past' nochi" (The Maw of Night) in *Zolotoe Runo* (January, 1906).
"Kust" (The Bush) in *Zolotoe Runo* (October, 1906).
"My zhdem ego vozvrashcheniia" (We Await His Return) in *Svobodnaia Sovest'*, I (1906).
"Gornaia vladychitsa" (The Mountain Queen) in *Pereval* (December, 1907).
"Adam. Zapiski naidennyia v sumasshedshem dome" (Adam. Notes Found in an Insane Asylum) in *Vesy* (April, 1908).
"Iog" (The Yogi) in *Sirena* (Voronezh, February–March, 1918).
"Chelovek" (Man) in *Znamia Truda*, I (Moscow, 1918).

"SYMPHONIES"

Severnaia simfoniia. 1-aia, geroicheskaia (The Northern Symphony. The First, the Heroic); Moscow, Skorpion, 1903. Also in his *Sobranie sochinenii*, vol. IV.
2-aia simfoniia. Dramaticheskaia (Second Symphony. The Dramatic); Moscow, Skorpion, 1902. Also in his *Sobranie sochinenii*, vol. IV.

Vozvrat. 3-ia simfoniia (The Return. Third Symphony) ; Moscow, Grif, 1905. 2d ed.: Berlin, Ogon'ki, 1922.
Kubok metelei. 4-ia simfoniia (The Goblet of Blizzards. Fourth Symphony) ; Moscow, Skorpion, 1908.

MEMOIRS

"Blok v iunosti" (Blok in His Youth) in *Golos Rossii* (February 26, 1922).
"Iz vospominanii o Bloke" (From My Reminiscences of Blok) in *Golos Rossii* (April 2, 1922).
Pamiati Aleksandra Bloka (In Memory of Alexander Blok). With R. V. Ivanov-Razumnik and A. Z. Shteinberg. Petersburg, Vol'naia filosofskaia assotsiatsiia, 1922.
"Vospominaniia o Aleksandre Aleksandroviche Bloke" (Reminiscences of Alexander Blok) in *Zapiski Mechtatelei*, VI (1922).
"Blok i Merezhkovskie" (Blok and the Merezhkovskiis) in *Posledniia Novosti* (April 7, 1922).
"Vospominaiia o Bloke" (Recollections of Blok) in *Epopeia*, I–IV (1922–1923).
"Iz vospominanii" (From My Memoirs) in *Beseda*, II (1923).
"Otkliki prezhnei Moskvy" (Echoes of Old Moscow) in *Sovremennyia Zapiski*, XVI (1923).
"Arbat" (Arbat) in *Sovremennyia Zapiski*, XVII (1923).
Odna iz obitelei tsarstva tenei (A Cloister in the Kingdom of Shadows). Leningrad, GIZ, 1925.
Veter s Kavkaza (Wind from the Caucasus). Moscow, Krug, 1929.

THEORETICAL, PHILOSOPHICAL, AND CRITICAL WORKS

Simvolizm (Symbolism). Moscow, Musaget, 1910.
Lug zelenyi (The Green Field). Moscow, Al'tsiona, 1910.
Arabeski (Arabesques). Moscow, Musaget, 1911.
Tragediia tvorchestva. Dostoevskii i Tolstoi (The Tragedy of Art. Dostoevskii and Tolstoi). Moscow, Musaget, 1911.
Rudol'f Shteiner i Gete v mirovozzrenii sovremennosti (Rudolph Steiner and Goethe in Contemporary Thought). Moscow, 1916.
Revoliutsiia i kul'tura (Revolution and Culture). Moscow, 1917.
Na perevale (At the Divide). Berlin, Grzhebin, 1923. Also appeared in parts: *I. Krizis zhizni* (I. Life's crisis) ; Petersburg, Alkonost, 1918. *II. Krizis mysli* (II. The Crisis in Thought) ; Petersburg, Alkonost, 1918. *III. Krizis kul'tury* (The Crisis in Culture) ; Petersburg, Alkonost, 1920.
Glossolaliia (Glossolaly). Berlin, Epokha, 1922.
O smysle poznaniia (On the Meaning of Knowledge). Petersburg, Alkonost, 1922.
Poeziia slova (Poetry of the Word). Petersburg, Epokha, 1922.
Sirin uchenogo varvarstva (The Sirin of Scholarly Barbarism). Berlin, Skify, 1922.
Ritm, kak dialektika i "Mednyi vsadnik" Pushkina (Rhythm as Dialectics and the "Bronze Horseman" of Pushkin). Moscow, Federatsiia, 1929.
Masterstvo Gogolia (The Art of Gogol). Moscow-Leningrad, GIKhL, 1934.

INDEX

Acmeism, 29, 121, 213
Agrippa of Nettesheim, 201
Alexander II, 3
Alexander III, 4
Andreyev, Leonid, 9, 123, 185
Anichkov, Yevgeni, 215
Annensky, I. F., 213
Anthroposophy, 86 ff., 93 f., 144, 193, 216
Apollo, 29, 121, 190, 213
Apukhtin, A. N., 7
Argonauts, 29, 69 f., 71, 75, 134, 155, 209, 210
Ariel, 65
Aseyev, N., 95

Bacon, 42
Bakst, L. S., 27
Balance, 28, 81, 104, 108, 114, 115, 116, 117, 119 ff., 142, 181, 184, 191, 210 f., 213
Balmont, Konstantin, 11, 21 ff., 111 f., 121, 167
Baratynsky, Yevgeni, 7, 69
Bartenev, P. I., 102
Baudelaire, 13, 68
Beardsley, Aubrey, 108, 132, 133
Beethoven, 38
Belinsky, V. G., 43
Benois, A., 27
Berdyayev, N. A., 84, 122, 137
Biely, Andrey, 29; childhood, 33–44; and the Solovyovs, 45–64; pseudonym, 52; as man and artist, 65–95; personality, 65 f.; and Russia, 78 f., 82, 87, 93 f.; and Bryusov, 99–127; and the Merezhkovskys, 128–145; and Blok, 146–196; and Ivanov, 197– 216; as a symbolist (summary), 217 ff.; *Armenia*, 93; *Art of Gogol*, 93; *Ashes*, 73, 79, 81, 93, 144, 212 f.; *Berlin Songbook*, 91; *Between Two Revolutions*, 93; *Christ Is Arisen*, 91, 193; *Crime of Nicholas Letayev*, 42 ff., 92; *Crises*, 84; *Epopée*, 92, 196; *First Meeting*, 63, 91; *Goblet of Blizzards (Fourth Symphony)*, 79, 81, 186, 187; *Gold in Azure*, 71, 73, 74 ff., 79, 210; *Kitten Letayev*, 37 f., 88, 92; *Masks*, 93; *Memoirs of an Eccentric*, 92; *Moscow Eccentric*, 93; *Moscow under the Blow*, 93; *On the Border of Two Centuries*, 92; *Petersburg*, 84, 85, 93, 125 ff., 191 f., 214 f.; *The Princess and Her Knights*, 88; *Reminiscences of Blok*, 92, 196; *Rhythm as Dialectics*, 93; *Silver Dove*, 81 f., 85, 122, 124, 190; *The Star*, 91; *Symbolism*, 81, 95; *Symphonies*, 51, 64, 71, 72, 74, 81, 105, 154, 155 ff., 196, 219; *Travel Notes*, 84; *Turn of the Century*, 92, 93, 94; *The Urn*, 73, 79 f., 81; *Wind from the Caucasus*, 93
Blake, William, 22
Blok, A. L., 147
Blok, Alexander, 29, 60, 61 f., 64, 65, 78, 86, 89, 104, 121, 122, 123, 124, 138, 142, 146 ff., 202, 209, 210, 211, 214
Blok, Lyubov, 78, 113, 138, 157 ff., 186 f.
Boehme, Jakob, 6
Brailovsky, A., 20
Bronin, A., 204, 205
Bryusov, Valeri, 16 ff., 22, 28, 29, 53, 64, 99 ff., 132, 181, 191, 202, 207, 210 f., 214 f.; *Fiery Angel*, 117 ff.

231

232 Index

Bugayev, Alexandra, 33 ff., 45, 48 f., 52
Bugayev, Boris. *See* Biely, Andrey
Bugayev, N. V., 33 ff., 46, 50, 77
Bulgakov, S. N., 57, 60, 122, 137
Bunin, I., 43

Campioni, V. K., 123, 188
Chekhov, A. P., 7, 10
Chopin, 38
Chulkov, Georgy, 28, 29, 137, 142, 180, 207 ff.
Clarism, 29, 121
Cohen, Hermann, 79
Coleridge, 22
Cooper, James Fenimore, 40

d'Alheim, P. I., 69, 143
Darwin, Charles, 4 f., 42, 68
Dawn, 9, 10
Dionysos, 204, 213
Divide, 29
Dobrolyubov, A., 24, 25 ff.
Dostoyevsky, 6, 43, 57, 63, 78, 85, 159, 172, 176
Dyagilev, S. P., 26

Eichendorff, Joseph von, 38
Ellis (pseud. of L. L. Kobylinsky), 179
Erasmus, 118
Eros, 204 ff.

Fet, A. A., 7, 43, 69, 102
Filosofov, D. V., 27, 129, 133, 136, 137, 142
Formalists, 81, 95
Forsh, Olga, 107
Freud, 113
Fuchs, Z. (pseud. of V. Bryusov), 17

Garshin, V., 6
George, Stefan, 68
Gershenzon, M. O., 84, 122, 195
Ghil, René, 108, 122
God-seeking movement, 14, 25, 26, 29, 138
Goethe, 43, 57
Gogol, 72, 82, 85, 93, 172
Golden Fleece, 28, 142, 181, 182, 209 ff., 213

Goncharov, I. A., 6, 43
Gorky (pseud. of A. M. Peshkov), 8, 182
Gorodetsky, Sergey, 213
De Gourmont, Rémy, 108
Gryphon, 29, 110, 114, 155
Gumilyov, N. S., 89, 142, 195, 213
Gurevich, Lyubov, 12 ff.
Gurvich, I., 204

Haeckel, E., 50
Hauptmann, G., 43
Hegel, 43, 50
Heine, 38
Heinrich, Count, 118
Helmholtz, 50
Hertwig, O., 50
Hippius, Natalya, 45, 136, 138
Hippius, Tatyana, 45, 136, 137, 138
Hippius, Zinaida (Merezhkovsky), 11, 24, 29, 43, 45, 64, 106, 121, 126, 128 ff., 170, 174, 176, 180, 207, 210, 213
Hitrovo, Sophia, 58
Hodasevich, Vladislav, 106, 110, 113 f., 165 ff.
Hoffman, V., 24
House of Song, 143, 210

Ibsen, 43, 69, 177
Imagists, 90
Ivanov, Yevgeni, 61, 167, 183
Ivanov, Vyacheslav, 28, 29, 60, 61, 104, 121, 125, 142, 144, 180, 197 ff.; "Wednesdays," 206 ff.
Ivanov-Razumnik, R. V., 85, 88, 104

Kant, 79
Karamazov, 6, 176
Karamazov, Ivan, 57
Kartashev, A., 133, 136, 137
Knowledge, 182
Kogan, P. S., 17, 90, 195
Konevskoy, I. (pseud. of I. I. Oreus), 24
Korolenko, V. G., 6
Krayni, Anton (pseud. of Z. N. Hippius), 129 f.
Kublitsky-Piottukh, Alexandra, 149, 156, 169 ff., 176

Kusikov, A., 90
Kuzmin, M. A., 205, 207, 213

Lady Beautiful, 60, 62, 157 ff., 181
Lensky, 204
Leopardi, G., 22
Lermontov, 102, 142, 219

Madiel (the "Fiery Angel"), 118
Maeterlinck, 16, 68, 101, 108
Makovsky, Konstantin, 34
Makovsky, Sergey, 213
Mallarmé, 5, 16, 22, 23, 68
Mamontov, Savva, 26
Martynov, Sophia, 58
Mayakovsky, Vladimir, 95
Maykov, Apollon, 7
Medtner, E., 83, 112, 127, 214
Medtner, N., 112
Mendeleyev, D. I., 157
Merezhkovsky, D. S., 13 ff., 20, 27, 28, 29, 64, 116, 121, 128 ff., 170, 197, 210
Messenger of Europe, 18
Mikhailovsky, N. K., 129
Minsky (pseud. of N. M. Vilenkin), 9 ff., 21
Miropolsky (pseud. of A. A. Lang), 16, 24
Mirsky, D. S., 65
Mommsen Theodor, 198
Moréas, Jean, 108
Morozov, Margarita, 45, 143
Musaget, 83, 123
Mystical anarchism, 28, 80, 180 f., 184, 185, 208 ff.

Nadson, S., 7, 43
Natorp, Paul, 79
Nekrasov, K. F., 125
Nekrasov, N. A., 9, 43, 79, 172
Neo-Christianity, 28, 128, 129
New Path, 29, 108, 135, 136, 155 f., 207
Nicholas II, 27
Nietzsche, 5, 68, 69, 70, 72, 79, 107, 108, 201
Northern Flowers, 29, 135
Northern Messenger, 11 ff., 26 f., 43
Notes of Daydreamers, 127
Novalis, 5

Index 233

Ostwald, Wilhelm, 68

Papini, Giovanni, 108
Pertsov, P. P., 19, 137, 155
Petrovsky, A. S., 68, 150
Petrovsky, Nina, 77, 110 ff., 141, 198
Plato, 48, 55, 61, 202, 211
Pleshcheyev, A. N., 10
Pobedonostsev, K. S., 4
Poe, E. A., 13, 22, 68
Polivanov, L. I., 41 ff., 46, 47
Polonsky, 7, 43
Polyakov, S. I., 21, 108, 120
Pozzo, A., 123
Pushkin, 7, 9, 37, 43, 72, 85, 93, 102, 142, 203
Pyast, Vladimir (pseud. of V. A. Pyastovsky), 106, 107

Questions of Life, 29, 208

Rabelais, 53, 55, 68
Rachinsky, G. A., 123
Radin, Belle, 40 ff., 44, 45, 48
Raisa Ivanovna, 37 ff., 45
Reade, Mayne, 40
Religious-Philosophical Society, 69, 129, 130, 143
Renata, 118
Rhythmics Society, 80
Rickert, H., 79
Rimbaud, 5, 16, 69
Rops, Félicien, 132
Rosetti, D. G., 22
Rozanov, V. V., 129, 133, 136, 137
Russian revolution (1905), 27, 78, 138, 174 f.
Russian revolution (1917), 125, 144, 193 f.
Russian Archives, 102, 104
Russian Thought, 119, 122 ff., 142, 192, 215
Russian Wealth, 43, 70
Russo-Japanese War, 27, 78
Ryabushinsky, N. P., 209 ff.

St. John, 72, 156, 165
Schelling, 5
Schlegels, The, 5

Schmidt, Anna, 59 ff.
Schopenhauer, 5, 39, 43, 70, 74, 79, 209
Scorpio, 21, 28, 29, 64, 69, 105, 108, 109, 110, 112, 115, 116, 119, 135
Scythians, 88 f., 193
Serov, Valentin, 27
Severyanin, Igor (pseud. of I. V. Lotaryov), 24
Shaginyan, Marietta, 108
Shakespeare, 160
Shelley, 22
Sirin, 125
Skitalets (pseud. of S. G. Petrov), 182, 185
Socialist Revolutionaries, 88
Society of Free Aesthetics, 69
Sokolov, S., 110, 114
Sologub, F. (pseud. of F. K. Teternikov), 24, 43, 121, 129, 215
Solovyov, Mikhail S., 43 f., 46 ff., 60, 62, 64, 66 f., 71, 77, 105, 109, 131 ff., 150, 155
Solovyov, Olga M., 44, 45 ff., 64, 71, 77, 131 ff., 134, 135, 143, 150 ff., 155, 170
Solovyov, Poliksena, 47
Solovyov, Professor S. M., 47
Solovyov, S. M. ("Seryozha"), 48 ff., 117, 148, 150 ff., 155, 157, 166 ff., 179, 186, 187, 210
Solovyov, Vladimir S., 18 f., 19, 20, 28, 48, 50, 52 ff., 69 ff., 74, 82, 90, 104, 132, 133, 142, 147, 148, 150, 154, 156, 158 ff., 160, 166, 168, 172, 188, 201, 204, 210; poetry, 54 ff.
Solovyov, Vsevolod S., 47, 59
Sophia (Divine Wisdom, Soul of the Universe), 57 ff., 62, 63, 90, 113, 154, 157, 164, 168, 187
Spencer, Herbert, 47
Stasyulevich, M. M., 53, 54
Steiner, Rudolf, 86 ff., 144, 215
Struve, P. B., 122 ff.
Sudermann, Hermann, 43
Symbolism, 3, 5 f., 8, 14 ff., 21, 27, 61, 63, 73 f., 80, 104, 110 f., 119, 120, 127, 190, 202 f., 217 ff.

Symons, Arthur, 17

Tenishev, Princess, 26, 29
Tennyson, 22
Tereshchenko, M. I., 125
Tolstoy, A. N., 215
Tolstoy, L. N., 6, 7, 21
Torches, 29, 142, 209
Tower, Ivanov, 28, 205 ff., 213, 214
Tsvetayeva, Marina, 65, 107
Turgenev, Anna A. ("Asya"), 45, 82 ff., 122 f., 143, 188, 191, 192, 215
Turgenev, I. S., 6, 43
Tyutchev, F. I., 7, 69, 102

Uhland, 38

Vasilevsky, L. M., 204
Vasiliev, Klavdia (Bugayev), 93
Velichko, V. L., 54
Verhaeren, 68, 103
Verlaine, 5, 16, 22, 68, 69, 101, 108, 109, 216
Verne, Jules, 40
Vladimirov, Anna, 69
Vladimirov, V. V., 68, 69, 71, 134, 180
Volfila, 89, 194
Volynsky (pseud. of A. L. Flekser), 11 ff.
Vrubel, M. A., 99

Whitman, Walt, 22
Wilde, Oscar, 22, 70, 108
Works and Days, 214
World of Art, 26 f., 108, 135, 136, 153
Wundt, Wilhelm, 50

Yasinsky, I. I., 9, 10
Yesenin, Sergey, 89
Yevreinov, Mme. A. M., 12

Zarathustra, 46, 72, 107
Zaytsev, Boris, 107
Zhukovsky, 172
Zinovieva-Annibal, Lidia (Ivanov), 205
Znosko-Borovsky, Yevgeni, 213

www.ingramcontent.com/pod-product-compliance
Lightning Source LLC
Chambersburg PA
CBHW021701230426
43668CB00008B/696